CHANGE YOUR MINDSET AND ACHIEVE ANYTHING

HOW TO CHANGE YOUR MINDSET

ARVIND UPADHYAY

ISBN 979-888521822-1

I'm here today to talk to you about overcoming the biggest obstacle you'll ever face. Let me take you on a journey.

It was the middle of the night, almost a year ago. I struggled to breathe. Each step taking longer than the last, I fought my way upward at the cruising altitude of a commercial airliner. "Focus," I thought, "keep pushing forward." The culmination of 130 days of consecutive climbing, the negative 60-degree windchill and the actual physiological state of my body fighting back at 28,000 feet on Mount Everest summit ridge was pushing me to my breaking point.

"Get ahold of yourself, Colin", I desperately tried to regain control of my mind. But doubts, fear, and pain swirled in my thoughts. "One step at a time," I thought. In an apparent daze a chair appeared in the snow in front of me blurring in and out of my vision. "One step at a time," I thought.

These labored steps reminded me of steps I had taken before — steps that had given me a new lease on life, steps that would bring me to my knees yet simultaneously teach me life's greatest lesson. My mind flashed back.

10 years ago, I had just graduated from college. It was time to let loose to see the world. I took my life savings from three summers painting houses, packed a backpack and a surfboard and set off into the world for an adventure with no itinerary. After all, adventure is just bad planning, right?

Three months into the journey, I found myself on a beach in rural Thailand. It was a beautiful evening. I was watching fire dancers in amazement and I decided to partake in the fun, jumping a flaming jump rope because you know I was 22 years old and invincible. In an instant my life changed. The rope wrapped around my legs and ignited my body completely on fire.

Survival mode kicked in when I needed it most and with one last breath and ounce of courage, I dove into the ocean a few steps away to extinguish the flames. Then darkness. Silence.

I woke in a one-room nursing station to look down finding my body completely bandaged. "What have I done?" I thought. I had been severely burned. Well, it must have been at least 24 hours later, I awoke leaving a surgery room in a small ICU where there was a cat running across my chest and around my bed, hammering home the fact that I was far from home and in a dire set of circumstances. Being in this unsanitary hospital could kill me and the pain — the searing pain was unimaginable, yet the morphine they kept giving me made it feel like there was insects crawling over my skin. I couldn't tell which was worse.

I just wanted to give up. I was downward spiraling fast, ready to quit. Thankfully five days in this ordeal, my mother arrived to be my protector. I know now she was just as afraid as I was but she chose to never show me her fear. Instead she came into my hospital room every single day with a smile on her face and an air of positivity, daring me to dream about the future.

She kept asking me questions like: "Colin, what do you want to do when you get out of here? Let's set a goal."

My immediate response: "Mom, I'm screwed. The doctors say I may never walk again normally. What hope do I have? Life as I know it is over."

But her positivity was unrelenting and infectious. In three days after she arrived, she was sitting on my bedside and I announced my goal: "Mom, when I get out of here, I'm going to one day compete in a triathlon." Not something I'd never done before and looking down at my legs it seemed rather unrealistic. But with a tear in her eyes, she nodded and wrapped me in her arms as only a mother can.

It was many more weeks until I was released from that Thai hospital. I still hadn't taken a single step. I was carried on and off the plane and placed in a wheelchair when I got back here to Portland.

The next morning, I was in my mother's kitchen. My mom said to me, "All right, Colin, now I know you've got this big triathlon goal but today your goal is to take your first step." She then grabbed a chair from our kitchen table and placed it one step in front of my wheelchair. "You need to figure out how to get out of your wheelchair and step into that chair." It took me three hours that day to work up the courage and strength to take that first step, but I did it.

The next day she had moved the chair five steps away, and the next day ten. Each day I could take a few more steps until finally after many weeks I regained my ability to walk.

And then one day jogged — jogging felt like flying but jogging was a far cry from running a triathlon. So for the next 18 months I grinded with my goal in mind and finally a year and a half after my accident, it was time for me to take a shot at my dream.

I showed up in Chicago to compete in the triathlon. I dove into Lake Michigan to swim the first mile. I got on my bike, rode 25 miles, put my shoes on and ran 6.2 miles to the finish, crossing the finish line. I had done it. I had achieved my goal.

And there was one more surprise in store for me that day. I hadn't just finished the race, I had won. Thank you. Placing first out of more than 4,000 other participants.

The first thing I thought about were those months in the hospital imagining what would have happened had my mom not forced me to look towards the future and set a measurable goal. Through his tragedy, I'd learned an invaluable lesson. I had learned that life will test us with setbacks but these situations aren't permanent. We have full control of our choices to keep moving forwards one step at a time. I had learned that we all have reservoirs of untapped potential that can achieve great things. The biggest thing standing in our way: our own minds.

For the next six years, I competed as a professional triathlete in 25 countries and then in the fall of 2014 I found myself at the summit of Ecuador's third tallest mountain with a diamond ring in my pocket asking my longtime girlfriend Jenna to marry me. I don't know if it was the lack of oxygen to her brain to the altitude but she said yes.

Awed and inspired by the mountains around us and wanting to set a goal larger than herself, we set a goal together. I would attempt to set a world record for the Explorers Grand Slam with the larger purpose of inspiring kids everywhere to dream big, to set goals, to live active healthy lives. We coined our project Beyond 7/2.

Now the Explorers Grand Slam includes climbing the Seven Summits which is the tallest mountain on each of the seven continents as well as completing expeditions to both the North and South Poles. Fewer than 50 people in history had ever completed the Grand Slam and I would aim to be the fastest.

Contents

Foreword

Change is inevitable. Accepting it--and learning to anticipate it--is not, and understanding that is a major mental hurdle for entrepreneurs as their businesses, customers and market shift over time.

But you can actually train your brain to get better at handling change through some simple mental exercises, from imagining your company's demise to learning how to meditate. It's not always pleasant, but it is possible.

I am a strong believer that success and happiness are all about mindset. Your mindset and belief system affect everything in your life from what you think and feel to how you act and react to the world around you.

In order to achieve your goals, your mindset needs to match your aspirations, otherwise, it might be holding you back from getting where you want to be.

Preface

Someone recently explained to me what changing your mentality really does. It's changing your beliefs. It's changing the patterns and energies that you attract. And ultimately, it's changing how you live.

No wonder it's difficult. You change beliefs that you have probably had for a long time, if not your entire life. It's beliefs that you probably grew up with.

Everything that's happened you have somehow found a way to use as a confirmation of your beliefs.

That's where the problem lies. In order to change your mindset, to think and act differently, you need to change your beliefs. And to change your beliefs, you need to start thinking of different reasons for the things that are happening in your life.

I held the belief that I wasn't good enough or worthy enough, and everything that would happen to me would fall into that pattern. My friend is upset because I'm not a good enough friend. I was lied to because I wasn't worthy of being told the truth. I wasn't good enough, disciplined enough, or strong enough, to pursue my dreams and live the life I want.

When in all honesty, there are many possible reasons for the things that have happened. But I chose to believe the one that hurt me the most, the belief that I have subconsciously carried with me the majority of my life.

It's the conclusion I came to after anything bad would happen to me.

It's toxic, and not true. We define our own truth. We all have our own truth that we act on and that is the concept that our actions and thoughts follow. We just have to choose to see a different side of things.

When you aren't given the truth from other people, we are left to make our own assumptions. And that is where I, and I think a lot of others, fall into the trap of confirming our own beliefs, however hurtful, damaging or downgrading they are. Those are the beliefs that should change.

My mentor described it to me as holding bars in front of you as if you were in jail, not able to get out, and feeling like your stuck. But those bars are only in front of you. But they're all you see because you're holding onto them. If you let go, and turn around, you're free. There's nothing and nobody stopping you but yourself. Your beliefs.

Change your beliefs and you live a different life. You can choose to live the life you want despite your fears and beliefs telling you that you can't.

You're in your own prison and the only person that has the key is you. You just have to find it by turning around and seeing a different side of things, liberating you from your own prison of negative beliefs and patterns.

CHAPTER ONE

Change your Self-Talk

CHAPTER TWO

9 Signs It's Time To Change Your Mindset

Today, you have the opportunity to transcend from a disempowered mindset of existence to an empowered reality of purpose-driven living. Today is a new day that has been handed to you for shaping. You have the tools, now get out there and create a masterpiece.

Steve Maraboli, The Power of One

At the heart of this quote, you will find that regardless of what is currently happening in your life, the way you perceive your life is what makes you happy or unhappy.

If negative assumptions or beliefs are consuming you, then you will be unhappy. On the other hand, if you have a positive mindset (even in when navigating tough times), then you will be happy. Ultimately, perception is your reality, so changing the way you look at your life can make the difference.

But how can you know when your mindset is faulty?

It can be hard to tell when the negative thoughts are outside yourself or inside your psyche. That's part of the problem with a negative mindset—it clouds your judgment.

Thankfully there are some red flags to alert you when it might be time improve your thoughts and mindset.

Here are 9 signs it's time to change your mindset...

1. You are constantly focusing on what's wrong

Do you always find yourself fixating on your worries and disappointments, but never thinking about the things that are actually going your way? This is a sure sign that your mindset is contaminated with negativity. There may be a lot of bad things happening right now, but odds are there are at least some aspects of your life that are in good shape.

Taking time to be thankful for those things is important, because it helps to keep the bad from completely overwhelming your perspective. If you become blind to the good things, you may lose them, or not use them to your advantage.

2. You mourn your failures but forget to celebrate your victories

The difficulties and struggles of today are but the price we must pay for the accomplishments and victories of tomorrow.

William J. H. Boetcker, Motivational Speaker

This is closely related to the sign above. Do you find yourself feeling angry and despondent whenever you suffer a loss, but glossing over your victories? When you do not take the time to celebrate the moment when something goes your way, it is because on a conscious or unconscious level, you do not believe in your victory. You believe underneath it is concealing the seeds of failure.

When you do this, you continuously are sending yourself a very negative message. You believe that you will always fail, and that you cannot celebrate victories because they are all just future failures in disguise. This is a really poor way to live your life, because not only do you miss out on all of life's precious, beautiful moments, but you spit on life itself, and on your own ingenuity, luck, and achievements.

"But I don't want to take anything for granted," you might reply. That is a good thing, but there is a third path, and that is gratitude. Remember, constantly casting doubts on your victories is as ungrateful as taking them for granted, because it isn't a real acknowledgment of them.

Believe you are capable of real victory. Some things do last.

3. You don't want to face the truth

Complaining about reality is not going to change it. You can rage all day about the rain clouds, but it is not going to bring out the sun. It is good to have a sense of justice, to appreciate what things should be.

But in a way, relentlessly complaining is a refusal to acknowledge and accept the truth. There are simply some things you cannot change. Not everything is under your control. And there is no bigger mistake than refusing to see the world for what it is, because that is the point where you can no longer tell fact from fiction.

Take action to change the things that you can. Speak the truth when you see an injustice, but accept that the world will never be fair, as much as maybe it should be. Until you can accept that fact and change your mindset, it will never be realistic, and you will always be plagued by resentment that your expectations are not being met.

4. You feel angry when your expectations are not met

This leads directly to another red flag. If you are constantly finding that the world or people in your life or even you yourself are not meeting your expectations, it most likely means your expectations are unrealistic to begin with. Our expectations are a huge part of our mindset. They are what we believe to be possible or necessary.

Expectations lay the groundwork for our experiences. If we have unrealistically high expectations, nothing ever satisfies us. For example, if you set out after college expecting to be a millionaire by age 30 and you find yourself nowhere near that benchmark by age 25, you will probably be pretty miserable. But are you really miserable because you are not a millionaire, or because you have not achieved what you expected to by that age?

This all comes back to seeing the world as it truly is. Maybe you are gifted and ambitious, and maybe in a perfect world, you would have your first million by now. But we do not live in a perfect world, and with all the gifts and ambition in the world, you cannot control every factor. That is why it is important to adjust our mindsets to survive and thrive in such a world.

5. You feel unsatisfied and unhappy with everything you have (or don't have)

The downside of ambition is that it often blinds us to the wonderful things and people we already have in our life. Maybe you want a bigger home or a more expensive car, but can you remember when you didn't even have the home or car you have now? Maybe you wish you had more friends, while disregarding the value in the friends you have now.

There is always more to strive for, but for this reason, more can never truly satisfy us. It always leaves a hole that is impossible to fill.

You will never stop wanting more until you allow yourself to have what you already have. To take it in. Savor it. Now is a good time to do that.

Geneen Roth, Author

6. You find yourself regularly coming to blows with the people you care about

If you are constantly disagreeing with the people you love, it is a good sign that your mindset may need some work, especially if you trust those people and respect and value their opinions. Your arguments with them may reflect more on you than on them. Try to see where they are coming from—it could change your mind for the better.

7. You think about what you "have to" do instead of what you "get to" do

When you find yourself viewing everything as an inconvenience instead of as a welcome opportunity, it usually means that you are no longer appreciating what you have. "I have to do all this work," is a tempting statement when you are tired, but you get to do all that work. Not everyone does!

Work feeds you and keeps you alive, and keeps the enjoyable things in your life accessible. So remember to appreciate your work, even when it feels burdensome!

8. You see yourself as a victim

The problem with seeing yourself as a victim doesn't come from the fact that it is necessarily inaccurate—sometimes you really have been victimized by bad people or unfortunate circumstances. However, constantly viewing yourself as the victim does not empower you to change or build a better life for yourself. Even if you were the victim, overcome this low self-esteem by making a decision to reject that role and start creating something better. You deserve it!

9. You hold onto the dramas of other people

Sometimes, the negative mindsets we find ourselves struggling with do not reflect us so much as they reflect the messages we have received throughout our lives. Maybe your parents told you that you shouldn't pursue your passions, or maybe you had a negative partner in your past who made you feel you were never good enough.

If the dramas inside your head sound familiar and you catch echoes of voices that are not yours, it may be time to let them go. Those dramas belong to those other people and reflect their judgments and perceptions, not yours.

To change your mindset is not easy—but it is one of the most powerful things you can do. Learning how to recognize a negative mindset is the first step. Once you do, you will be empowered to make those changes and start seeking out the positive. Doing this can often turn your entire life around!

CHAPTER THREE

steps to change your negative thoughts and feelings Develop a winning mindset

What do you do when you start feeling down or when you start having negative thoughts?

Do you just want to hide under your duvet from the whole world and watch movies hoping you might feel better tomorrow?

Or

Does one negative thought lead to another and before you know it you cannot get out of negative thinking and you feel anxious, fearful and down?

Do you think your current ways of dealing with negative thoughts and feelings serve you?

As much as it might feel that sometimes we have no control over our thoughts and feelings, we do have control!

I would like to share with you some techniques to use when you feel down and when you feel you have no control over your negative thinking. These techniques work wonders with me and I am sure they will help you.

1. Focus on what you want, not on what you don't have

It is so easy to compare ourselves to others and feel like a victim as there are so many things we want in life that we don't currently have. BUT thinking this way will only make you more upset. Where focus goes, energy flows. The more you focus on something the more it grows so don't focus on what you don't have, focus on what you want to achieve instead.

Focus on things you want to achieve and your brain will automatically go into a problem-solving mode. It will think "How can I achieve this?". Identify ways in which you can achieve your goals and you will see that your goals are within your reach. This will fuel your optimism and motivation and encourage you to take action. Before you know it, you will have achieved it!

2. Visualise and get your vision board up

Sometimes we feel negative and down because we are not getting what we want. Take the time to re-connect with your vision.

Close your eyes and visualise what you wish to achieve. For example, "I want to feel happy, motivated and optimistic." Picture yourself experiencing these emotions, feel them. Visualise what life would look like once you felt this way? Don't worry if you can't picture the scenario clearly – just feel. Visualise in as much detail as possible. Where are you? What can you see? Who is with you? What can you smell? What can you hear?

Now visualise what type of person you need to become (your ideal self) to achieve your goal. How do you think? How do you act? What are your beliefs?

Create a vision board with photos/pictures that represent your ideal life or anything you want to achieve, including how you wish to feel. Put it in a visible place and visualise the achievement of your goals every time you see your vision board.

3. Gratitude

Gratitude is such a powerful tool. Did you know that you cannot feel negative emotions and feel grateful at the same time? Choose to feel grateful.

Every time you feel down, think about all the things you are grateful for. Learn to find beauty and gratitude in small things. You can be grateful for your family, friends, house, for having an income, food on a table or you can simply be grateful for the sunshine.

Find gratitude in your challenges. For example instead of thinking "I hate my job, I want to quit as soon as possible but I can't" think "I am so grateful for the opportunity to create my business whilst I am receiving a monthly salary". It is not all as bad as we think it is.

4. Keep a worry list

The minute you start to worry, write it down and keep the list for 2 weeks. This not only helps release the heavy energy that weighs us down, but at the end of 2 weeks you will notice that none of these worries were warranted. Your brain will have a proof that worry is a waste of time.

5. Negative self-talk

Start watching the way you talk to yourself. Self-talk is important because it has a big impact on how you feel and what you do. What is your self-talk like? Is it positive and empowering or is it negative and disempowering? What type of self-talk would serve you more? What can you do to develop this self-talk? Below are some ideas to get you started.

Tip: Turn negative self-talk to a positive one. For example, every time you hear yourself say "I can't do this", change it to "What can I do to be able to do it? Who can I ask for help? What can I learn that will enable me to do it?"

Tip: What sort of self-talk would your ideal-self have? Commit to developing the same self-talk as your ideal-self would have.

Tip: Affirmations are positive mental repetitions that can reprogram your thinking patterns so that, over time, you begin to think and act differently, with accordance to your affirmations. Affirmations are successful at managing your negative self-talk. An example of an affirmation could be "My business is growing and thriving" or "I am successful and never give up".

Write down your affirmations and repeat them every day. You will be amazed how quickly they lift your spirits.

Tip: Say 'STOP' straight after a negative thought appears in your mind. You may not be able to control the first thing that pops into your head, but you can control the second.

Remember, as much as we want to believe that we have no control over how we feel and what happens to us, we do have control over our lives. What we think directly impacts how we feel and how we act. So if you think you are a failure, you will feel like a failure and you will act like one which will only reinforce your belief that you are a failure. We don't need to feel like a victim and take whatever our mind throws at us. We can choose to take back control, work on training our mind so we can create the life we want.

You view the world through your mental attitude. If that attitude is predominantly negative, it can impact everything, including health, career, family, and more. Furthermore, negative thinking can have a spiraling effect that attracts more negative thinking.

1. Have Daily Negative Thought Time

A paradoxical strategy to gain control over negative thinking is to commit to 10 minutes a day ruminating and reviewing them over and over again. Negative Thought Time (NTT) must be 10 minutes and must be every day. When you have a negative thought during the day, jot it down, and tell yourself that you'll review them during NTT. Over time, you will gain control and negative thinking will stop. – Julie Kantor, PhD, JP Kantor Consulting

2. Replace the Negative Thoughts

We don't overcome negative thought patterns, we replace them. For most of us, those negative thought patterns are well-worn neural pathways. Four simple steps:

1. Notice when you have started the pattern.
2. Acknowledge that its a pattern you want to change.
3. Articulate what you want to be different.
4. Choose a different behavior — one that serves your goals.

– David Taylor-Klaus, DTK Coaching

3. Be Your Own Best Friend

We are mean to ourselves. Nearly 90% of self-talk is negative. Three steps:

1. Release it. Let it out to help process, not to dwell. Three minutes, then the pity party is over.
2. Track it. Identify when you have negative thoughts. Awareness will enable reframing.
3. Reframe it. Once you know why you are being mean, consider what your best friend would say to you. Then tell yourself what you need to hear.

– Michelle Tillis Lederman, Executive Essentials

4. Write Instead Of Think

Write down why the negative thought is present. Writing versus thinking helps purge the thought out, and when you can see the words on paper or a screen it is easier to make sense of it and move forward. – Steven Cohen, Meyvn Global

5. Make A Conscious Effort To Find Things To Love, Like And Appreciate

Instead of fighting negative thoughts, consciously reach for better feeling thoughts. One powerful way to do that is to speak (out loud if you can) to what you love, like and appreciate. Heading into a tough talk? "I love the way the coffee tastes today." "I like the way this chair feels at my back." "I appreciate the chance to process ideas with my team." Reach for the relief, and you'll find it. – Wendy Pitts Reeves, C2C Consulting, PLLC

6. Ask Yourself Some Tough Questions

Reflect on your answers to some tough questions. 1. What do I get from having negative thought patterns? What's the reward for me? 2. What do I lose by engaging in negative thoughts? What are the costs? 3. What benefits would I receive from engaging in positive thoughts? What costs are associated with thinking more positively? 4. What in my past made me think negatively? 5. What will I do now? – Bill Gardner, Noetic Outcomes Consulting, LLC

7. Establish New Habits

Rather than thinking of it in terms of "overcoming" negative thought patterns, think of it in terms of establishing new habits. You do that by directing your attention to subjects where there's nothing to "overcome": subjects that you already feel good about, and therefore think positively about. That could be your pet, your painted toe nails, being outside, the beach... Start with something easy. – Christine Meyer, Christine Meyer Coaching

8. Stop Watching The Morning News

Research has shown just three minutes of negative news in the morning will significantly increase your chances of a negative experience over the course of the day. Research has also shown that positive mindset increases productivity and satisfaction while reducing errors rates. Mindset is a choice, but not always an easy one. Look to eliminate negative influences and stop watching morning news! – Dr. Woody Woodward, HCI

9. Use Affirmations

When you wake up, open your eyes and feel gratitude for the new day. Write down daily affirmations: "I love the people I work with," "I make positive contributions every day," or "I am open to inspired thoughts." If a negative thought creeps in, think of a success you've had and the feeling that went with it. Positive thinking is a daily task, but worth it. – Erin Kennedy, Professional Resume Services, Inc.

10. Develop Your Success Routine

Every morning for fifteen years, I've done a process I created called "Quantum Programming." It involves taking time each morning as you wake to meditate and focus on the person you want to be and the quality of life you want to live. You also set a few important goals to keep your momentum building toward your dreams. When you know what you want and are driving at it daily, negativity will fade. – Brett Baughman, The Brett

Baughman Companies, Inc.

11. Channel Those Thoughts Into Something Constructive

Negative thought patterns can easily take over, but a fantastic (and constructive) trick is to identify what the negative thought pattern is and a project you're excited about. Then, consciously commit to this: Every time you find yourself focusing on the negative, refocus your thoughts for five minutes on your exciting project. I did this recently and a new initiative is now ahead of schedule! – Emily Kapit, MS, MRW, ACRW, CPRW, ReFresh Your Step, LLC

12. Focus On Gratitude

Gratitude is underrated by most but is essential to a happy life. Life doesn't get easier, but we become stronger as we reframe difficulties by recognizing all of the little good things going on around us. Keep a Good List and refer to it daily. Also, focus on what you really want and be very specific. A focused, positive mind will attract what it is seeking over time. – Jen Kelchner, TeenTrep.co

13. Try Movement And Meditation

As a registered yoga teacher (RYT-200) and a writing coach and author, I know that you can't escape negative thoughts without physically disrupting them. To get out of your head, get into your body. A few minutes of deliberate breath work (seated 10-15 minute meditation) or body movement (like a yoga class)can disrupt those thinking patterns. To get out of your head, move more. Feel more. – Dave Ursillo, The Literati Writers

CHAPTER FOUR

How to Turn Negative Thoughts Into Positive Actions

We've been through the wringer this past year and it's fair to assume that we've all had some dark moments. As an introvert, I have a running monolog in my head all day, constantly analyzing situations and other people's words and actions.

I have to manage the floodgates, to stop negative thoughts ruling my day. Some days, it's exhausting. I'm still learning as I go.

I've struggled with negative thoughts my whole life. Sometimes I've looked enviously at other people who didn't seem to struggle at all.

However, it turns out that little voice in our heads is completely natural, whether you're an introvert or not. Some people have just learned to manage it.

Quiet the Negative Inner Voice

When our brain senses imminent danger, it triggers the release of stress hormones. Adrenalin and Cortisol help keep us safe in an emergency, but we're not running from saber-toothed tigers anymore, and too much of these powerful chemicals can make us ill.

Don't get me wrong, at times this little negative voice can actually be good, "No, I should not eat that entire packet of biscuits and call it breakfast."

That little voice can also keep us motivated toward goals. But, sometimes it says things like, "I'd never be able to do that," or "It's so obvious they all hate me."

Coping Under Negative Pressure

I remember my first time project-managing a huge and complicated web build for a client. I was out of my comfort zone, and every little hurdle triggered, "I'm really screwing this up" thoughts.

Those thoughts knocked my confidence and put me off my game, almost becoming an evil self-fulfilling prophecy. At times, I felt utterly paralyzed by them.

On the last day, once everything had gone live, our account director Neil called me into his office. My heart was in my throat, I was physically shaking as I sat down.

I was certain that he was about to confirm how I'd let everyone down. Just like I'd been telling myself all these weeks. Instead, he told me what an incredible job I'd done and how well I'd coped under all the pressure. He even apologized for not helping more.

Are Negative Thoughts Impacting Every Area of Your Life?

Perhaps those negative thoughts are always there, perhaps they come and go. Sometimes they're a day-ruiner. Sometimes, when they get out of control, you begin to realize that they're a life-ruiner.

Negative thoughts will fester and stop you going for promotions, jobs, friendships, relationships, adventures, and opportunities. They can stunt personal growth, cause us to make bad decisions, and drive us to become the worst versions of ourselves.

They can warp our perception of experiences and even cause us physical and mental damage, feeding mood and anxiety disorders.

I don't know about you, but the worse I feel, the less likely I am to take positive action. I sink into a pit. My sister Laura is a psychotherapist and told me to start writing down every single negative thought I had, as soon as I had them. After a couple of days, I was horrified. It felt like I had no control over my brain; like I was poisoning myself.

Getting to Know Your Inner Chimp

When talking with my friend Ellen about writing this blog, she told me that her negative thoughts have increased in strength and frequency since the start of the pandemic. That's understandable – we've all been working from home, with our personal spaces functioning as workspaces. We've felt bored, isolated, lonely and sluggish. All of which increase stress, anxiety and negative thought patterns.

It was Professor Steve Peters who coined the "Chimp" concept. We all have a Chimp, a part of our subconscious, with us since birth. It told us when to cry for attention. Now it tells us when to get angry at drivers who don't indicate.

It stored our emotional memories and tries to help us avoid emotional pain. The Chimp has its hand hovering above the big red button of anxiety, ready and waiting with a catalog of negative thoughts.

And because it pre-dates the development of our logical minds, the Chimp has cemented beliefs into our internal computers. They can take us over before our logical minds can reassure us that spending a whole afternoon watching Netflix does not mean we will never amount to anything.

Negative Thoughts Can Take Many Forms

The thing about negative thoughts is that they don't usually reflect reality. In the 1960s, U.S. psychiatrist Aaron Beck recognized specific patterns to negative thinking, which he called "Cognitive Distortions" or "Distorted Thinking."

They're common, entirely normal, and not our fault. Beck's pioneering research formed a central part of his cognitive theory of depression and, later, Cognitive Behavioral Therapy (CBT).

Since then, researchers have developed his ideas and identified at least 10 common distorted thinking patterns. Below are some examples from my own life – how many sound familiar?

1. Polarized Thinking

When I was in high school and thought, "If I don't get straight As, I've essentially failed."

2. Overgeneralization

When I went through break-ups and told myself, "This always happens, I'll never find anyone," or when I burn the fishfingers and think, "Why does nothing ever go right?"

3. Mental Filtering

When I was a year into having started my own business and filtered out the fact that I'd managed to achieve that, had wonderful clients, great friends, and a supportive partner. I was only focusing on why I wasn't yet making £x p/a.

4. Discounting the Positive

When I was in a slump last Tuesday and caught myself saying, "Yes, I might be a decent copywriter, but anybody can learn how to do that."

5. Mindreading

When my partner introduced me to his friends and I spent the entire journey home thinking, "They all hate me, I told that stupid story and now they all think I'm boring." A couple of hours later he showed me their group chat, where everyone had been singing my praises.

6. Catastrophizing

The time a client of mine hired a full-time writer and I lost their business and automatically assumed, "I'm going to lose all my other clients, then I'll have to move out and live in my parents' shed."

7. Emotional Reasoning

The time my ex-manager, Steph, suggested I go for a copywriting position, and I thought, "I'm so worthless, there's no point in even trying – I'd never get the job anyway." Spoiler: I got the job.

8. "Should" Statements

When I'm rigid with my ideas about how I should and shouldn't be spending my free time, "I should be getting up early to start every morning with yoga." I then feel anxious and blame myself when I'm too tired to manage it.

9. Labeling

The time I assumed that my ex-colleague Lara was a horrible person because she was a bit "short" with me when we first met. Spoiler: she was just having a nightmare Monday and we became really good friends.

10. Personalization and Blame

When my ex-boss Jo used to look annoyed and I'd instantly shrink into myself and think, "I must have done something wrong, I can't do anything right."

NOTE: If you're constantly experiencing negative thoughts, it's important to seek advice from a mental health professional. People suffering from depression and anxiety often experience destructive thoughts, that can become incessant and painful.

12 Tips to Turn Those Negative Thoughts Into Positive Actions

It was only when I was first getting to know my partner Leo, and he said, "It feels really great to be around a positive person all the time," that it hit home. My efforts had turned into habits.

Over time, due to the process of neuroplasticity, habitual negative thinking patterns wear such a path that they become physical neural traits in your brain. Scientists say that our brains are always looking to make habits because they're always looking for ways to save effort.

But a habit cannot be eradicated; only replaced. You have to go back to the very beginning of the stimulus/response cycle and replace the current response with a different one.

How many times have you listed all the positive steps you're going to take, then not acted on them? That's because the longer you think about doing something, the less likely you are to do it. Negative thoughts will talk you out of it.

Don't make negative thinking a lifelong habit. Here are some tips for getting your brain and mind to work with you. Your actions will prompt more positive thinking too!

1. Start a Journal

Acknowledge negative thoughts, don't try to push them away. You want them resolved, not buried like seeds, ready to rear their ugly heads again. Every day, I record every negative or positive thought, where it happened, why it happened, and who it happened with. It helps me identify triggers and turn negative thoughts around next time.

2. Always Ask Yourself, "What Would I Say to a Friend?"

We tend to find it easier to be kinder to others than ourselves. There's a simple exercise developed to aid children in reframing cognitive distortions, teaching them to recognize "BLUE" thoughts – Blaming myself; Looking for the bad news; Unhappy guessing; and being Exaggeratedly negative.

It also works for adults. Turn those "BLUE" thoughts into true thoughts by imagining that your friend has this problem. You'd probably reassure them. What advice would you give?

3. Say "Stop"

Becoming aware of your Chimp and its patterns takes time. When you spot it, say "Stop," out loud, and tell the Chimp how to behave.

4. Change Negativity to Neutrality

It's a lot easier to turn down negativity than switch it off. Ask yourself, "Is this thought helping or hindering me in my journey to become my best self?" If it's hindering, be gentler with your language. For example, change, "This is impossible," to "Let's try a different approach." Interestingly, when you do this, your brain will come up with answers to your questions.

5. Create an SOS File of Positive Praise

I compile positive emails and comments from clients and friends, to dig out when I'm feeling insecure. Some days it's a lifesaver. I'm always pleasantly surprised at how quickly I bounce back.

6. Breathe

In the words of Mr Miyagi, "When you feel life is out of focus, always return to the basic of life. Breathing. No breath, no life." Every day, I use the 4-7-8 breathing technique that NAVY Seals use. You can do it throughout the day for maintenance, or as an SOS. It'll quickly get you into a calmer state, where you can be more rational.

7. Talk to Somebody

Whether it's a therapist, close friend, or colleague, with an understanding of the exact boat you are in. As long as it's someone supportive, who will identify the positives, and put any negative thoughts into perspective.

8. Follow a Healthy Lifestyle

I do three 10-minute workouts daily. Exercise positively affects mood and reduces stress. I'm also thankful that my dog Colin gets me outside. More oxygen to the brain improves concentration and memory. Exercise can also lower blood pressure and releases chemicals in the brain that help you feel happier and more relaxed.

9. Identify Areas to Change

Which areas of your life do you most often think negatively about? Perhaps it's work, a relationship, your downtime. Start by focusing on one small area and on how you can approach that in a more positive way.

10. Surround Yourself With Positive People

Negative people will likely increase your stress levels, make you doubt your abilities, and make it harder to manage negative thinking in healthy ways. Instead, seek supportive people who you can depend on to give grounded advice and feedback.

11. Practice Self-Compassion

It's taken me years, but it's never too late to begin. Tara Cousineau's 2017 book, The Kindness Cure points out that self-criticism just makes you feel stuck. But, she says, replacing disapproval and self-judgment with self-compassion allows you to accept in a gentle way that you are flawed – strengthening your mental wellness.

12. Practice Positive Self-Talk Out Loud

Use your name, not "I." Creating emotional distance in our self-talk can help to calm us down, see things more clearly, and think more rationally, according to University of Michigan psychologist Ethan Kross.

"Stop," Breathe and Be Kind to Yourself

A few weeks ago, I was so tired by the end of Friday that almost all my weekend plans quickly flew out the window. I saw a friend for breakfast the next day, but there was not a lot of anything else. By Sunday night, my brain was awash with negative thoughts, "I've wasted the whole weekend."

So, I told myself out loud to, "Stop." I practiced some 4-7-8 breathing and thought about what I'd say to my friend Sarah if she were in this position.

I could feel my heart rate slow back down to normal as I began to reframe negative thoughts into more caring ones, "It's OK, you needed the rest. Perhaps you worked a bit too hard? Let's think about how you can practice some more self-care." I felt calmer, lighter, and more clear-headed.

Positive Impact of Positive Change

It was a bit of a wake-up call. Now, I'm stricter about when my working days end, and I don't feel so burned out by the weekend.

I've stopped skipping lunches on busy days and started eating healthier food. I feel more creative and confident at work and have the energy to exercise daily and use my free time in a reinvigorating way.

Take it from me – and countless scientists and therapists – changing how you behave will help you to change how you feel. Changing your thoughts will physically alter your brain over time.

Realistic thinking will eventually become second nature, as your brain starts to view you and your talents fairly. Maintain positive actions, and you'll soon notice your confidence increase – along with your achievements and opportunities.

Which negative thoughts do you struggle with most? How have you been coping? What actions are you going to take today to turn negative thoughts into positive action, and create real change? Let us know your thoughts and experiences in the Comments section below.

Do you always remember criticisms and never compliments? Do you spend hours mulling over previous mistakes? You may be in the grip of negative thinking — but there is a way to escape the pattern.

For some people, happiness doesn't seem to last long before a return to less positive thoughts and feelings. But if your focus is more negative than you'd like, don't assume it's simply a bad habit — negative events tend to stay longer with everyone than happy ones. It's simply human nature to spend time working through the reasons why something went wrong, in order to learn for the future. So don't tell yourself you're paranoid, just realistic.

However, if negative thoughts are casting a shadow over your life, there are skills you can learn to stop them in their tracks.

To take control of negative thoughts:

Counter them. Remember a situation in which you felt assured and calm. Bring that feeling to the front of your mind.

Keep your perspective. Things are rarely as bad as they seem at first. Avoid jumping to conclusions.

Segregate the thoughts. Stay clear on each separate issue instead of letting them become a jumble.

Stay rational. Don't let panic get the better of you. Use the energy to find solutions.

Look for the positive. Often there's an opportunity to turn the situation around.

Understanding Negative Thinking

Scientists say there's a neurological reason for the cycle of negative thinking we all sometimes fall into. When the amygdala — the part of the brain believed to play a key role in emotions — becomes aroused, it remains in that state for a long time. At the same time, a memory of the situation becomes imprinted in the brain. The more emotional the situation, the stronger the memory will be.

Over time, specific memories become attached to certain emotions. For example, feeling nervous may bring back the memory of being fired from a job years ago, and the feeling is perpetuated. This can continue too long, known as "flooding," and every negative event you've experienced comes to mind suddenly and overwhelmingly.

The process probably evolved to help us survive and prepare us for the worst, as negative emotions ring alarm bells demanding attention and alerting us that something's wrong. Meanwhile, the body produces "fight or flight" hormones and we feel tense.

Negativity doesn't have to be all bad, however. Some psychologists believe that pessimism has its advantages. Those who expect the worst often are more resourceful because they are better prepared when things go wrong.

Feeling down can encourage us to be alone for a while, allowing insight and giving us the chance to gather our strength. Depression tends to make people more cautious and slow to act. It may become clear later that the feeling was a signal that the time wasn't right. Decisions and actions can be taken later on when we are feeling more confident.

How Negative Thinking Develops

Our upbringing may be at the core of a tendency to experience negative thoughts more frequently than others. Parenting styles vary widely. Some parents explain all the possible dangers of a situation in an attempt to keep their child safe. This may work, but as a side effect, the child can grow up with anxiety, expecting the worst in any situation and developing an overall negative view of the world.

Another factor is excessive criticism from parents, which can lead to the adoption of a negative mental framework. It may be that you've grown up with a long list of "shoulds" and "musts," so relaxation is difficult. When life becomes a series of chores it is hard to break out and adopt a new outlook.

Common negative thinking traps:

Shoulds and musts. Telling yourself not to do something actually makes it more likely that you will do it. The "command" voice belongs to your parents and teachers. Remember you are now in charge.

All-or-nothing thinking. One failure does not mean you will always fail, or that life's out to get you. Avoid overgeneralizing with words like "always" and "never."

Personalization. You may feel responsible, but take a step back and often you'll realize that you weren't the cause of the negative event. Think calmly about how the situation arose, sticking to the facts.

Moving Forward

Altering your outlook toward positive thinking can be life-changing but also takes some effort. However, the benefits are enormous — greater creativity, patience, calm and problem-solving skills. Your relationships are likely to improve too, because disputes will be resolved more easily if both parties feel there is a good chance of a solution and believe the outcome will be worthwhile.

Overthinking is not in itself a medical term, but research shows the habit can have real impacts on our well-being. Oftentimes, overthinking involves focusing on the negative — rehashing the past, dwelling on bad experiences or worrying about the future.

Ashley Carroll, a psychologist with Parkland Memorial Hospital, says when we ruminate on a certain thoughts, it can snowball into bigger, more extreme negative thinking. Carroll says overthinking becomes a problem when it starts to affect everyday life.

"When it becomes destructive to our life or really impairs our daily functioning, so for example, if you're having trouble sleeping at night because you can't turn these thoughts off, that's impacting your daily functioning," Carroll said. "If it's affecting your appetite, if you're so lost in your thoughts you're starting to isolate from other people..."

Carroll says ruminating on the worst possible scenarios and outcomes can be a misguided form of self-protection.

"For some people, it can be kind of like a defense mechanism," she said. "'So I'm going to automatically assume that everyone is unworthy to be trusted, so that way I won't get close to anyone, so I'm protecting myself.'"

Overthinking can also affect physical health, Carroll says. Some of her patients who deal with negative thoughts and anxiety have also experienced headaches, body aches and stomach problems, she said. Overthinking is also often associated with mental health issues like depression, anxiety, post-traumatic stress and borderline personality disorder.

To break the habit, Carroll says a good first step is to take note of what triggers your overthinking. It might stem from a past trauma, or something in your life that's currently a source of stress. Once you identify those triggers, Carroll says you can start finding ways to overcome them.

"Whenever patients kind of get in that cycle of ruminating, I always encourage controlled breathing exercises," she says. "It helps them shift their focus to their breathing and calming down their central nervous system. And then, [activities] like journaling really helps them express and process the thoughts that are in their head. So any type of mindfulness activities where you're really focused on present moment can keep you out of your thoughts about the past or about the future."

CHAPTER FIVE

Change your mindset, change your life

Change your mindset, change your life. It sounds so easy, yet many of us tell ourselves it's too late to change careers or that we don't have enough time to learn something new. Living with these limiting beliefs creates a self-fulfilling prophecy: we believe we can't, so we don't. If we instead lived in terms of "I can" and "I will", imagine what we could achieve!

I believe our thoughts have incredible power over our everyday lives, and that our moods and behaviors are a reflection of how we think. Over the years, I've developed 7 hacks to ensure I'm always in the right frame of mind to be successful and happy — and it starts with imagining possibilities instead of focusing on roadblocks.

Ask people to imagine the impossible and you'll be surprised what you can achieve.

Anyone can transform their mindset and learn to ask "Can You Imagine?" too. Here are the 7 mindsets of highly successful (and happy) people.

1. Ditch the Fixed Mindset and Go For Growth

Let's say you feel like you're not getting ahead at work. A fixed mindset says the situation is the way it is, and it will never change no matter what you do. A growth mindset says you can create change if you work hard, adapt to feedback and implement strategies for personal development. It goes without saying which type of people go further in their careers.

It comes down to the difference between limiting and empowering beliefs. If you believe your growth is confined to its current state indefinitely, you're unlikely to develop. But if you start to believe in your capacity to achieve greatness, you'll find that everything in your life will follow suit.

2. Adopt An Abundance Mentality, Not Scarcity Mentality

About 6 years into 1-800-GOT-JUNK?, my top employee resigned. This wouldn't have been the end of the world ... except he was leaving to start a competing junk removal business. At first, I was gutted — then, I wanted revenge. I became obsessed with shutting his business down, to the detriment of my own company.

Now I know that I was stuck in a scarcity mentality: I thought there was only enough success for one of us. I've since learned that this kind of thinking breeds a culture of paranoia where everyone lives in fear. Now, our company thrives on an abundance mentality: we believe that everyone benefits when we share ideas, even with the competition. By recognizing that there's more than enough success to go around, we've freed ourselves from limitations.

3. Stop Fearing Failure. Instead, Be Willing to Fail

The number one reason entrepreneurs don't succeed is because they're afraid to fail — that fear can even keep them from starting something in the first place.

The fact is, no one ever fell to the top of the mountain; you can't reach the peak unless you take the first step. We believe in the philosophy WTF (Willing to Fail) because the only way to grow is to make mistakes. Risk is scary, but stagnation is worse — and the more you believe you'll fail, the more likely it is that you will. Remember: if you're not progressing then you're failing anyway, so you're better off taking the chance.

4. Create a Long-Term Vision Instead of Only Short-Term Goals

You can't reach a destination if you don't know where you're going. Same goes if you're climbing the corporate ladder, switching jobs, or starting a new business. Before you can create a strategy and set your short-term goals, you first need to write a long-term vision of success.

I've always been more concerned with where our company is going than how we'll get there. I'm a visionary entrepreneur, so for me, it's not a matter of blindly putting one foot in front of the other — it's about shooting for the moon and working backwards to bring our vision safely back to earth. We call our vision our Painted Picture: a crystal-clear snapshot of how our business will look, feel and act every five years. It's a way of keeping everyone aligned and motivated to succeed as a team.

5. Don't Be Afraid to Break the Rules

Growing up, I was a bit of a rebel. But despite what my parents and teachers told me, this didn't hold me back. If anything, my affinity for troublemaking made me a better entrepreneur.

Risk-averse people who stay in their comfort zones rarely lead the pack. It's the people who move fast, break things and defy convention who change the world. Success is all about grit, guts and gumption — so if you want to progress your career, you better get comfortable colouring outside the lines.

6. Listen to Your Gut

We all overthink things every once in awhile and that's okay — but if you second guess every decision you make, you'll never get anything done. Over thinking also leads to rumination, the destructive and potentially career-ruining process of dwelling on the past.

After twenty-eight years in business, I've learned how important it is to make quick (and tough) decisions, and that to get ahead you need to avoid unproductive indecisiveness. Stop letting your lizard brain control your thoughts and actions — instead, take charge and start acting on instinct. In most cases, your intuition will steer you in the right direction.

7. Let Positivity Flow Into Everything You Do

If you're only going to change one thing about the way you think, this should be it. It's scientifically proven that optimists are happier and more successful than pessimists (provided they're realistic about goals and outcomes). As an eternal optimist, I always try to see the good in every situation. If we're falling short on some aspect of the business, I don't see it as impending doom — I know it's only a temporary obstacle we need to overcome.

The best part is that positivity breeds positivity; when you adopt a glass-half-full attitude, it will start to guide everything you do. The truth is success doesn't automatically bring happiness — but a positive frame of mind will invite success into your life. All it takes is a few simple tweaks to your thinking to become your happiest, most fulfilled self.

As a life planner, I've got more than a little interest in mindset.

Because mindset is what ultimately determines your attitude and approach to the myriad of challenges you'll face over your lifetime.

In your financial life, your money mindset has been carefully erected from early childhood. That's because we take in what we hear and see from our parents and create a belief system around money and what is "normal."

What we don't always get is that sometimes, our beliefs and our "normal" work completely against our values and best interests. But what you may not realize is that your mindset is absolutely changeable.

And the right mindset will change not only YOUR life, but can influence those around you.

So it was with great relish that I devoured "The Code Of The Extraordinary Mind" (Rodale 2016), that carries the idea of mindset to a whole new level.

Author Vishen Lakhiani (the founder of Mindvalley), states that our beliefs are constructed from our "Culturescape"—that our culture and living situation teach us that following “the rules” provides safety and acceptance.

But he argues that the only rules we SHOULD be accepting as truths are the absolutes: fire is hot, water is wet, we need air to breath. Beyond indisputable facts, the Culturescape’s bulls**t rules—or "Brules"—are EXACTLY what we need to question to become who we were meant to be.

A few Brules you may have heard along the way: you need to go to college to guarantee success; you must marry within your religion or ethnicity; you can only be successful by working hard 24/7.

If you’ve been drilled with these beliefs, they become your mindset and will limit the scope of your thinking and experience. Challenging these installed ideas can be frightening if you’ve not done it before—it can feel tantamount to challenging your parents and the authority figures in your society. It pushes hard against our universal need to belong and presses on our internal insecurities.

But if you can successfully push back and question these "Brules", there are a multitude of possibilities and growth opportunities just waiting for you to break free.

The "Code" is a how-to book that shows you how to examine your mindset, offering options and opportunities to alter your beliefs to lead you to a more fulfilling, meaningful and values-based life.

It shows you that you are not stuck being who you are, but that a better version is available if you’re willing to open your mind to the possibilities.

Think about the last time you made a significant change.

Chances are, it was sparked by something that was deeply unsatisfying.

Maybe you committed to get in shape and lose twenty pounds. Or you decided you were done living with debt collectors calling constantly. Perhaps you chucked working for a big company to start your own business.

You challenged your beliefs and created a new path to change—you worked into a better, more authentically satisfying version of you. You changed how you see yourself in relation to the world around you—you changed your mindset.

Those mindset alterations allowed you to make substantial changes in your life that brought you greater joy and meaning.

It's all in your mindset. It's the key to a better you, a better life and yes, a better world.

You see life through your own unique lens. This is your mindset – the assumptions and expectations you hold about yourself, your life and the situations around you. Research shows that mindsets play a significant role in determining life's outcomes. By understanding, adapting and shifting your mindset, you can improve your health, decrease your stress and become more resilient to life's challenges.

To learn more about mindsets and how to change them, BeWell spoke to Dr. Jacob Towery, adjunct clinical instructor in the department of psychiatry at Stanford University.

Mindsets help you to simplify.

Mindsets are a set of assumptions that help you distill complex worldviews into digestible information and then set expectations based on this input. For example, you may believe that becoming sick with cancer would be catastrophic or that going on a diet would be challenging and depriving. These belief systems help you set expectations, plan for the worst and guide decisions based on these assumptions.

While mindsets can be helpful for distilling information and managing expectations, they can also be maladaptive, lead to interpersonal problems and feelings of guilt, inadequacy, sadness and anxiety. Dr. Towery observes that it is common to hold onto mindsets that were adaptive at one point in life but have since become maladaptive. For example, it might have been helpful to believe that others cannot be trusted if you were betrayed at a young age, but this belief may lead to interpersonal issues at a later stage of life.

Dr. Towery assures, "the good news is mindsets are highly changeable, and if you are willing to learn the technology of changing your mindset and defeating your distorted thoughts, you can have significantly more happiness."

Having a fixed or growth mindset affects your worldview.

You may have heard of "fixed" and "growth" mindsets. These terms were coined by Stanford researcher and professor Carol Dweck, Ph.D. to describe belief systems about your ability to change, grow and develop over time. If you believe your qualities are essentially unchangeable or "fixed," you may be less open to mistakes because setbacks are seen as inherent, and impinging on future success. For example, if you have a fixed mindset and have trouble connecting with others at an event, you may see this as evidence that you will never be able to socially connect, leading to social anxiety and avoidance.

With a growth mindset, you know that you can change over time, and therefore you are more open to reflect, learn and grow from challenges. Because failure is less threatening, you are more willing to embrace life's challenges, take feedback as a learning opportunity and continue to learn and grow throughout life. With a growth mindset, you are also less likely to personalize setbacks. For example, in the scenario above, you might reflect that the cause of your social difficulty had more to do with the environment at the event than a personal inability to socialize.

With a fixed mindset, it can be hard to find motivation to work through perceived weaknesses, because the ability to change may seem as hopeless as changing your eye color. In contrast, with a growth mindset, you'll see your perceived weakness as a challenge that can be motivating — and even fun — to overcome.

As Dweck writes in "Mindset," "...as you begin to understand the fixed and growth mindsets, you will see exactly how one thing leads to another — how a belief that your qualities are carved in stone leads to a host of thoughts and actions, and how a belief that your qualities can be cultivated leads to a host of different thoughts and actions, taking you down an entirely different road."

Dr. Towery gives a personal example, "In my own life, I was dissatisfied with my singing abilities and decided to take singing lessons for nine months. While you won't be hearing me on the radio any time soon, my singing is remarkably less terrible than it used to be before the lessons." He describes that it was fun to learn that singing is a skill that can be cultivated rather than something innate and immutable.

Mindsets can impact your reality.

Mindsets can impact your outcomes by determining the way you think, feel and even physiologically respond to some situations. A 2007 study revealed that increased awareness of physical activity resulted in health benefits like weight loss and decreased blood pressure. To further investigate this phenomenon, a 2011 study was conducted to test physiological satiation in relationship to mindset around certain foods. The study revealed that participants' satiety aligned with their mindset around the food they were consuming more than the food's nutritional content.

Another example of how mindset affects physiology was shown in a 2012 study on the association between stress perception, health and mortality. Kelly McGonigal references the study in her 2013 TED talk, explaining that participants who experienced high levels of stress had an increased risk of death, but only if they believed stress to be harmful. Those who experienced high stress levels but did not see it as harmful were no more likely to die. McGonigal encourages developing more positive mindsets around stress, and to perceive your body's physiological responses to stress – like a pounding heart and racing mind – as your body's natural response to rise to the challenge and overcome it, as opposed to a signal that something is wrong.

Dr. Towery points out the impact of mindset on the effect of medications. "There is a powerful phenomenon in medicine known as the placebo effect, in which if someone believes they are going to derive benefits from taking a particular medication, they often do. In fact, regardless of the disease or condition, about 30-40% of people can have significant improvement in their symptoms even when taking a placebo (sugar) pill, if they believe that the pill is going to be helpful."

"Equally fascinating," Towery observes, "is the 'nocebo-effect,' a psychological response based on a person's expectations around side effects. When a physician emphasizes the potential side effects of a medicine, and the patient believes they will develop those symptoms, even if given a sugar pill, these patients can develop the adverse side effects, just based on what their mind expects."

Science is just beginning to validate the power of the mind-body relationship. Mindset matters, so it is important to pay attention to your belief systems—where they come from, how valid they are, and how they impact your quality of life.

You can change your mindset.

Although your mindset about topics like appearance and success are largely influenced by outside factors, the brain is neuroplastic, meaning neural networks can continue to grow, change and reorganize throughout the lifespan. By challenging yourself with new experiences and perspectives, you can form new neural connections — or mindsets — at any point in life.

Even a fixed mindset is not set in stone. You can change your mindset by learning and consciously choosing to believe that your characteristics are not predetermined and that you can continue to grow over time.

According to Towery, "The exciting news about mindsets is that they are absolutely changeable. The entire field of cognitive therapy is based on the idea that thoughts determine feelings and that you can learn powerful techniques to modify distorted thoughts and self-defeating beliefs. For those that want to learn how, I recommend reading the book "Feeling Great" by David Burns, MD and doing all of the writing sections. A competent cognitive therapist can also teach you how to change your mindset, even in a small number of sessions."

Dr. Towery says that the most rewarding part of his work is helping people transform distorted beliefs like "I'm a failure" to more realistic thoughts like "I didn't perform well, but I can better prepare next time and it will probably go much better."

Towery encourages questioning self-defeating thoughts and creating new narratives that are more self-serving. If you develop a growth mindset, setbacks can become learning opportunities and there is always another chance to improve and feel better.

Possibly more than any other single factor, your mindset determines your success.

What you think is what you become.

Internal dialogue--the ongoing conversation we all have with our mindset--is the driving force behind every success story, and also behind every failure.

The difference between who you are and who you want to be stems from your mindset. Once you start to change your mindset, you will immediately start to change your behavior.

Here are seven mindsets that will radically improve your business and your life.

1. Self-trust mindset.

To do anything great, you have to be able to trust yourself and believe in your capabilities. Success is not something that just happens but something you create. You have to have the confidence to banish any negative voices in your head. Don't give up on the things you believe in--and most important, don't give up on yourself.

2. Goal-setting mindset.

Knowing what you want and willing yourself to reach it are two different things. When you know your goals, they motivate you. Remember, if it doesn't challenge you, it won't change you. Set high goals and don't stop until you reach them.

3. Patient mindset.

There's a fine line between moving forward and standing still. The most successful people do all they can to move forward, but they also have the patience to wait and watch. Those who are impatient tend to lose out on great opportunities. Sometimes you have to wait for the right thing.

4. Courageous mindset.

Doing anything great requires courage, but fear always has a way of showing up. Courage does not mean being unafraid; having courage and showing courage means facing your fears, saying "I am scared and I am moving forward anyway." Courage is like a muscle you can strengthen with use.

5. Focused mindset.

One of the worst setbacks that can happen is losing focus and allowing procrastination to step in. Important as it is, it's difficult to be focused and disciplined. The best way is to stay in the here and now and to concentrate on everything going on in this particular moment. Distraction wastes time, and procrastination keeps you from moving forward. Discipline is the bridge between goals and accomplishment, and a mindset of focus builds that bridge.

6. Positive mindset.

Choosing to be positive and having a good attitude will determine a lot about your life. If you set your mind to positivity it can go a long way. Be positive, not passive. Instead of giving yourself reasons why you can't or shouldn't, give yourself reasons why you can and permission to go for it. Happiness doesn't come from circumstances but always from within.

7. Learning mindset.

Just because you are struggling, that doesn't mean you're not learning. Every failure has something to teach you, and everything you learn helps you grow. If you are unwilling to learn, no one can help you; if you are determined to learn, no one can stop you.

Every great success requires some kind of struggle, and good things really do come to those who work hard and struggle to pursue their goals and dreams they believe in. To radically change your life, you have to change yourself. Start building your new mindset today--think the thoughts that will help you move toward your goals right now.

CHAPTER SIX

Self-trust mindset.

Relations imply relata, and so interpersonal relationships require distinct persons, at least two, among whom they hold. One person, for example, might come to the aid of, befriend, joke with, deceive, bargain with, trust, take interest in or respect another person, or one person might have any of these relationships to several other persons who might or might not reciprocate. Similarly, interagential relations require distinct agents, at least two, among which they hold; for example, two chess programs might creatively play each other, or a human and Watson might compete at the game Jeopardy, or human passengers might trust (or distrust) their plane's automatic pilot, or a family might benefit from being driven somewhere by a self-driving smart-car or living in a smart-house that recognizes and serves each individual inhabitant. For interpersonal and interagential relations, it is generally the nature of the relation that is questioned; it is clear who or what the two or more required relata are. The same requirement exists for intrapersonal relations but in this case the relata, again at least two, are not as obvious as they are in the case of interpersonal or interagential relationships. Self-esteem, self-respect, self-acceptance, self-control, self-doubt, self-deception, self-confidence, self-trust, bargaining with oneself, being one's own worst enemy, and self-denial, for example, are thought to be deeply human possibilities, yet there is no clear agreement about who or what forms the terms between which these relations hold. Philosophers who work in the area of intrapersonal relations have devised two strategies for dividing one person into the required multiplicity such that these are (i) sufficiently diverse for these kinds of self-relations to hold, yet (ii) sufficiently unified to constitute one person – a single self. A problem, of course, is equally satisfying both conditions (but that's another story). One strategy, Humean in spirit if not by direct influence, is to conceive a person as an aggregate of interests, each a coherent assembly of epistemic and practical abilities and accomplishments; each rich enough to be considered a kind of "sub-self" having its projects, goals, duties and "life." Some of these interests conflict while others are mutually supportive; some function on a base-level while others function on higher-orders; some dominate others and some as it were "voluntarily step aside"; some tend to impulsiveness, some are timid; some take a longer while others a shorter view of issues the person confronts, some are critical of others and some are defensive. But there is no super-interest that 2 manages, coordinates, or referees all the others. This conception presents a person as more a set of systems each with a degree of independence, rather than a system of sub-systems. A person is left internally "messy," subject to inner struggles, self-defeating projects and failed attempts at selfmanagement, as well as subject to self-agreements, self-improvement and self-satisfaction. Intrapersonal relationships, on this model, are relations between and among such "parts" of the self. Self-doubt for example has this structure: one of a person's interests questions or rejects an accomplishment(s) of some other interest of that same person. Take someone, upon driving away from her house for a long vacation, who says to herself, "I remember locking the door, I know I did; but I'd better go back and check just to be doubly sure." Here, this person's epistemic interest (seeking assurance) doubts her practical interest's accomplishment (locking her doors as a responsible homeowner). It is self-doubt in so far as the relata are different interests within one and the same person. Donald Davidson, in several influential essays on problems of practical agency, works within this framework. 1 Trudy Govier, in her seminal essay on self-trust, likewise appears to accept such a model of the self.2 Jon Elster offers a vivid illustration: "I wish that I didn't wish that I didn't wish to eat cream cake. I wish to eat cream cake because I like it. I wish that I didn't like it, because, as a moderately vain person, I think it is more important to remain thin. But I wish I was less vain."3 Another illustration: suppose a long-time smoker decides for health reasons to quit smoking. Based on past efforts, he knows that he will have a craving to smoke for a long time after quitting and will end up giving in to the temptation. To manage this un-steadfast interest in quitting, he turns to snacking which does the trick – it overcomes the craving. But now he experiences weight gain that, in his case, has as serious health consequences as his smoking. To manage his weight, he starts an exercise routine; but this takes time, commitment, and dedication if it is going to work. And in the interest of health, his exercise can't lead to injuries, ... It is noteworthy that this concept of a person as a population of diverse interests, because of its formal similarity to the world of interpersonal relations, is able to draw on and apply to intrapersonal relations insights from the study of human interactions. A second strategy, Lockean in spirit if not by direct influence, divides a person into stages within a unit of time. A person is conceived as an aggregate, a composite, of temporally earlier and later selves, each a "snap-shot" of the whole person at a time or at a phase/stage of an epistemic or practical undertaking. Intrapersonal relations are understood as holding between and among earlier and later selves or temporal stages of a person during his or her undertaking. At each stage or "snap shot" a person is a complex assembly of epistemic and practical capacities, interests and accomplishments; stages or selves have access to each other, and each has the ability for reflection, that is: to see another stage of itself both from its vantage point in time, and to see itself from its other stage's point in time. For example, self-doubt might have the structure of a later self questioning or rejecting the accomplishment of an earlier self of the same person and that earlier self accepting its later self's judgment. The self-doubter who says to herself, "I remember locking the door, I know I did; but I'd better go back and check just to be doubly sure." is analyzed as a later self doubting her memory and her certainty of her earlier self's action of locking her door, and her earlier self agreeing with, not rejecting, this doubt. George Ainslie, Elster, and Thomas Schelling have worked out this model of an agent as a population of time-indexed selves who negotiate a variety of interactions and relationship with each other, in great detail in their different explorations of practical rationality, especially preference instability, self-binding 3 (precommittment), and self-management. 4 Edward Hinchman's analysis of self-trust and its failures insightfully employs this model.5 Each conception of a person or a self as a collection of interacting parts and powers has, of course, a long and varied philosophical history. And each strategy for dealing with intrapersonal relationships is open to (and has received) a variety of criticisms, each resting on several controversial metaphysical assumptions. Granting this, I find the second strategy less problematic and more manageable than the first for my topic and will use it as my framework for distinguishing between self-trust and selfconfidence. 6 In what follows, then, I will explore self-confidence and of self-trust, and suggest some distinctions between them, that use temporally earlier and later selves of the same person as relata for these two (easily confused) self-relations. It will help my efforts to be limited by two restrictions, one pragmatic and the other conceptual. First, to keep my topic manageable, I will focus on these two intrapersonal relations in the context of practical agency and neglect them in the epistemic context (to the degree that these two areas of human effort can be treated separately). Self-confidence and self-trust will here be examined as operating within a practical agent's abilities, rationality and actions, and not examined as operating within an agent's epistemic projects, goals or rationality. The territory of practical agency is vast and complex. A schematic is needed to locate where selfconfidence and self-trust enter the picture. The rational choice view of a practical agent – an ideal rational individual-decision maker who, in pursuit of a goal, calculates the expected utility of her options, each an act-state-outcome trio, and chooses the best option – leaves little room, as far as I can see, for self-trust or self-confidence; so I put this conception aside. For my purposes, then, let a practical agent be composed of the following five capabilities: 1) Cognitive – the ability to form and hold beliefs, including the ability not to believe (withhold belief) about what is or what is not the case; the ability to form and hold expectations, including the ability not to form or to cancel expectations, about what should or should not be the case or what ought or ought not happen. Expectations, then, are normative and are not just anticipations or predictions. I will assume that beliefs can be more or less strongly held, and that: to believe that something is not the case = to disbelieve that it is. 2) Emotive – the ability to desire or not desire that (positively) something be the case or happen, or (negatively) that something not be the case or happen. I take an agent's positive desire to have the power to make the object of desire appear subjectively valuable (that is: desirable) to the agent, and negative desire the power the make its object subjectively dis-valuable (undesirable) to the agent. Having no desire that something happen or that it not happen, then, is not the same as (negatively) desiring it not happen. 3) Volitional – the ability to form an intention, or withhold from doing so, to do or to refrain from doing something. Not intending to refrain from doing an action is not equivalent to intending to do it. I include here the ability to make a decision, and will assume that intentions are formed and decisions make with greater or lesser commitment and resolve. 4 4) Physical – the ability to act as well as the ability not to act (that is: to hold back and refrain from action) on an intention or on a desire. The "inability" to so act or refrain, then, is not in the sense that an agent physically can't, but in the sense in which the agent who says, "I can't" means "I can't get myself to do it" even though the agent is physically able to do so. 5) Rationality – the ability to bring reason and standards of reasonableness to bear on one's practical agency, to reflect critically on the exercise of and the products of one's practical abilities, and a practical agent's responsiveness to the norms and requirements of rationality with regard to principles of justification, coherence, consistency, and means-ends coordination. This capacity includes the failure of an agent to be rational: to be unreasonable, to have inconsistencies and to be irrational within an undertaking. This general profile of a practical agent, we see, makes no assumption one way or the other that a practical agent is a morally good person. The next step is to set out a general framework for a unit of practical agency. I will take a practical agent's undertaking to start at t1 with an emotive state and end at t3 with an action, and between the emotive state and the agent's action comes a volitional state at t2: (t1 emotive state ----------------> t2 volitional state ----------------> t3 agent's action). There are 64 possible combinations. For example: at t1 Jack desires to lose weight by exercising, at t2 Jack intends to exercise at t3, and at t3 Jack fails to exercises. Or: at t1 Jill desires not to go to the dentist at t3, at t2 Jill decides to go to the dentist at t3, and at t3 Jill goes to the dentist. Or: at t1 Jack wants to watch TV at t3, and at t2 Jack intends not to watch TV at t3, but at t3 Jack ends up watching TV. Or: at t1 Jill does not desire not to hurt her friend's feelings, at t2 she does not form an intention not to hurt her friend's feelings at t3, and at t3 Jill (says something that) hurts her friend's feelings. Or: at t1 Jack desires not to play video games at t3, at t2 Jack intends not to play video games at t3, at t3 Jack does not play video games. Only some of the possible combinations will be used to explore self-confidence and selftrust. Between an agent's desire stage at t1 and the agent's intention-forming stage at t2 of an undertaking, additional practical capabilities might, and typically do, operate: beliefs, expectations, other intentions, rationality or other desires. Likewise, between t2 and t3 stages of the above unit of practical agency, beliefs, desires, rationality or expectations might, and typically do, operate. This picture of a practical agent requires the assumption of constancy or stability of these capabilities and their contents. So, a t1 desire to do something is assumed to continue to operate when a t2 intention to do it is formed, and both still operate at t3 when the agent performs an action, thereby both discharging the earlier intention and satisfying the earlier desire. Within a unit of practical agency, then, we have a single agent distributed over – "spread-out" into –

a series of time-indexed "selves," each with the full capacity for practical agency; each "self" represents an event of composition – another layer built up or stage added on – in the agent's undertaking. In this model of a person self-confidence and self-trust are intrapersonal relations to the degree that they are analyzed as relations between and among one agent's earlier and later selves. 5 The second restriction is intended to avoid a conceptual (logical) problem of self-reference. If the scope is global, then both self-confidence and self-trust apply to themselves; an agent would be confident about her self-confidence, and be trusting about his self-trust. In the affirmative, such self-reference seems to be conceptually harmless even though practically it might be self-reinforcing to the point that it becomes too difficult for an agent to examine critically and skeptically his excessive self-confidence or to question and escape her excessive degree of self-trust (and why would you, if you are self-confident and self-trusting compounded up several higher orders?)7 However, if their opposites (as opposed to just their absence) are given the widest scope, self-non-confidence and self-distrust are unsustainable; they are self-undermining. If an agent lacks confidence in his lack of self-confidence, or if an agent distrusts her self-distrust, then the original (base-level) lack of self-confidence or self-distrust are weakened and undermined; they become conceptually as well as practically impossible for an agent to have. Yet it is obvious that agents do experience a lack of self-confidence and are self-distrusting. To block this problem, I will narrow the scope of self-confidence and self-trust to local domains of action and to specific practical capacities. An agent will be described as self-confident or not, self-nonconfident or not, about a given action or course of action that the agent performs or intends to perform, but not described as self-confident or not about everything within the agent's realm of possibility. Likewise, an agent will be described as self-trusting or not, self-distrusting or not, about certain of her abilities and projects, but will not be described as self-trusting or not tout-court. Give these two restrictions within the theory of a person as an aggregate of temporally relativized selves, I believe self-confidence operates between an agent's intention and action, and will be seen to run primarily from an earlier self to a later self with respect to an action and only derivatively from a later self back to an earlier self (see note 16). In contrast, I will argue that self-trust operates primarily between an agent's desire and intention-formation, even though self-trust carries through to an action. Also, self-trust, in contrast to self-confidence, will be seen to involve a core of abilities that continue from an earlier to a later self and as such are closely connected to the person's identity through time; a self-trusting practical agent is a specially constituted person, a self-confident agent isn't. As a final introductory remark, I note that the philosophical literature on self-trust – to the degree I'm aware of it – generally treats this intrapersonal relation as something good and self-distrust as a bad thing. I suspect the same about self-confidence and its lack, especially within the psychological literature, though I'm less familiar with the literature on this topic. 8 I believe this is one-sided; self-trust might be a good thing in some circumstances, but it can also exist in, and tend to strengthen the resolve of, the murderer, the terrorist, and the tyrant. In such cases, self-distrust is far better morally than selftrust. And I'm sure that a Hitler or a Stalin had accurate self-confidence, not just over self-confidence, in many of their horrible undertakings; too bad, we might wish, they didn't have much less of it, better none at all. In distinguishing between self-trust and self-confidence, I will try to separate for each form from content; it is only with respect to their content, I will argue, that we can judge self-trust and selfconfidence a morally good or bad relationship a person can have with him-or-herself. 6 2. The problem Why distinguish between self-trust and self-confidence? In every-day language these two are used interchangeably in many contexts, apparently without any harmful results. One might even argue that conceptually they must be close, for we often think of self-doubt as the equally opposite attitude to both self-confidence and self-trust. Also, it is difficult to separate them conceptually; examples of cases in which a person has one and not the other don't readily come to mind. Doesn't this indicate that they imply each other, even if they are not simply two ways of saying the same thing? Philosophers who work in the area of self-trust have argued powerfully and insightfully for the importance of this self-relation to a number of features and capabilities they consider central to our humanity. Govier, for example, argues that self-trust is a necessary condition for autonomy and self-respect, and a sufficient condition for selfesteem. 9 Keith Lehrer likewise argues that self-trust is foundational for both epistemic rationality and practical wisdom.10 Hinchman considers self-trust the basis of our exercise of practical reason.11 Given that these philosophers are correct that self-trust is something central to human agency, to the exercise of our autonomy, to our epistemic and practical sense of self, and perhaps to a person's overall sense of self-worth, it is essential that it not be confused with other intrapersonal relations; even if some are closely related to self-trust, they might not have the core importance that it is argued to have. Yet when following the arguments and analyses of these philosophers, one gets the feeling that they are sometimes referring to self-confidence not to self-trust, or are using “self-trust” and “self-confidence” interchangeably as if they were two expressions for the same thing. Here, for example, is Govier: Nor on the present account is self-trust to be valued absolutely. A person may in several different senses have too much self-trust. One may have more confidence in one’s own character and capacities than past experience and evidence would warrant, thus having “too much” self-trust in an epistemic sense. 12 Hinchman, for another example, considers two situations: in one is an agent who is not confident about her memory of an earlier action, and in the other the agent is not confident about an earlier decision; for Hinchman, if these cases of lack of confidence in an earlier self’s action or decision are reasonable, then the agent’s mistrust in her earlier self’s action and of her earlier self’s decision are reasonable. But, Hinchman argues, if the lack of confidence in her earlier self’s action or decision are unreasonable, the mistrust in each case is “pathological.”13 In these representative passages, I am not questioning the claims or the arguments being made; I only mean them to show that here we have insightful and influential work on self-trust – argued to be at the very core of practical agency – in which the target concept of self-trust is sometimes linked to, or interchanged with, or “blended” with that of self-confidence as if there were no problem in doing so, no argument needed. Contrary to this impression, I believe that self-trust and self-confidence can and should be distinguished; that even though they might have structural and dynamic similarities (making them subject to being confused) there are nevertheless important differences between them as to their role in and value for practical agency. 7 3. Self-confidence: a proposed analysis What exactly does an agent who lacks self-confidence lack self-confidence about (or in)? The answer “everything” has been ruled out as unsustainable, if not impossible. It must be something specific to the agent in question, not someone else, for it would then be a case of lack of confidence (in someone else) and not a case of lack of self-confidence. Let’s consider some typical examples. -- a business manager must make a presentation to his staff and his superiors, and worries he is not fully up on the topic and will do poorly -- a teenager plans to lie to her parents about her use of drugs; as she thinks up the perfect story, one she is sure her parents will accept, she starts to worry that she won't be able to pull off her elaborate deception in a convincing enough manner -- a competitor in an athletic contest has just witnessed a stunning performance, and starts to feel that when it's her turn she will do badly and won't "measure-up" -- a recent college graduate is about to be interviewed for a desired job, and is afraid he will make a poor impression -- a student in a communication class must make a class presentation, and experiences stage-fright at the thought of doing poorly in front of her classmates and her teacher -- an admirer wants to ask that attractive and popular person for a date, but loses nerve at the thought of being turned down -- a new driver plans to go on a long car trip, but feels too inexperienced and worries about highwayspeed driving on unfamiliar roads and gives up her plan -- an elderly person has been given a new computer and believes she'll be confused by this technology, and is afraid that she'll do something wrong and damage it. -- a homeowner has purchased an item of furniture that requires assembly; told the assembly would be easy, he now finds the instructions confusing and the task daunting and fears he will fail to put it together correctly It seems natural to describe these examples as in each case a lack of self-confidence, but it seems odd to call them instances of self-distrust or even failures of self-trust. Given that these count as typical cases of lack of self-confidence (or self-non-confidence), what is their common form? In each we have: (i) an agent who intends to, or has committed to, or is required to perform an action. Prior to forming the intention the agent might or might not have a desire to do the intended action; having a prior desire is, thus, not necessary and will be left out of my analysis. (ii) the agent believes that the action in question is "public" in the sense that there are social, perhaps official, norms/standards for judging how well or poorly the action is performed, that it is not solely up to the agent who is to do the action to determine how well or poorly or correctly 8 it is done, (iii) the agent desires to do well: that is, to have the action judged "successful," or "good," or "acceptable" or "correct" by the applicable norms, and (iva) the agent believes (for various reasons) he will fail (or will be judged to have failed) to perform as the agent desires, that is, well by the applicable norms. I take these four conditions to be the core of a lack of self-confidence, even though a variety of emotions and physical symptoms – worry, fear, stage-fright, nervousness, panic, loss of nerve, avoidance, sweat, stomach in knots – would typically accompany an agent's belief that she will "publically" fail to do well at something she desires to do well, and believes might be desired or expected by others who matter to the agent that she do well. (We will see below that self-distrust is not accompanied by such symptoms.) Given that conditions (i)-(iii) hold, self-confidence requires a change in condition (iva)to: (ivb) the agent believes (for various reasons) that s/he will perform the intended action as the agent desires to perform it; that is, to perform well and be judged a success by the applicable norms. There are two variables here: the strength of the agent's belief that s/he will do well, and how well the agent believes s/he will perform the intended action as judged by the applicable norms. Which do we consider self-confidence: an agent who weakly believes s/he will perform exceptionally well, or an agent who strongly believes s/he will perform minimally well? I think it is intuitively clear that the latter has more self-confidence than the former. Thus, the stronger an agent holds a belief that his intended action, if done, will be (judged) good, even if this belief is false, the more self-confident the agent will be. The crucial (iva) and (ivb) beliefs, I note, are self-predictions that need not be justified by evidence; self-confidence or its lack need not satisfy epistemic norms of justifications, much less truth, to operate within practical agency. So, on this analysis it is possible for an agent to be self-non-confident even when by her own reflection she finds that there is no (good) reason for her to be. I now examine more closely and argue for each of these four conditions on self-confidence. Condition (i) seems necessary; if an agent has no intention of doing anything, then it is hard to see how the agent could have (or lack) self-confidence about anything. And if an agent decides not to do a given action (A), and to do something else (B) instead, it is equally hard to see how the agent could have any confidence in herself doing A well (or doing A at all, for that matter). Thus, it follows that if an agent has self-confidence, then the agent intends to perform an action (even though the agent may change her mind at a later point and revoke her intention, perhaps out of a loss of self-confidence). Intending to do an action, of course, implies the belief that the action intended is physically possible for the intending agent to do; I will assume that the intending agent has formed this belief. The connection in this context between an agent's intention to perform an action and the action the agent ends up doing, assuming it is performed, isn't clear. For one, the action an agent intends to do must be in the agent's future, it can't in the agent's past, for it must be possible that the action an agent intends to do never gets done. (It will have to be seen in what sense an agent could have self- 9 confidence about a past action the agent performed. See note 16.) Thus, we have in condition (i) an agent who at one time intends or decides that at a future time this same agent will perform an action. I see no reason why the intended action must be completely voluntary (that is, internally motivated); the agent might conceivably be under some external obligation, duty, or even coercion to perform it (say, if the agent legally contracted to do it and will now be subject to legal coercion to perform as contracted). Another point to note is that the action an agent intends to do and the action the agent performs should match14 ; if not, the action couldn't carry out that earlier intention, though it might carry out some other earlier intention. In "matching," the earlier intention to do it becomes at the later time when it is performed, so to speak, the "identifying or guiding principle" or set of constraints that keeps the action being done identical (within bounds) to the action that was intended – if type, then to type; if token, then to token. If the action performed is to execute the earlier intention to perform it, then the intended action must be done as it was intended, if not also because it was intended (the "because" case, for example, might be an agent who does something merely because they intended to do it; say, merely to prove a point in answer to someone who doubts this agent's intentions are "for real"). Also, if this match or link didn't happen, the action performed couldn't serve as the measure by which the agent's earlier degree of self-confidence was too-much, too little, or accurate. Consider this case: suppose an agent (S) at t1 (i.e., the t2 point in the basic unit of agency in part I above) forms an intention to deliver a speech to an audience at t3 and is confident at t1 that her performance at t3 will be a huge success, and suppose that at t2 S has a mini-stroke that causes her completely to forget her t1 intention, and as it happens S ends up for an entirely different reason delivering a speech to an audience at t3 but it is not the speech S at t1 intended to deliver. What connection does this agent's t3 self, the one giving the speech, have to this agent's t1 confident self? These are an earlier and a later stage of the same agent, but there seems to be no connection, or at least not the right connection, between S's confidence at t1 in her future t3 self and S's performance at t3, because there is no longer the right match between the action that is intended at t1 and the action that is performed at t3. Even if at t3 S delivered the exact same speech word-for-word, to the same audience to which S intended to talk at t1 (say the mini-stroke destroys all short-term awareness S has of her t1 intention, but not her long-term memory of that speech given countless time to countless audiences); at t3 S's action would be the one intended at t1, but it could not be "identified" as such by the agent applying her earlier t1 intention, and so performed "under the guidance of" that intention. What connection, in this case, exists between S's t1 confidence in her t3 self and her t3 performance? Again, because the link between S's t1 intention and her t3 action has been disturbed, if not completely broken by the stroke, S's t3 performance can't retroactively confirm or falsify this agent's t1 level of confidence in her t3 self; the performance would be as if the earlier intention never existed – it would not be that action and the constancy requirement assumed above has been broken for her intention. Condition (ii) seems necessary; if an intended action is not subject to norms or standards of performance, then there is no way the action can fail; it couldn't fail even if it were not done, for there would be no norm even of completion. And if an intended action is not subject to norms, then it can't be judged or evaluated as to how well or poorly or correctly it is performed; it might comparatively be judged, say, to have been completed faster or slower than another action, but couldn't comparatively 10 be better or worse unless speed was normative. If an agent believes an action cannot succeed or fail and cannot be normatively evaluated, even if not done, then there is nothing about the action about which an agent who intends to do it could be confident or lack confidence. It follows that if an agent has selfconfidence, then the agent believes the intended action is subject to evaluation by norms of performance. The question that condition (ii) raises is: why must the norms or standards of performance be "public"? Why can't an agent's intention be (or contain) the only norms by which an action succeeds or fails to execute that intention, or be judged to have? Why condition self-confidence (or the lack of it) on anything beyond an agent's will or on anything outside an agent's control? The answer, I believe, has something to do with fear and the difficulty understanding self-fear. If there is nothing about performing an action that can make an agent worry or be concerned about, if an agent has "nothing to fear" in doing something, then it would seem that any standards of success and failure – any norms of performance – would have to be completely private, subjective, determined and controlled solely by that agent: that is to say, easily manipulated by the agent. Given that there is no such thing as fear without an agent-relative uncontrollable power or force of some kind, it follows that there can't be selffear without an inner force or power, some part of the self, the agent can't control. Now, an agent's intentions can't be such an uncontrollable power or force without making agency (at least rational agency) itself impossible. It would seem to follow, then, that self-confidence, as well as the lack of it, requires norms of performance that are in some sense "external" to the agent; that is, "public" in the sense of not completely determined or controlled by the self-confident agent. So, for instance, an agent answerable only to self-created and self-imposed norms of performance could, and would be foolish not to, simply change the norms to fit the performance, thereby making every intention successfully executed. Self-confidence and self-non-confidence become meaningless in this case; they would not be "felt" by the agent as "operating." Condition (iii) is necessary; if an agent did not desire to act in a way that satisfies the applicable norms of performance, if an agent who intends to perform an action doesn't care about and has no interest in its success or failure, then there is no basis or motive within the agent for worry or concern about failure, and no basis within the agent for performing according to the norms in question. Condition (iii) brings the norms of performance, as it were, into the agent's circle of interests, motivations, and goals. Thus, a self-confident agent is an agent who does not only believe that there is such a things as doing well in an intended action, and not only predicts that she will do well, she also wants to do well even if prior to forming the intention the agent does not desire (or desires not) to do the intended act. But an agent who wants to do well need not be a self-confident agent. Thus, condition (iii) is necessary for selfconfidence. Desire of course implies awareness of what is desired; if an agent who intends to do something desires that it be done well, the agent must "know" – have some idea of – what a successful doing in that case is, or believe that someone able to evaluate its success or failure knows what the standards are. That is to say, the agent must either be aware of the norms of performance in order to desire to act in a way that satisfies them, or believe that there are such norms of which someone is aware who will be able to evaluate the agent's performance. 11 Condition (ivb) is necessary for self-confidence; it seem impossible for an agent to intend to perform an action and at the same time believe s/he will never do (or try to do) the intended action. To believe the intended action will at some point be attempted, if not completed, by the agent seems part of what it means for an agent to intend to do an action. Thus, if an agent satisfies condition (i), then the agent believes s/he will at least try to do the action the agent intends to do. And, if an agent satisfies condition (iii), the agent desires to do that intended action well. But the content of the agent's desire [I am judged to do the action I intend to do well] and the content of the agent's belief [I will do the action I intend to do] can't generate self-confidence unless these contents match. Given that degrees of confidence attach to beliefs and not to desires, the agent's belief content must match the agent's desire content, not the other way around. Thus, it follows that if an agent has self-confidence, then the agent believes that s/he will do the intended action as s/he desires to do it – that is, judged a good or correct performance by the applicable norm (and this is condition (ivb)). Given that an agent satisfies conditions (i)-(iii), condition (iva) is necessary for lacking self-confidence. The argument parallels that for condition (ivb). In brief: the agent's basic belief content [I will perform the action I intend to perform] must conflict with – can't match with – the agent's desire content [I am judged to do the action I intend to do well]. The belief content, then, must be [I will fail to perform the action I intend to perform as I desire to perform it]. And the agent, we see, can't in this case change her lack of self-confidence into self-confidence simply by making her belief fit her desire, because the agent believes that the norms of performance by which her action will be judged are "out of her hands." By way of clarification, condition (iva) harbors a potential confusion. We would not accept an agent who says, "I intend to pay back the loan and I desire to pay back the loan, but I do not believe I will pay back the loan"; this doesn't make sense. But we would accept an agent who says, "I intend to pay back the loan and I desire to pay back the loan, but I believe I will not (be able to) pay back the loan." We wouldn't lend this honest agent money precisely because what the agent says makes sense. Thus, condition (iva) for a lack of self-confidence says: the agent believes s/he will not perform the intended action well and will do poorly by the applicable norms of performance. It does not say: the agent does not believe s/he will perform the intended action well, for a state of non-belief cannot provide a place for a lack of self-confidence (or, for that matter, self-confidence) to operate. We might ask at this point: doesn't condition (iva) clash with condition (i)? Why would an agent who lacks self-confidence ever even form an intention to perform an action in the first place? Doesn't lacking self-confidence operate prior to intending, and doesn't it block forming an intention to do something the agent would be self-non-confidence about doing? Clearly, this can't be the case. As argued here, self-non-confidence is not a belief an agent has about everything the agent might do, it is a belief an agent has about himself relative to a specific performance and its "public" evaluation. Often, the agent has no choice about the action at issue, it is something the agent is required to do by the agent's circumstances or it is something the agent has already made a commitment (perhaps legally binding) to do. Where this is not the case, the agent's self-non-confident belief must still be about something; minimally the agent must, prior to the operation of any lack of self-confidence, consider or present to himself the action at issue as something "I might intend to do." The agent in this case, as it were, imaginatively form the intention to do it in order to be able to discover if this is a performance about 12 which the agent would lack self-confidence. Without some such prior "intention," there couldn't be anything about which the agent would have a self-non-confidence belief. An added problem for an agent under condition (iva) is that in the case of lack of self-confidence the agent who can escape from acting will probably try to do so. An agent who lacks self-confidence, then, might believe that she will be more severely judged for lacking self-confidence, or for opting out, than for performing the action poorly. This creates a dilemma that the self-confident agent does not face. I note that both conditions (iva, b) do not require that the intended action is actually performed by the agent; self-confidence and its opposite are beliefs, by this analysis, not properties of actions. But in cases in which the intended action never gets done, the self-confidence (or its lack) does not operate counterfactually. By the above analysis, the person who never swims yet claims, "If I were to swim, I would be (judged) a very good swimmer." counts as a boastful agent, perhaps, or a bragger, but cannot count as a self-confident agent; likewise, the agent who never swims and claims: "If I were to swim, I would be (judged) a terrible swimmer." might be mistaken or might be correct in attributing this possibility to himself, but couldn't qualify as lacking self-confidence about swimming well. In contrast, we will see below that self-trust and self-distrust supports counterfactuals. How, then, do conditions (i)-(ivb) fit together to form an account of self-confidence? I have argued that each condition is separately necessary for self-confidence, that (i)-(iii) are each necessary for conditions (iva,b), and that (i)-(ii) are necessary for condition (iii). Schematically, we have the following analysis of self-confidence for agent (S) and action (A): S has self-confidence about A'ing iff: (i) S intends to A, (ii) S believes A'ing will be evaluated by "public" norms and expectations of performance, (iii) S desires to A in a way that satisfies its norms and expectations (ivb) S believes S will, in A'ing, satisfy S's desire. S has a lack of self-confidence (has self-non-confidence) iff S satisfies conditions (i)-(iii), and: (iva) S believes S will fail to satisfy S's desire (by doing A poorly or by opting out if possible). This analysis still leaves it unclear (at least to me) why an agent who meets all 4 conditions has selfconfidence as opposed to just confidence that others will judge his/her A'ing in a certain way, or confidence that A will be done well by an agent with whom s/he identifies. To see more clearly how this concept of self-confidence (I leave out self-non-confidence) might develop – be built up layer-by-layer in a unit of agency – as an intrapersonal relation, I apply the model of a person as a series of time-relative selves, each possessing the capacity for practical agency. For person (S), we have S's t1, t2, t3, ... tn selves. For any given tn self, higher number selves represent S's later selves and lower number selves represent S's earlier selves within a given unit of practical agency. Person S is, under this conception, a composite of selves developing over a given length of time within a unit of agency, unified by the access each self has as a practical agent to S's other selves and the influence each self has as a practical agent over the practical capabilities of S's other selves. For person (S) and action (A) the analysis above (with added commentary) becomes dynamic: 13 (i) S's t1 self forms the intention that S's t2 self perform action A. And, S's t2 self agrees to accept and to be bound by S's t1 self's intention that S's t2 self do A. (That is: at t1 S's intention serves as a directive, perhaps even a command or a "telling," to S's t2 self that commits or binds S's t2 self to doing A.15 And S's intention is consistent and coherent; when S intends to do A, S believes: that future agent, me, who is to do A consents to do that action and will not when the time comes for no good reason refuse to do it; and S believes this because S believes that the agent who forms the intention and the agent who carries it out by doing A are the same practical agent, S, who is not agential self-destructive or selfdefeating, inconsistent or incoherent.) (ii) S's t1 self believes that S's t2 self's A'ing is perceived by others, and that when or after S's t2 self performs A, they will evaluate – judge – S's t2 self's A'ing by norms and expectations of performance that neither S's t1 self nor S's t2 self can manipulate at will. 16 (iii) S's t1 self desires that S's t2 self performs A in a way that is evaluated positively and not judged negatively. (That is: in desiring that one's future actions meet the norms and expectations that are to be applied, S is "saying" that it matters to S that S's future performance will be perceived and be judged, and it is of value to S that it be judged a good or a correct performance.) (ivb) S's t1 self believes (with variable strength) that S's t2 self performs A as least as well as S's t1 self desires S's t2 self to perform A. (That is: this belief depends on the above three conditions being fulfilled, and it is this special belief that carries the confidence (of variable strength) in one's future self that makes it self-confidence. It is natural to think of self-confidence, in this model, as varying with the strength of S's t1 condition (ivb) belief: the stronger this belief, the more self-confident the agent.) The above analysis of self-confidence and lack of self-confidence has these beliefs operating in a unit of practical agency between the points of forming an intention to do an action (point t2 in the general structure of practical agency described in part I above) and the agent's attempt to perform the action (t3 in this general structure, assuming the intended action is attempted). I would like to note several features about this analysis. First, it is formal in the sense that S and A are variables: "S" ranges over practical agents as its values and "A" over actions that practical agents are able to perform. In its formal structure and dynamics, we see that self-confidence is morally neutral; neither a good nor a bad thing. As stipulated above, it allows well-intentioned as well as evil-intentioned persons to have self-confidence or to lack it. Any given instance of self-confidence or its lack, however, has content; who S is, what A'ing is, and what the practical context or situation is, are specified. Instances of self-confidence or its lack, in this case, are open to moral evaluation either by the agent himself or by any other interested party. So, for example, the terrorist's, the murderer's, the tyrant's self-confidence are, I will assume, morally reprehensible, and their lack of self-confidence a source of hope that these agents might back down. The surgeon's, the trial lawyer's, the student's self-confidence can be judged morally praiseworthy or not, and their lack of self-confidence perhaps a cause for worry. Being "open to moral evaluation," of course, does not mean that such instances are morally evaluated; there is no part or moment in the structure or the dynamics 14 of self-confidence or its lack (that I can see) that represents, necessitates, or motivates its moral evaluation. It might even be the case that strong self-confidence, and all-the-more over-self-confidence, makes moral reflection both more important and more difficult for the agent to undertake. Another point of interest is that according to this analysis, self-confidence is not essential to practical agency. It is a self-relation that depends on the capacity for intrapersonal relations, a capacity no doubt essential to our humanity, but it itself appears to be a contingent as opposed to an essential property of agency. The absence of self-confidence (as opposed to self-non-confidence) is clearly not destructive or essentially limiting to practical agency and its presence does not provide an essential link between an agent's intention and the agent's action that carries out that intention. It is possible that the pleasure and assurance that typically accompanies self-confidence, and the trouble, added weight and sense of insecurity of action that typically accompanies self-non-confidence, can help or hurt the agent in performing the intended action, but are not necessary to perform or fail to perform it well; it is easy to imagine the self-non-confident agent's being judged to have done well and the self-confident agent's being judged to have done poorly. And, it would seem, in much of meaningful human life the actions of rational practical agents are done successfully without self-confidence and without self-non-confidence; done perhaps out of habit, routine, automatically and with minimal conscious forethought. And on average we seem to get by. So then, where might the value of an agent's self-confidence or lack of it be found, if not within practical agency itself? Perhaps their value is more social than intrapersonal; to the degree that interagential (including interpersonal) relations require actions and interactions that are (a) governed by norms of performance and (b) performed well, there seems to be an important role for self-confidence, and its lack can be significant. I note, as a third point of interest, that this analysis allows for the possibility for both self-confidence and lack of self-confidence to become self-sustaining. Take an agent who lacks self-confidence and who performs A well. The fact that the norms of performance are in some sense "public" might go a long way toward overturning S's false negative prediction about how well she A's. S, perhaps after several such well-done A's, could gain increasing self-confidence about A'ing. But now, as typically happens, suppose that disturbing emotions accompany S's lack of self-confidence – S worries about A'ing, becomes nervous, or experiences anxiety, stage-fright or panic, becomes unfocused and easily distracted, and perhaps physically stressed – such that these states interfere with S's doing A well. The probability could well increase that S does A poorly for situations in which S has no choice about not A'ing, and that S fails to do A at all for situations in which the original intention to do A can be overridden by a later decision. And doing poorly would tend to confirm and perhaps even increase S's lack of self-confidence. Self-nonconfidence can become, as it were, a self-fulfilling prediction, a self-reinforcing self-relation, to the detriment of the person, as practical agent, who lives with it (but, I should add, may be a benefit to the agent's society for cases in which A is morally condemnable). The same self-sustaining loop is possible for self-confidence. The accompanying emotions typical of self-confidence – feeling secure, calm, focused, on-top of the situation and in control, feeling mentally sharp, perhaps being physically sharp – could tend to enhance S's performance and increase the probability of a favorable evaluation. This, in turn, would confirm and perhaps even increase S's self-confidence in the given domain of action (which, in the case of the terrorist, for example, is to be regretted, feared and condemned). 15 Finally, this analysis provides a way to understand the overly self-confident agent, the agent whose selfconfidence is too-little, and the difference between having too little self-confidence and having a lack of self-confidence (self-non-confidence). We see that too-much self-confidence is not a problem within condition (iii): the agent's desire to do well by the applicable norms of evaluation; rather it is a mismatch between conditions (ivb) – the agent's belief that the agent's future self will A in a way that satisfies condition (iii) – and how well the agent actually A's or the evaluation that future self receives for A'ing. Being overly self-confident is either to perform less well than the agent's former self believes the agent's future self will perform, or to believe more strongly that the agent's future self will A well than is warranted (say, it was a stroke of luck that S does A that well, not to be repeated). The greater this mismatch is, the more overly self-confident the agent. Under-self-confidence, then, is mismatch in the other direction: the agent's future self performs better, by the norms of performance the agent accepts, than the agent's earlier self believed his future self would perform. Under-self-confidence, on this understanding, is quite different from a lack of self-confidence. An agent who has self-non-confidence satisfies condition (iva); but an agent who has too little self-confidence satisfies condition (ivb), only in a way that mismatches her future self's performance evaluation. 4. Self-trust: a proposed analysis The concept of a practical agent as a set of time-indexed selves among which intrapersonal relations hold allows, as was mentioned above, insights, mechanisms and techniques from the world of interpersonal relations to be used in the area of self-relations. So, as people can bargain and negotiate with each other, we can bargain and negotiate with ourselves; as we have ways of justifying our beliefs or actions to others, we can use these to justify our beliefs or action to ourselves; and, as people have certain techniques and means by which they seek to manage or govern others, a person might be understood to use similar techniques and means in seeking self-management or self-government.17 Philosophers who have worked on the problem of trust as an interpersonal relation have used their insights, analyses and models to understand self-trust. Here, for example, is Govier: Usually we think of trust in interpersonal terms, as an attitude one person has toward another, or as an important aspect of a relationship between people. To show that self-trust is a kind of trust, I seek to explain central features of interpersonal trust and then show that these features are also present in an attitude toward oneself that can properly be called "self-trust."18 Hinchman, likewise, models self-trust on trust in others based on their analogy: It is revealing that self-trust runs the same risk of pathology as trust in others. In each case, I'll argue, reasonable trust presupposes trustworthiness in the trusted. But reasonable mistrust equally presupposes untrustworthiness in the mistrusted, or evidence thereof. That's why the exercise of practical reason is incompatible with baselessly failing to trust your earlier intention forming self. Yet earlier selves are not inherently more trustworthy than other people. If it is ever reasonable to act on the basis of self-trust, it must sometimes be reasonable to act on the basis of trust in others.19 16 I accept this methodology and in what follows try to apply certain features of interpersonal trust to the case of self-trust.20 However, there is an important feature in one's relation to oneself that isn't found, and cannot exist, in one's relationships to other people: a special kind of intimacy, degree of transparency and expectation. In the area of self-relations, it is hard to shake the "Cartesian insight." When all is said and done, one person can't "know" another person as well or as deeply or as closely as a person can "know" herself (even though in both cases there might well be more confusion than clarity, more ignorance than insight); one person's expectations about another person do not have the same kind of force as one's self-expectations, and thus the realization of frustrated or violated expectations in each case are not equally disturbing or disturbing in the same way; one person's rightful powers over another person are not as sweeping as one's rightful powers over one's self, and so self-resistance and self-rebellion and failures of self-control are not the same as interpersonal resistance and rebellion; a person for whom another is a problem is in a very different position than a person who is a problem to themselves; it is one thing to dislike or to be fed-up with or disgusted with or ashamed of someone else, but it a very different thing to dislike or to be fed-up with or disgusted with or ashamed of one's self. These vaguely stated truisms are meant to underscore the deep disanalogy between inter- and intrapersonal relations.21 Applying results from the study of trust in other agents to the study of selftrust, therefore, can only go so far. At some point, the exploration of self-trust must part ways with that of interagential trust if it is going to reveal the place trust has in a practical agent's relation to his-orherself. There are three points of disanalogy that I believe are important.

First, in interpersonal trust (but not in interagential trust, for example when human agents trust autonomous smart-machine agents such as the fully self-driving car), it is always possible for the one trusted to betray the trust placed in them. The betrayal of trust is a different type of trust-risk in trusting other persons from the risk that the trusted turns out to be untrustworthy and one's trust is disappointed; betrayal is a violation of trust, not just a let-down of trust. In contrast, self-betrayal does not seem possible; a self-trusting agent may be untrustworthy and let herself down, but the "Cartesian insight" does not seem to allow in self-trust for the opacity, lack of inner access, secrecy, and perhaps malice, between different persons that are required for betrayal. The impossibility, then, of self-betrayal in the case of self-trust and the possibility of betrayal in the case of trusting other (human) agents make these two kinds of trust significantly different. In this respect, self-trust is closer to interagential trust than it is to interpersonal trust. The second dissimilarity between intra- and interagential trust (including interpersonal trust) centers on control and autonomy. Trust in other persons and non-person agents implies that the trusted agent is autonomous, at least in the domain of activity in which s/he or it is trusted; if one agent completely controls the actions of another agent such that the latter has no autonomy (in the sense of the ability to weigh options and act on its own, without being controlled by other agents) there is no room for the one to trust the other to do an action or for the other to function as trustee. However, an agent can't have self-autonomy without making agency impossible; an agent (whether a human or a smartmachine) requires a degree of self-control or self-regulation, s/he or it can't be "beyond control" or "out of control" with respect to the scope of its own powers or s/he couldn't trust themselves – and it couldn't be trusted – to do anything. The impossibility of self-autonomy in the case of self-trust and the 17 necessity of trustee autonomy in the case of trusting other agents make for an important disanalogy between these two kinds of trust. The third significant disanalogy involves the kinds of thing interagential (including interpersonal) trust and intrapersonal trust are. I believe (and have argued: see Carr 2012) that trusting other agents, when it is rational to do so, are individual decisions based on justified beliefs. Trusting or distrusting another agent is a choice an agent makes, an act of good or bad judgment founded on beliefs about the other agent but not itself another belief. For example, when you enroll in a retirement fund that periodically re-balances you investment profile automatically as you age, you trust this autonomous e-agent to make financially responsible re-adjustments of your retirement savings within the bounds of financial risks that apply. You don't just believe this about the fund and the algorithms controlling it, for you can believe this without enrolling in the fund; the decision to enroll is a decision to trust. Justified trust in another agent is a good decision, and unjustified trust a bad decision. In contrast to this, in what category do we intuitively (the argument comes below) place self-trust? It seems wrong to say that you decide to trust or to distrust yourself; self-trust and self-distrust are more in the nature of beliefs you have about yourself then they are choices you make about yourself. When it comes to one's self, the interdependence between trusting yourself and belief in your own trustworthiness is more intimate than in the case of trusting other agents; the psychic space that separates them in interagential trust, making room for the needed decision, collapses in intrapersonal trust. Trusting one's self, when there is good reason to do so, is not evaluated as an "a good choice" based on belief, it is itself believing something about one's self (or an enduring self-attitude for ongoing self-trust). If this is correct, then – as a decision and a belief are importantly different – there is an important third disanalogy between interagential trust and self-trust. When an agent is self-distrusting, what is it about the agent that is distrusted? "Everything" has been ruled out as an unsustainable, if not conceptually impossible; and the target of distrust can't be something about someone else, for then the distrust wouldn't qualify as a self-relation. Consider the following examples: -- an elderly person explains his new hearing aid by saying, "I didn't want to admit it, but I could no longer trust my hearing, I reached the point where I was misunderstanding everyone." -- a student is taking a final exam on topics she feels weak in, and is sitting next to someone who has mastered the material; during the exam she thinks: I know I shouldn't peek, but I can't trust myself not to glance over at his exam to see what his answers are; I can't resist looking. -- a person who works around money has gotten into debt and thinks: I know I shouldn't, but it would be so easy that I can't trust myself not to take some of this money when no one is looking; I can't keep from taking some, I really need it. 18 -- a person who can't stand the sight of blood and feels faint in its presence is asked at a traffic accident to help stop an injured person's bleeding; he thinks: I want to help, but I can't trust myself not to get sick or maybe faint if I do; I just can't help it. -- late at night on a long drive home alone, a tired driver thinks: I want to make it home for a good night's sleep, but I don't trust myself to stay awake; I'm not able to fight my drowsiness. -- a suicide bomber, as the time of her act of martyrdom draws near, starts to feel she lacks the courage and conviction to go through with her mission, and secretly worries: can I trust myself to go through with this? These are examples for which self-distrust seems the right description; it would be odd and unnatural to describe them as instances of a lack of self-confidence. If we add in the typical and sensible mechanisms and strategies people use to cope with their self-distrust, many more examples come to mind:22 -- the late-sleeper doesn't trust himself to get out of bed for work in the morning and not be late again, so he moves the alarm clock away from the bed and makes it as loud as it will go -- the cigarette addicted mother doesn't trust herself to keep her promise to her children to stop smoking, so she flushes an expensive stock of cigarettes down the toilet -- the overweight man doesn't trust himself to keep to his exercise plan, so he joins a health club that charges a stiff fee for failing to show up for sessions in the program in which he enrolled. -- the suicide bomber doesn't trust himself to follow through with his mission, so he boosts his courage with another exposure to the propaganda of his cause and takes drugs as the time approaches. Such strategies, it seems to me, do not make up for a lack of self-confidence, and they don't provide the agent with self-confidence; they are better understood as ways for an agent to substitute external mechanisms for internal areas of self-distrust. Granted, then, that these are all acceptable examples of self-distrust, consider their common form. In each we see: (i) an agent who desires to perform or refrain from performing an action "A" (e.g. hear others, not copy answers, not take money, stay awake, not get sick, exercise, commit an act of terrorism, etc.); (ii) the agent believes that satisfying this desire (i.e. doing or refraining from doing the action) is in some way challenging, difficult or minimally not easy for the agent; the agent believes it requires the agent to be capable: to have an ability, skill, resolve or to make an effort, or to have a certain strength of ability, skill, effort or resolve, and that this capability is not just enabling with respect to A'ing or refraining from A'ing, it is also productive of A'ing or refraining from A'ing; (iii) the agent believes s/he should possess the requisite capability: the (strength of) ability, skill, effort or resolve to satisfy condition (i) desire; the agent values possessing this (strength of) ability, skill, effort or resolve and normatively expects it of him or herself; 19 (iva) the agent believes s/he does not possess the capability in question; the agent believes s/he is not sufficiently capable to meet his or her own expectations; as a result, (va) the agent does not form an intention to satisfy condition (i) desire, or intends not to satisfy it, or – if possible – turns to an external mechanism that substitutes for the missing capability so that condition (i) desire is satisfy "with assistance" (e.g. a hearing aid, a loud alarm clock, destroying opportunity to back out, threats of a fine, drugs, etc.) I will take these 5 conditions to capture the core form of self-distrust. The distrust, we see, comes primarily with conditions (iva), a consequence of which yields condition (va). To capture self-trust, then, we must change (iva) to: (ivb): the agent believes s/he possesses the capability: the (strength of) ability, skill, effort or resolve, and consequently change (va) to: (vb): the agent forms an intention to satisfy condition (i) desire, with no external assistance needed. I now argue for each of these 5 conditions and examine each more closely. Condition (i) is necessary; if an agent did not desire to do an action (A) or refrain from doing an action (not-A), then there would be no internal reason (no motive internal to the agent) to consider whether or not the agent was up to the task of A'ing or not-A'ing (though there might be a theoretical reason). 23 But self-trust and self-distrust, by analogy with trusting and distrusting other human or non-human agents, intuitively involve accessing an agent's ability to A or to not-A; an agent not able to A can't be trusted to A. Thus, if an agent is self-trusting (or self-distrusting), then the agent desires to perform or refrain from performing an action. Why, it may be asked, say that the agent desires to A or desires to refrain from A'ing? Why not state condition (i) as the agent intending or deciding to A or refrain from A'ing? One reason is the logical coherence of the 5 conditions: unlike desire, intending or deciding to A implies belief in the ability to A; this conflicts with condition (iva) for the case of self-distrust, and duplicates condition (vb) for the case of self-trust; the set of 5 conditions wouldn't be coherent. The other reason is phenomenological: self-trust and self-distrust seem to be experienced as based on a belief about the ability or lack of ability to do something an agent wants to do – and would like to be able to do – rather than on what an agent might intend or decide to do without any accompanying desire to do it, or perhaps with a desire not to do it.24 Condition (ii) is necessary; we would have to believe that "desiring = its own satisfaction" – to believe that "to want is to get" – in order to consider condition (ii) unnecessary. Clearly, this is only the case for a human agent who desires to desire: the desire is automatically self-satisfied and the issue of trust or distrust doesn't arise. Otherwise, this seems true: if (a) an agent who desires to A is the agent who satisfies that desire by doing A, then (b) that agent must possess any ability, skill, resolve or strength of effort necessary to do A or refrain from A'ing and at least one that is sufficient to do A or refrain from A'ing. Now if an agent satisfies condition (i), then the agent satisfies the antecedent (a) of this conditional; we have an agent who desires that s/he, not someone else, satisfy her desire by doing A or by refraining from A'ing. It follows this agent satisfies the consequent (b); that agent must have the 20 capability to A or refrain from A'ing. But why would this agent make this into a belief? What would internally motivate forming such a belief? If, for example, A'ing or refraining from A'ing takes courage or alertness or perseverance, then why would an agent who desired to A or refrain from A'ing form the belief that s/he must possess that courage or alertness, or perseverance? Why would such a belief be formed by the same agent who satisfies condition (i)? The reason, I believe, is that the agent considers A'ing or refraining from A'ing in some sense challenging or difficult for the agent. Self-trust and selfdistrust wouldn't operate in a unit of practical agency that an agent found easy to do or refrain from doing, something the agent ordinarily does. Any agent who believes a task would be difficult for that agent to do, and who also desires to do it, would also form the above consequent (b) as a belief; and this is an agent who satisfies condition (ii). Thus, condition (ii) is necessary for self-trust and for self-distrust. Condition (iii) is necessary; by condition (iii) a self-trusting and a self-distrusting agent evaluates him-orherself with respect to a capability; namely, the capacity the agent believes (by condition (ii)) is required to A or to refrain from A'ing. Importantly, the agent does not evaluate his or her present or future behavior; it is a judgment about capability, not performance. 25 If the agent did not believe that the (strength of) ability, skill, effort or resolve (hereafter shortened to "ability" or "capability") needed to satisfy the condition (i) desire should be part of his-or-her powers of practical agency, it would be difficult to see how the condition (i) desire could be anything more than an empty wish. All the more: if the agent believed that the required ability should not be part of her powers of practical agency, this belief would clash with and undermine practical agency by rendering the condition (i) desire moot. We would not readily accept an agent who says, "I desire to do A, and believe x ability is needed to do A, and I believe I should not have this ability." This makes no sense, unless we could charitably interpret this agent as desiring to do something he wishes he not be able to do, perhaps an agent trying to keep himself from doing a (believed) wrong he uncontrollably desires to do.26 Thus, it follows that if an agent is either self-trusting or self-distrusting, then the agent believes s/he should be capable of satisfying his or her condition (i) desire. We can see two dimensions in this self-evaluation: one concerns the ability the agent believes is required and productive to satisfy condition (i) desire and the other concerns the agent's normative selfexpectation with respect to possessing this ability. With regard to the first, the agent clearly values the capability, and believes it is something good. In the context of practical agency, this value is minimally instrumental (whatever additional value the ability might have for the agent) and subjective; the capability in question, then, is good in the agent's eyes as a means to do or refrain from doing A – that is: valuable as a means to satisfy the desire of condition (i).27 With regard to the second, an agent who believes that she should have a given capability to do or refrain from doing an action imposes or applies a normative expectation on herself as a practical agent. She, as it were, holds herself up to a certain standard of practical agency with regard to doing or refraining from doing the action. The agent judges herself, we might say, from the vantage point of an ideal that she holds, and this ideal is normative for this agent to the degree that she applies it to herself; that is, the agent agrees with this ideal's "command" that she ought to be the kind of practical agent who has that ability.28 By what right or on what grounds, we might ask, does the self-trusting or the self-distrusting agent impose such a normative self-expectation? What if the self-expectation is unrealistic? Clearly, 21 desires alone can't justify self-expectations. Just because an agent desires, say, to run a marathon does not justify this agent expecting he should have the ability to do so. The answer, I believe, is that the basis for a normative self-expectation lies in the agent's autonomy and is constrained by the agent's practical rationality. A reasonable practical agent will have realistic self-expectations; unrealistic selfexpectations, in turn, indicate an "imperfectly rational" practical agent. 29 An autonomous practical agent will, by definition we might say, have the right to self-govern. A non-self-governing agent can't be an autonomous agent. Thus, if an agent is self-trusting or self-distrusting, then the agent satisfies condition (iii); and any agent who satisfies condition (iii) is – or at least takes him-or-herself to be – with respect to the capability required to satisfy condition (i) desire, a sufficiently autonomous and reasonable practical agent. Condition (iva) is necessary for self-distrust; this condition says that the agent finds an inner weakness in his practical agency, a sort of psychic incapacity or "moral" disability. This is not an inability to perform an action due to "external" causes; the agent sees himself deficient in something the agent reasonably expects he should possess, something obligatory by his own standards. A practical agent who believes that he is not in fact capable in a way that he believes a practical agent in his situation ought to be, (1) can't – and shouldn't – trust himself to be a practical agent who can exercise that ability, and (2) must distrust himself to act on the basis of that capability. This agent, in other words, believes – i.e., judges or evaluates – himself to be untrustworthy in a domain of activity. This belief is special in two important ways. First, it is general: an agent who satisfies conditions (i)-(iva) must consider himself not worthy of anyone's trust when it comes to exercising a capability he believes he does not possess (strongly enough). Second, it is counterfactual: an agent who is self-distrusting in this way believes that he would be equally untrustworthy in every similar unit of practical agency were they to arise (but in fact don't), for he believes he still can't trust himself to do what he desires to do even when – because of his selfdistrust –he intends not to do it and in fact doesn't do it; self-distrust lasts through an action that doesn't get performed, it does not cease with a decision not to A or not to refrain from A'ing. Thus, a self-distrusting agent is one who believes himself untrustworthy in a given domain of exercising an ability and associated range of possible action. An agent, then, who is self-distrusting clearly satisfies condition (iva), but an agent who satisfies condition (iva) need not be a self-distrusting agent, for this agent might not satisfy any of the other conditions on self-distrust. Thus, condition (iva) is necessary for self-distrust. Why would an agent who satisfied conditions (i)-(iii) also satisfy (iva)? Why wouldn't such an agent just refuse to form or accept a belief about such a perceived inner deficiency? This is of course a possibility, but I believe unlikely. For one, it is doubtful that will or decision or even desire governs belief; doubtful, that is, that practical reason can dominate epistemic reason "at will." But I grant that this is controversial. However, given that the agent is (or takes herself to be) rational (see condition (iii)), the agent will have evidence that s/he is deficient in the ability in question. If we return to the representative examples at the beginning of this section on self-trust – the elderly man, the student, the sleepy driver, the late-sleeper, the overweight person, etc. – we see that they are practical agents whose beliefs in their own lack of ability or lack of inner strength are typically epistemically justified by a degree of self-knowledge based on, say, a history of experiences in which the incapacity or lack of inner 22 strength were made manifest. In this case, self-distrust is justified by the agent's accurate belief in her own untrustworthiness. Refusing to believe in one's inner weakness given such evidence would make for a very unusual, confused and troubled practical agent, and if this agent were to intentionally (falsely) presents himself to others as not internally "disabled" in this way, he thereby acknowledges his belief that he is agentially deficient. A bigger problem, I believe, is that this self-belief might be inaccurate, it might "miss the mark" and an agent could distrust herself to a lesser degree (or possibly greater degree) than she is untrustworthy. I take this to be self-mistrust: the possibility of being overly self-distrusting or too-little self-distrusting; the agent's degree of self-distrust does not match the evidence the agent has of her untrustworthiness; equivalently, the agent is more or less untrustworthy than she distrusts herself to be with respect to the capability at issue. So, for example, an agent who believes he lacks the strength to stay awake when driving at night – who believes he won't be able to fight off his sleepiness – and who believes he ought as a practical agent, undertaking a night-driving task, have the ability to keep awake and successfully fight off such drowsiness, considers himself untrustworthy to continue driving and arriving home, which is what he desires. But this agent might get it wrong; he might be able to stay awake with strength of effort he does not realize he has, based on a history of too-quickly giving in to his sleepiness. This agent is self-mistrusting in the sense that his self-distrust is excessive; he is somewhat less untrustworthy than he believes himself to be with respect to the ability to stay awake on his late night drive home. (But, we recognize, this might be a fortunate case of being wrong in a good way, erring on the side of caution, a case of inaccurate self-distrust that qualifies as "better safe than sorry.") Condition (ivb) is necessary for self-trust; condition (ivb) stands to self-trust as condition (iva) stands to self-distrust. (ivb) says in effect that the agent believes herself sufficiently capable in an agential quality that the agent believes she ought (as a practical agent in that given task) to possess. A practical agent who believes that she does in fact possess the ability she believes a practical agent in her situation ought to possess, (1) can – and should – trust herself to be a practical agent who can exercise that capability, and (2) can and should trust herself to act according to that capability (given that the agent also believe that circumstances have not changed so as to create unanticipated problems). This agent, then, believes – judges or evaluates – herself to be trustworthy.

We can see that this belief is both general and counterfactual. An agent who satisfies conditions (i)-(ivb) must consider herself worthy of anyone's trust when it comes to exercising that ability she believes she possesses, and is self-trusting in the range of possible action that would depend on that capability were any to be desired and intended. It follows that a self-trusting agent is one who believes herself trustworthy in a given domain of exercising an ability and range of associated possible action. A self-trusting agent, then, satisfies condition (ivb); but an agent who satisfies condition (ivb) need not be a self-trusting agent, for example if this agent did not satisfy any of the other conditions on self-trust. Thus, condition (ivb) is necessary for self-trust Because self-trust is typically taken to be a positive part of practical agency (by the agent herself as well as others who might benefit from her actions), there is not the worry that arose in the case of selfdistrust that a practical agent might not want to admit she is self-trusting, and resist this belief; there is instead the opposite worry: a practical agent might be disposed to holding a false belief that she is trustworthy in the exercise of an ability when she isn't. Thus, there is the rational requirement that the 23 agent justifies her self-trust and critically reflects on its accuracy; that is, it should be supported by evidence that the agent is trustworthy, and such evidence would presumably come from the agent's self-knowledge based on a history of experience exercising the ability at issue. As with self-distrust, selftrust might "miss the mark." It is possible for an agent to be self-mistrusting, that is: overly self-trusting or too-little self-trusting, because there is the possibility that the degree of self-trust does not match the agent's degree of trustworthiness with respect to exercising that ability. The chain-smoking mother, for example, who doesn't destroy her stock of cigarettes because she (overly) trusts herself to keep her promise to her children to quit, perhaps believing that her love for them and her promise to them are much stronger than her smoking habit (and in her experience have always proved to be much stronger than most things in her life), may regret she didn't destroyed them when her resolve approaches the breaking point in its clash with her addiction, and her children discover her sucking on an unlit cigarette. Given that conditions (i)-(iva) have been satisfied, the agent is self-distrusting; a reasonable consequence is condition (va). Similarly, given that conditions (i)-(ivb) are satisfied, the agent is self-trusting and condition (vb) would result. It is reasonable to conclude that a self-distrusting reasonable agent will form the intention not to exercise a capability she believes herself untrustworthy to exercise. Thus, the sleepy driver does not continue driving but pulls over for a rest; the elderly person whose hearing is going gets a hearing aid and does not continue to struggle making out what folks are saying. Likewise, the selftrusting reasonable agent will form the intention to satisfy her condition (i) desire by A'ing or refraining from A'ing, but of course might fail to do so for various external or internal reasons. Of the above 5 conditions on self-trust, then (i), (ii), (iii), and (ivb) have been argued to be necessary for self-trust and (vb) argued to be the result. And for self-distrust: (i)-(iva) are each necessary conditions and (va) would result, or so I've argued. In sum, where "S" ranges over practical agents, "A" ranges over actions, and "X" ranges over an agential capability (an ability or strength of ability, skill or strength of skill, effort or strength of effort, resolve or strength of commitment) S is self-trusting with respect to X and A iff: (i) S desires to A or to refrain from A'ing, (ii) S believes that A'ing or refraining from A'ing requires X, (iii) S normatively expects, as a reasonable autonomous practical agent, that S should possess X, (ivb) S believes that S does possess X (and as such is trustworthy with regard to A'ing or refraining from A'ing); consequently, (vb) S forms an intention or makes a decision to A or to refrain from A'ing. S is self-distrusting with respect to X and action A iff S satisfies conditions (i)-(iii) and: (iva) S believes that S does not possess X (and as such is untrustworthy); consequently, (va) S does not form an intention to A or refrain from A'ing, and might form an intention not to A or not refrain from A'ing, or might when possible intend to substitute "external" assistance for S's inability/incapacity. 24 Given that these 5 conditions get at the structural core of self-trust, I would like to turn to the dynamics of self-trust as an intrapersonal relation. How does self-trust get built up, what are its layers, and function in a practical agent's temporally forward and backward coordination of its multiple time indexed selves, and function to unify these selves such as to form a relationship one has with one's self? Using the above analysis as a base and adding comments, I offer the following: for practical agent (S), agential capability (X), and action (A), at times t1, t2, t3,..., tn, S is self-trusting with regard to X and to A'ing or refraining from A'ing iff: (i) S's t1 self desires to A or to refrain from A'ing, such that S's t1 self desires that S's t3 self desires to A or to refrain from A'ing, and S's t1 self desires that S's t3 self, not anyone else, satisfy S's t1 self's and S's t3 self's desire by A'ing or by refraining from A'ing at t3. (That is: it is not simply that S desires to do something, it is that S desires that S satisfies S's desire, not some other practical agent, and that S's later self still desires what its former self desires. The late sleeper, for example, who desires at night to get up in the morning in time for work, desires at night that (a) in the morning it is she, not someone else, who gets herself up in time for work, and that (b) in the morning she still desires to get up in time for work and not that in the morning she no longer desires to and instead desires that it is her partner, not she, who wants her to get up in time for work (even if this is true). Condition (i) establishes a practical agent's desire that forms the base for self-trust and that has stability over the unit of time during which practical agency is exercised.) (ii) S's t1 self believes that S's t3 self must have X for S's t3 self to satisfy S's t1 self's desire, and S's t3 self accepts this belief. (That is: S's later self who attempts to A or to refrain from A'ing does not reject as false S's earlier belief that S's later self requires capability X in order to A or refrain from A'ing, but shares that belief. There is constancy to the agent's belief about X from its earlier to its later self and back.) (iii) S's t1 self normatively expects that, as a practical agent, S's t3 self have X, and S's t3 self believes that S's t1 self is both reasonable and autonomous in normatively expecting this of S's t3 self. (That is: S's earlier self expects that S's later self ought to be capable or ought to be sufficiently disposed, as a functioning practical agent of a certain kind, to A or to refrain from A'ing; and S's later self believes that its earlier self has every right – is completely justified – in imposing on and obligating it with this expectation; from the viewpoint of S's later self, S's earlier self is within its rights to tell it how things should be with it.) (ivb) S's t1 self believes that S's t3 self in fact possess X and thus meets its expectations, and S's t3 self believes that S's t1 belief is correct. (That is: S's earlier self believes with good reason that S's later self is (sufficiently) trustworthy with respect to A'ing or refraining from A'ing, and so trusts S's later self to do so. And S's later self believes with good reason that its earlier self is (sufficiently) trustworthy with respect to the normative expectation it places on it and with which it binds it, and so trusts its earlier self in having done so.) Given these conditions, (vb) S's t2 self commits or enlists S's t3 self to do or refrain from doing A by forming the intention that S's t3 self do or refrain from doing A, and S's t3 self by accepting this commitment attempts to A or refrain 25 from A'ing within the constraints and guidance of S's t2 self's intention. (That is: an earlier and a later self of the same agent, in holding reciprocal justified beliefs in each other's trustworthiness on the matter of A'ing (though not with respect to the same thing), have a relation of mutual trust holding between them. As stages of the same practical agent's undertaking, this qualifies as self-trust. From the earlier to the later self, it is trusting the agent's ability and determination – i.e., capability – to A or to refrain from A'ing; from the later back to the earlier self, it is trusting the agent's intension that it satisfy a desire. It is as if in forming the intention one says to the other, "Don't worry, you are in good hands, I will not get you into trouble." and the other says back to the one, "And don't you worry, you are in good hands, I will not let you down." except that it is one person "talking" to himself, so it means: "I trust myself, and I am trustworthy, on the matter of A'ing or refraining from A'ing." This t2 intention, then, is founded on the agent's self-trust) Self-distrust and degrees of self-mistrust can likewise be understood as dynamic intrapersonal relations by putting conditions (i)-(v) into this same framework: that of a practical agent as a composite of coordinated time-indexed selves, interrelated by their access to, their ability to see themselves from the other's perspective, and their effect on each other's capabilities for practical agency. However, I leave this step undone and, before moving to a discussion of some distinctions and relations between selftrust and self-confidence, turn to the following noteworthy points about self-trust. 1) Self-trust, on this analysis, is at the center of the exercise of a certain important form of practical agency, but is not essential to all forms of practical agency. It seems possible for an agent to act with no prior desire or even intention to so act, and by "automatically" and "thoughtlessly" acting produce a result such that this qualifies as a unit of agency (perhaps the agent can in some sense even be held legally responsible for that result) – no self-trust operating or needed. However, given that prior to acting there is desire, belief, and intention, which form the typical unit of practical agency, self-trust has been argued here to play an essential part of successful agency. 2) On the level of form, self-trust as integral to practical agency is not inherently morally good or bad, as practical agency itself is formally neither necessarily morally good nor bad. The moral dimension, we see, enters with content, but not with formal structure and dynamics. Once we specify what A'ing or refraining from A'ing are, what exactly the agent desires and intends, what the context of a given instance of agency is, and perhaps who the agent is, it becomes possible to evaluate any instance of selftrust, self-distrust or self-mistrust from a moral point of view. So, for example, we (and perhaps the agent himself) would judge it morally good for someone who tends to weaken at the sight of blood to distrust himself to stop the bleeding of a seriously injured party; his weakness could result in the injured party bleeding to death, so he shouldn't even form the intention to stop the bleeding much less try to do so, even though he might strongly desire to do so. The terrorist's self-trust might help make her an efficient killing instrument, but (we assume) this is not a morally good thing even if it's for a good cause. 30 I note that the rationality requirements in self-trust for belief justification and reasonable expectations certainly allow for, but they do not themselves represent, moments of moral reflection on the agent's part. 26 3) Self-trust, as presented here, parallels a special case of interpersonal trust: 2 trustworthy people trusting each other to A or to refrain from A'ing. In game theory, this is the standard 2-person outcomedominant Nash-equilibrium in the stag-hunt; if agents trust each other, they decide to cooperate or to continue to cooperate in the iterated stag-hunt. Self-distrust tracks the parallel case: 2 untrustworthy agents distrusting each other to A or to not-A. This is the risk-dominant Nash-equilibrium in the staghunt and the maximin rational choice; if agents distrust each other, it is rational to defect. These gametheoretic models can help the analysis of intrapersonal trust and distrust because of the partial analogy between intra- and interpersonal trust. Such areas of analogy, however, are generated by the metaphysical theory of the self or person as an aggregate or composite of time-distributed sub-selves, the accumulation of stages of an event. The assistance, then, is purchased at the cost of opening the above analysis to all the philosophical controversy and criticism to which this theory of the self is open, especially those concerning personal unity and identity through time. 4) Self-trust and self-distrust, by condition (iii), are seen to depend on the agent's autonomy and rationality. If a later self couldn't believe that its earlier self was both autonomous and reasonable in placing it under a normative expectation, it surely couldn't trust that earlier self and that earlier self would not be trustworthy in its eyes. Govier (1993, p. 111), however, argues that the relation between self-trust and (procedural) autonomy is the reverse; she argues that an agent's autonomy depends on self-trust. I believe Govier is too quick here; an agent's autonomy is not the same as an agent acting with autonomy, just as deciding is not the same as acting on one's decision. Self-trust might well be necessary for acting with (and perhaps even without) autonomy, but autonomously (and reasonably) placing one's self under a normative expectation is not, in the usual sense, an action – a behavior; it is more in the nature of inwardly exercising the right of self-government. Thus, I don't see my analysis of self-trust clashing, in this respect, with that of Govier.

Importantly, the rationality constraint in condition (iii) is epistemic not practical; it concerns evidence for a belief, not deliberation for a decision. Thus, there is a stage of practical self-trust that imports epistemic norms for belief, but not for truth; that is, norms for justifying: (a) a future self's belief that its former self, whose "rule" it agrees to live by in the undertaking at issue, is trustworthy in its expectations for that future self, and (b) an earlier self's belief that its future self is sufficiently capable to carry out its intention to A or refrain from A'ing while confronted by countervailing forces. A selftrusting agent, just as much as an other-trusting agent, should not be epistemically gullible or biased; one would expect an important place for epistemic norms of self-examination and self-criticism within the dynamics of self-trust. The above analysis allows for this. 5) Hinchman (2003) sees self-trust as the "rational link" between intending and acting. The problem he addresses is: why should (not: why does) an agent carry out (be "intention-executing" in his terminology) an intention formed by its former self? That is: what reason does the agent have at the time of execution to execute its earlier intention, given that there is no reason not to. It can't be, for example, because at the time of action the agent re-deliberates and reaffirms its earlier intention; for Hinchman this just moves the same problem forward in time, as does claiming the explanation lies in intention-constancy by way of a memory at the time of action of the agent's earlier intention. Hinchman argues that self-trust is the solution; a relationship of trust runs from the later intention-executing self 27 back to the earlier intention-forming self, and this trust functions as a "pre-emptive reason" to act on the intention, providing the agent's later self judges its earlier self to be trustworthy. 31 This self-trust is essential to rational practical agency for without it, in Hinchman's view, there looms an un-bridged gap of reason between intention and action. There are two points of disagreement between Hinchman's and my analysis of practical self-trust. First, I see self-trust as rationally bridging the space between a practical agent's desire to do or refrain from doing something and the agent's intention to do or to refrain from doing it. Why should an agent who desires to do something form an intention to do it? Why not just live with the desire? One explanation might be self-distrust; a self-distrusting agent does just that, or when possible seeks external assistance strategies, for she believes (rightly or wrongly) – prior to forming an intention – that she does not have what it takes to do what she desires to do. If there is a form of practical self-trust that links intention with action – and Hinchman's analysis convincingly shows that there is – it is further downstream in practical agency and would have to presuppose the earlier self-trust that I have analyzed here: that leading to forming an intention in the first place to do what the agent desires to do. Self-trust, as I see it, first (because practical agency typically begins with a desire) and foremost (because practical agency is primarily a matter of the power and limits of practical reason) is a link between a desire to do something and an intention or decision to do it – an intention formed with sufficient belief in one's self and resolve that the agent has little room to fret, hesitate, or re-consider either when forming it or when the time comes for carrying it out. And, this is why self-trust is a sometimes dangerous thing. The second disagreement between Hinchman's conception of self-trust and the one suggested here is that for Hinchman the trust seems to run in one direction: from a later self at the time of action to an earlier intending self whom that later self believes (with good reason) to be trustworthy (see note 31). But isn't this just part the picture? It would seem that a person's earlier self, in believing that it should appear – and be – trustworthy to its future self, must to a degree still trust that future self to then act (as intended) on the reason of trustworthiness and not sink into "pathological" hesitation, forgetfulness, procrastination, self-doubt, self-non-confidence or over-scrupulosity. This is the case, I believe, because even self-trust as a "pre-emptive reason" is no guarantee. Nor should it be; it would be deeply troubling if an agent were so bound by its self-trust that it couldn't freely, even whimsically, at the very last moment of action spontaneously ignore her earlier intention, rebel against it, or give up for no good reason. This may be irrational (even though externally fortunate should a last minute whimsical opt-out means a great harm doesn't get done), and perhaps frightening to an agent's earlier self who then must be deeply uncertain and always vulnerable to risk even about self-trust – about the kind of person s/he will discover themselves to be in some future circumstance – but we wouldn't accept an account of selftrust that made it impossible. The trust that runs from the earlier intending to the later executing self would acknowledge trust-risk: that the agent's freedom to "change my mind" has not disappeared, even at the very last moment of action, nor the possibility to "surprise myself" in acting. It would seem that some forward self-trust, then, is always needed; an agent's future intention-executing self ought to appear trustworthy to the earlier self, as much as its earlier intending self appears trustworthy to the self that is about to act. Hinchman's account of self-trust, in other words, gives us deep retrospective insights about agency: how in a unit of practical agency the reasonable agent is, so to speak, "pushed" 28 to act by its self-trust. Yet, at least intuitively, practical agency is also – if not primarily – a future oriented rationality: an agent also needs to be "pulled" in its journey by its self-trust. Granted, the problem on which Hinchman sets his sights is inherently backward looking, so the unevenness of his account (granting that it is) may well be justified by the bounds of his topic. Still, the account of self-trust offered here provides, I believe, a fuller picture than Hinchman's. 5. Some connections and some distinctions between self-trust and self-confidence Based on the analyses of self-confidence and self-trust offered here: (1) what are some of the ways in which these two intrapersonal relations are importantly different for the exercise of practical agency? Also, (2) how are these two intrapersonal relations conceptually related? (1) First, self-confidence depends primarily on an agent's belief as to how well the agent's action will be performed and be judged, given the expectations of others. The self-confident agent intends to (or must) do something, desires to do it well, believes she will, and expects to receive recognition for satisfying norms of performance not only her own. An agent's self-confidence or lack thereof, then, is about the agent's performance; the agent's beliefs about the agent's body – e.g., voice and speech, bodily actions and appearance, how the agent looks, and what results from these – and beliefs about how it will be perceived and judged by others should the agent perform the intended action, are integral to self-confidence or its lack. Self-confidence is only indirectly about the person: to the degree, perhaps, that a performance would be evaluated as reflecting qualities of the person who performs such as dedication to prior preparation, training, practice, seriousness of effort, etc. For most actions done with self-confidence, however, doing well or poorly says little or nothing about the character or the inner qualities, much less the value, of the person. The exception might be the case of the overly selfconfident or the overly self-non-confident agent, mistakes in self-knowledge that are typically judged to be flaws in the person. For the most part, the self-confident (or opposite) agent believes s/he is being judged qua performer, not qua person; in failing to act well, the self-confident agent believes she primarily lets others down regarding their expectations about her actions, who then think less of her as a performer but not (or at least shouldn't) as a person. This dimension of the "eyes of others" and "public expectations" the self-confident or self-non-confident agent believes she faces is the basis, I suggest, for any emotional or physiological states that typically accompany these self-relations and their potential beneficial or harmful effect on the agent's performance. It is reasonable, for example, for the coach and for the athlete both to be concerned about the athlete's self-confidence or lack of selfconfidence in a future competitive sports event, and in my (granted somewhat limited) experience they are, only if they believe that these will affect the athlete's performance. In contrast, self-trust depends primarily on an agent's self-evaluation regarding the agent's capability to satisfy a self-imposed normative expectation. The agent desires to do something, believes this takes being a certain kind of person (qua practical agent), expects of herself that she ought to be that kind of person, believes that she is, and consequently forms an intention to do what she wants to do. Self-trust, 29 then, is primarily about how one views one's self and the kind of person one takes one's self to be: namely, capable and trustworthy in regard not just to a given undertaking, but also in the domain in which a "moral strength" – a virtue – might be exercised. Self-trust, then, is not just about the agent's specifically intended action; it is about enduring practical capabilities, within and beyond any particular unit of agency. In failing to act as intended, the self-trusting agent primarily lets himself down; selfdisappointment is the important result and only incidentally the disappointment of others. This aspect of "in my own eyes" central to self-trust and self-distrust, in contrast to the "eyes of others" central to self-confidence and self-non-confidence, I suggest, is a step toward explaining the lack of similar emotional and physiological states in the case of self-trust/distrust that we typically associate with selfconfidence/non-confidence. In my experience, neither the coach nor the athlete, for example, show concerned about the athlete's self-trust or self-distrust in a sports event; if this analysis is correct, they shouldn't if it's the athlete's performance and not her character that matters. A second distinction is that self-confidence does not itself contain normatively; it involves an agent's intensions, desires, and beliefs. There is no action that an agent can intend to do that the agent can't be self-confident about doing (or lack self-confidence about doing). The norms of performance the agent is challenged to satisfy and is confident about meeting are necessary as "public" and "external" to the agent; but even in the case where the agent alone applies them to evaluate his performance they are "internally" part of – constitutive of – the agent's self-confidence as an "external" expectation. An agent's self-confidence, then, might be summed up by the words "I will show them I can do it" – the selfconfident agent is not trying to prove something to herself. Self-trust, however, contains normativity: the ideals of autonomy, reasonable expectations, belief justification, and trustworthiness are integral to self-trust. These serve to constrain an agent's self-trust; there are many actions an agent might desire to do that the agent can't be self-trusting about doing, and many the agent should be self-distrusting about doing. Self-trust, perhaps, can be summed up by the words "I should be and can be believed in, by myself, to do it." A third distinction is that, typically, it is commendable but not necessary to the exercise of effective practical agency that the agent desires to do something well, or even that it be done well, just that it be done sufficiently to achieve its end even though this might be judged a mediocre performance. 32 In fact, there are no norms of performance for many (most?) actions; and, there are human activities that apparently don't even have norms of completion, such as counting the natural Arabic numerals, parenting one's child, or appreciating a great work of art. It follows that in such cases self-confidence plays no role in successful practical agency. Self-trust, however, is an essential part of successful practical agency of an important form. Self-trust and self-distrust operate between the t1 point of desire and the t2 point of forming an intention in the general structure of a unit of practical agency described in part I above. A desire to do something (whether morally good or bad) can't reach the point of forming an intention to do it without self-trust and self-distrust will cut it off, or so I've argued. And without an intention to do something, it is hard to imagine an agent acting successfully on desire alone; at any rate, it certainly would not qualify as rational practical agency, and without a lot of luck wouldn't be successful action. Without self-trust, then, an important form of practical agency – though not all practical agency – breaks down in its earliest stage.

There are several more distinctions between self-confidence and self-trust that follows from the above analyses: -- that self-confidence tends to eliminate the agent's risk aversion and sense of vulnerability even in high-stakes performances, but self-trust remains open to a sense of risk and vulnerability, -- that even though both self-confidence and self-trust are intrapersonal relations, neither selfconfidence nor its lack can exist in a universe containing only one person whereas self-trust and selfdistrust can, -- that while both self-confidence and self-trust are beliefs, and as such share the basic propositionalattitude structure: subject-content-object, the general content and object of each type of belief are importantly different, and they are not subject to the same epistemic norms. However, the first three argued points of contrast are sufficient, I believe, to show that these two intrapersonal relations, though they might have some structural and dynamic similarities, turn out to be quite different aspects of practical agency. It follows that "self-confidence" and "self-trust" are not just two ways of referring to the same thing about a person, even if they might be used this way in everyday language. 2) How are self-confidence and self-trust, as these are defined above, conceptually – as opposed to empirically or causally – related? They are logically compatible if it is possible to imagine one practical agent in one unit of agency of whom both sets of conditions are true – that is, a practical agent who is both self-trusting and self-confident with respect to the same action – and incompatible if this is not possible. It is easy to show that they are compatible. Imagine practical agent Jill (=S) who desires to exercise well (=A), say for reasons of health, and who believes that to exercise well she must have a strong, long-term commitment to good health (=X). So: let S at t1 desire to A at t3, and let S at t2 intend to A at t3, and let S perform A at t3. In the interval between t1 and t2 let S believe that capacity X is required and productive of A'ing, and let S normatively expect that S has X at t3, as a result of which S forms her t2 intention to A at t3. And in the interval between t2 and t3 let S believe that to A is to be evaluated by public norms of performance (e.g. an exercise coach or readouts on an exercise machine) as having A'ed , and let S desire to meet these norms of performance at t3, and finally let S believe that at t3 she does A according to the norms of A'ing. Whether we further imagine S A'ing or not A'ing at t3, this is so far a possible scenario in which all the conditions for self-trust and for self-confidence are true. Thus, self-trust and self-confidence are compatible; a practical agent can be both within one unit of agency. I note, however, that this model does not show that this imaginary agent is either trusting about her self-confidence or confident about her self-trust, only that it is possible to be both self-trusting and self-confident within a single practical undertaking. Self-distrust and self-non-confidence, however, are mutually exclusive; it is impossible for an agent to be both with respect to the same practical undertaking, and the presence of one implies the absence of the other. We see this in the contradiction between condition (i) for lacking self-confidence (an agent must form an intention to A: the action about which the agent lacks self-confidence) and condition (va) for 31 self-distrust (after satisfying conditions (i)-(iva) the agent does not form an intention to A). For any given action A, an agent cannot both form and not form an intention to A in a single unit of agency;

thus, an agent cannot be both self-distrusting and self-non-confident – a self-distrusting agent does not reach the point in practical agency for a lack of self-confidence to take effect, thus an agent lacking in selfconfidence can't also be self-distrusting. 33 Self-trust and self-confidence are logically independent if it is possible for a practical agent to satisfy one set of conditions without satisfying the other. So, is it possible to imagine: (a) a self-trusting agent who has no self-confidence, and (b) a self-confidence agent who has no self-trust? (a) While it may be part of human psychology for a self-trusting person to tend to have self-confidence, the issue here is whether conceptually self-trust implies self-confidence. Clearly it does not. Imagine Jack who desires to swim back to shore against an increasingly strong ocean undertow after swimming a bit too far from shore. Jack has no desire to swim well and doesn't care about being judged a poor swimmer, and does not believe that his efforts will be evaluated; he simply wants to make it back to shore. He believes this will take determination and strength of effort, and the ability to fight panic and stay focused in case the undertow becomes stronger and he should start to tire. He normatively expects that, as a swimmer in his situation, he ought to have such determination and ability, and personally believes that he does; he is trustworthy in his own eyes to make it back and not to give up. As a result he forms the intention to swim back to shore and begins the effort. All of the conditions for self-trust are true of this agent's undertaking, but only the first condition for self-confidence, forming an intention to perform an action, is true; the others are false of Jack. Therefore, this practical agent trusts himself to swim back to shore, but is not confident about his performance (which is not to say that Jack is confident that he won't make it). It follows that for a person within a given unity of practical agency, self-trust does not imply self-confidence. (b) If an agent is self-confident, must the agent be self-trusting? Imagine Jill is asked by an elderly neighbor for a small favor: drive to the local pharmacy and pick up her medication. Jill is neutral about the favor; she has no desire to drive to the pharmacy and no desire not to, no desire to help her neighbor and no desire not to. Jill agrees and says she'll do (Jill forms the intention to do) the errand in an hour. The neighbor is grateful. Jill believes that there are norms for good driving involving speed, safety, road courtesy, etc. and norms of doing favors and neighborliness. Given her intention, Jill desires to drive to the pharmacy and back in a way that satisfies these norms of good driving and neighborliness, and would like to be judged as having done so. Finally, Jill believes that in an hour she will drive and complete the favor according to these norms; she believes that she will be a good driver and a good neighbor in this easy task she has agreed to do. In other words, Jill has complete selfconfidence in carrying out her intention well and being a good neighbor in doing this small favor, yet self-trust does not enter the picture. All the conditions on self-trust fail to hold in this scenario, and all the conditions on self-confidence are satisfied. Thus, self-confidence does not imply self-trust. 32 We see that self-trust and self-confidence do not imply each other and are, therefore, conceptually independent. What of self-distrust and a lack of self-confidence (self-non-confidence)? Given that these two self-relations are incompatible, as argued above, it follows that an agent who is self-distrusting can't also be self-non-confident. Scenario (c) offers an example of a self-distrusting agent who has no lack self-confidence. I note that not lacking self-confidence is not equivalent to having self-confidence; an agent could do something easy and automatically, for example get out of bed in the morning, without any self-confidence and without any self-non-confidence (without a lack of self-confidence). (c) Imagine Jack who desires to continue driving late at night in order to reach home. He feels tired and sleepy. He believes that it will take special effort to keep from falling asleep at the wheel, and he normatively expects that a driver in his situation ought to be capable of keeping awake and fight-off such drowsiness. But Jack believes he does not have the capability to do this; he distrusts himself to keep awake while wishing that he was the kind of person who would not be untrustworthy in such situations. Jack has no "external assistance" to turn to, to make up for his perceived agential weakness: no drugs, for example, or no external source of sensory stimulation. As a result, Jack forms no intention to keep driving home; instead, he forms the intention to pull off the road into the nearest rest-stop. All the conditions on self-distrust are true of Jack in this scenario, but none of the conditions on lacking selfconfidence hold. Given that self-distrust and self-non-confidence are mutually exclusive, it follows that an agent who lacks self-confidence can't also be self-distrusting within the same unit of agency. Scenario (d) provides an example. I note that not being self-distrusting is not equivalent to being self-trusting; an agent could do something easy and automatically, for example get into bed at night, without either self-trust or selfdistrust. (d) Jill, a recent college graduate who still lives at home, believes her mother (a dominant figure in Jill's life who worries about Jill's life-style and future) is overly-critical of her choices, actions, and "lack of long-term planning." One day Jill's mother asks her to do some food shopping at the local market. Jill has no desire to do this simple task, and believes that doing it takes no special capability or strength that Jill normatively expects of herself and further believes that she possesses or fails to possess. Thus, neither self-distrust nor self-trust operates in Jill's unit of agency: shop for food. Feeling obligated to accept her mother's request, Jill agrees and forms the intention to go food shopping. On the way to the market, Jill both desires to fulfill her mother's request in a way that leaves no cause for criticism from her mother, and believes that no matter what she purchases, her mother will still find fault and be critical of Jill's "performance." Jill experiences a lack of self-confidence about carrying out her intention to shop for food in the way she desires; that is, in a way that satisfies her mother's (perhaps perfectionist) norms and expectations. In this scenario all the conditions for lacking self-confidence are met by Jill, but none of the conditions for self-distrust hold.

CHAPTER SEVEN

Goal-setting mindset.

Goal setting is a powerful process for thinking about your ideal future, and for motivating yourself to turn this vision of the future into reality. The process of setting goals helps you choose where you want to go in life. By knowing precisely what you want to achieve, you know where you have to concentrate your efforts. You'll also quickly spot the distractions that would otherwise lure you from your course. More than this, properly-set goals can be incredibly motivating, and as you get into the habit of setting and achieving goals, you'll find that your self-confidence builds fast. Achieving More with Focus Goal setting techniques are used by top-level athletes, successful business-people and achievers in all fields. They give you long-term vision and short-term motivation. They focus your acquisition of knowledge and help you to organize your time and your resources so that you can make the very most of your life. By setting sharp, clearly defined goals, you can measure and take pride in the achievement of those goals. You can see forward progress in what might previously have seemed a long pointless grind. By setting goals, you will also raise your self-confidence, as you recognize your ability and competence in achieving the goals that you have set. Starting to Set Personal Goals Goals are set on a number of different levels: First you create your "big picture" of what you want to do with your life, and decide what largescale goals you want to achieve. Second, you break these down into the smaller and smaller targets that you must hit so that you reach your lifetime goals. Finally, once you have your plan, you start working to achieve it. We start this process with your Lifetime Goals, and work down to the things you can do today to start moving towards them. Your Lifetime Goals The first step in setting personal goals is to consider what you want to achieve in your lifetime (or by a time at least, say, 10 years in the future) as setting Lifetime Goals gives you the overall perspective that shapes all other aspects of your decision making. To give a broad, balanced coverage of all important areas in your life, try to set goals in some of these categories (or in categories of your own, where these are important to you): ? Artistic: Do you want to achieve any artistic goals? If so, what? ? Attitude: Is any part of your mindset holding you back? Is there any part of the way that you behave that upsets you? If so, set a goal to improve your behavior or find a solution to the problem. ? Career: What level do you want to reach in your career? ? Education: Is there any knowledge you want to acquire in particular? What information and skills will you need to achieve other goals? ? Family: Do you want to be a parent? If so, how are you going to be a good parent? How do you want to be seen by a partner or by members of your extended family ? Financial: How much do you want to earn by what stage? ? Physical: Are there any athletic goals you want to achieve, or do you want good health deep into old age? What steps are you going to take to achieve this? ? Pleasure: How do you want to enjoy yourself? – you should ensure that some of your life is for you! ? Public Service: Do you want to make the world a better place? If so, how? Spend some time brainstorming these, and then select one goal in each category that best reflects what you want to do. Then consider trimming again so that you have a small number of really significant goals on which you can focus. As you do this, make sure that the goals that you have set are ones that you genuinely want to achieve, not ones that your parents, family, or employers might want (if you have a partner, you probably want to consider what he or she wants, however make sure you also remain true to yourself!) Starting to Achieve Your Lifetime Goals Once you have set your lifetime goals, set a 25 year plan of smaller goals that you should complete if you are to reach your lifetime plan. Then set a 5 year plan, 1 year plan, 6 month plan, and 1 month plan of progressively smaller goals that you should reach to achieve your lifetime goals. Each of these should be based on the previous plan. Then create a daily to-do list of things that you should do today to work towards your lifetime goals. At an early stage these goals may be to read books and gather information on the achievement of your goals. This will help you to improve the quality and realism of your goal setting. Finally review your plans, and make sure that they fit the way in which you want to live your life. Staying on Course Once you have decided your first set of plans, keep the process going by reviewing and updating your to-do list on a daily basis. Periodically review the longer term plans, and modify them to reflect your changing priorities and experience. Goal Setting Tips The following broad guidelines will help you to set effective goals: ? State each goal as a positive statement: Express your goals positively – 'Execute this technique well' is a much better goal than 'Don't make this stupid mistake.' ? Be precise: Set a precise goal, putting in dates, times and amounts so that you can measure achievement. If you do this, you will know exactly when you have achieved the goal, and can take complete satisfaction from having achieved it. ? Set priorities: When you have several goals, give each a priority. This helps you to avoid feeling overwhelmed by too many goals, and helps to direct your attention to the most important ones. ? Write goals down: This crystallizes them and gives them more force. ? Keep operational goals small: Keep the low-level goals you are working towards small and achievable. If a goal is too large, then it can seem that you are not making progress towards it. Keeping goals small and incremental gives more opportunities for reward. Derive today's goals from larger ones. ? Set performance goals, not outcome goals: You should take care to set goals over which you have as much control as possible. There is nothing more dispiriting than failing to achieve a personal goal for reasons beyond your control. In business, these could be bad business environments or unexpected effects of government policy. In sport, for example, these reasons could include poor judging, bad weather, injury, or just plain bad luck. If you base your goals on personal performance, then you can keep control over the achievement of your goals and draw satisfaction from them. ? Set realistic goals: It is important to set goals that you can achieve. All sorts of people (employers, parents, media, society) can set unrealistic goals for you. They will often do this in ignorance of your own desires and ambitions. Alternatively you may set goals that are too high, because you may not appreciate either the obstacles in the way or understand quite how much skill you need to develop to achieve a particular level of performance. Achieving Goals When you have achieved a goal, take the time to enjoy the satisfaction of having done so. Absorb the implications of the goal achievement, and observe the progress you have made towards other goals. If the goal was a significant one, reward yourself appropriately. All of this helps you build the self-confidence you deserve! With the experience of having achieved this goal, review the rest of your goal plans: ? If you achieved the goal too easily, make your next goals harder. ? If the goal took a dispiriting length of time to achieve, make the next goals a little easier. ? If you learned something that would lead you to change other goals, do so. ? If you noticed a deficit in your skills despite achieving the goal, decide whether to set goals to fix this. Failure to meet goals does not matter much, as long as you learn from it. Feed lessons learned back into your goal setting program. Remember too that your goals will change as time goes on. Adjust them regularly to reflect growth in your knowledge and experience, and if goals do not hold any attraction any longer, then let them go. Key Points Goal setting is an important method of: ? Deciding what is important for you to achieve in your life. ? Separating what is important from what is irrelevant, or a distraction. ? Motivating yourself. ? Building your self-confidence, based on successful achievement of goals. If you don't already set goals, do so, starting now. As you make this technique part of your life, you'll find your career accelerating, and you'll wonder how you did without it!

SMART Goals: A useful way of making goals more powerful is to use the SMART mnemonic. While there are plenty of variants, SMART usually stands for: ? S Specific ? M Measurable ? A Attainable ? R Relevant ? T Time-bound For example, instead of having "to sail around the world" as a goal, it is more powerful to say "To have completed my trip around the world by December 31, 2015." Obviously, this will only be attainable if a lot of preparation has been completed beforehand!

A good way of getting going with this is to use the Mind Tools Life Plan Workbook. Supported by worksheets and advice, this guides you through a simple 5-step process for setting your life goals and for organizing yourself for success. Locke's Goal Setting Theory Understanding SMART Goal Setting Goal setting is a powerful way of motivating people. The value of goal setting is so well recognized that entire management systems, like Management by Objectives, have goal setting basics incorporated within them. In fact, goal setting theory is generally accepted as among the most valid and useful motivation theories in industrial and organizational psychology, human resource management, and organizational behavior. Many of us have learned - from bosses, seminars, and business articles - to set SMART goals. It seems natural to assume that by setting a goal that's Specific, Measurable, Attainable, Relevant, and Time-bound, we will be well on our way to accomplishing it. But WHY is this really the best way of setting goals? To answer this, we look to Dr Edwin Locke's pioneering research on goal setting and motivation in the late 1960s. In his 1968 article "Toward a Theory of Task Motivation and Incentives," he stated that employees were motivated by clear goals and appropriate feedback. Locke went on to say that working toward a goal provided a major source of motivation to actually reach the goal - which, in turn, improved performance. This information does not seem revolutionary to most of us some 40 years later. This shows the impact his theory has had on professional and personal performance. In this article, we look at what Locke had to say about goal setting, and how we can apply his theory to our own performance goals. Goal Setting Theory Locke's research showed that there was a relationship between how difficult and specific a goal was and people's performance of a task. He found that specific and difficult goals led to better task performance than vague or easy goals. Telling someone to "Try hard" or "Do your best" is less effective than "Try to get more than 80% correct" or "Concentrate on beating your best time." Likewise, having a goal that's too easy is not a motivating force. Hard goals are more motivating than easy goals, because it's much more of an accomplishment to achieve something that you have to work for. A few years after Locke published his article, another researcher, Dr Gary Latham, studied the effect of goal setting in the workplace. His results supported exactly what Locke had found, and the inseparable link between goal setting and workplace performance was formed. In 1990, Locke and Latham published their seminal work, "A Theory of Goal Setting and Task Performance." In this book, they reinforced the need to set specific and difficult goals, and they outlined three other characteristics of successful goal setting. Five Principles of Goal Setting To motivate, goals must take into consideration the degree to which each of the following exists: 1. Clarity. 2. Challenge. 3. Commitment. 4. Feedback. 5. Task complexity.

Let's look at each of these in detail. 1. Clarity Clear goals are measurable, unambiguous, and behavioral. When a goal is clear and specific, with a definite time set for completion, there is less misunderstanding about what behaviors will be rewarded. You know what's expected, and you can use the specific result as a source of motivation. When a goal is vague - or when it's expressed as a general instruction, like "Take initiative" - it has limited motivational value. To improve your or your team's performance, set clear goals that use specific and measurable standards. "Reduce job turnover by 15%" or "Respond to employee suggestions within 48 hours" are examples of clear goals. When you use the SMART acronym to help you set goals, you ensure the clarity of the goal by making it Specific, Measurable and Time-bound. 2. Challenge One of the most important characteristics of goals is the level of challenge. People are often motivated by achievement, and they'll judge a goal based on the significance of the anticipated accomplishment. When you know that what you do will be well received, there's a natural motivation to do a good job. Rewards typically increase for more difficult goals. If you believe you'll be well compensated or otherwise rewarded for achieving a challenging goal, that will boost your enthusiasm and your drive to get it done. Setting SMART goals that are Relevant links closely to the rewards given for achieving challenging goals. Relevant goals will further the aims of your organization, and these are the kinds of goals that most employers will be happy to reward. When setting goals, make each goal a challenge. If an assignment is easy and not viewed as very important - and if you or your employee doesn't expect the accomplishment to be significant - then the effort may not be impressive. 3. Commitment Goals must be understood and agreed upon if they are to be effective. Employees are more likely to "buy into" a goal if they feel they were part of creating that goal. The notion of participative management rests on this idea of involving employees in setting goals and making decisions. One version of SMART - for use when you are working with someone else to set their goals - has A and R stand for Agreed and Realistic instead of Attainable and Relevant. Agreed goals lead to commitment. This doesn't mean that every goal has to be negotiated with and approved by employees. It does mean that goals should be consistent and in line with previous expectations and organizational concerns. As long as the employee believes the goal is consistent with the goals of the company, and believes the person assigning the goal is credible, then the commitment should be there. Interestingly, goal commitment and difficulty often work together. The harder the goal, the more commitment is required. If you have an easy goal, you don't need a lot of motivation to get it done. When you're working on a difficult assignment, you will likely encounter challenges that require a deeper source of inspiration and incentive. As you use goal setting in your workplace, make an appropriate effort to include people in their own goal setting. Encourage employees to develop their own goals, and keep them informed about what's happening elsewhere in the organization. This way, they can be sure that their goals are consistent with the overall vision and purpose that the company seeks. 4. Feedback In addition to selecting the right type of goal, an effective goal program must also include feedback. Feedback provides opportunities to clarify expectations, adjust goal difficulty, and gain recognition. It's important to provide benchmark opportunities or targets, so individuals can determine for themselves how they're doing. These regular progress reports, which measure specific success along the way, are particularly important where it's going to take a long time to reach a goal. In these cases, break down the goals into smaller chunks, and link feedback to these intermediate milestones. SMART goals are Measurable, and this ensures that clear feedback is possible. With all your goal setting efforts, make sure that you build in time for providing formal feedback. Certainly, informal check-ins are important, and they provide a means of giving regular encouragement and recognition. However, taking the time to sit down and discuss goal performance is a necessary factor in long-term performance improvement. See our article on Delegation for more on this. 5. Task Complexity The last factor in goal setting theory introduces two more requirements for success. For goals or assignments that are highly complex, take special care to ensure that the work doesn't become too overwhelming. People who work in complicated and demanding roles probably have a high level of motivation already. However, they can often push themselves too hard if measures aren't built into the goal expectations to account for the complexity of the task. It's therefore important to do the following: ? Give the person sufficient time to meet the goal or improve performance. ? Provide enough time for the person to practice or learn what is expected and required for success. The whole point of goal setting is to facilitate success. Therefore, you want to make sure that the conditions surrounding the goals don't frustrate or inhibit people from accomplishing their objectives. This reinforces the "Attainable" part of SMART. Key Points Goal setting is something most of us recognize as necessary for our success. By understanding goal setting theory, you can effectively apply the principles to goals that you or your team members set. Locke and Latham's research emphasizes the usefulness of SMART goal setting, and their theory continues to influence the way we set and measure performance today. Use clear, challenging goals, and commit yourself to achieving them. Provide feedback on goal performance. Take into consideration the complexity of the task. If you follow these simple rules, your goal setting process will be much more successful and your overall performance will improve. Golden Rules of Goal Setting Five Rules to Set Yourself Up for Success Have you thought about what you want to be doing in five years' time? Are you clear about what your main objective at work is at the moment? Do you know what you want to have achieved by the end of today? If you want to succeed, you need to set goals. Without goals you lack focus and direction. Goal setting not only allows you to take control of your life's direction; it also provides you a benchmark for determining whether you are actually succeeding. Think about it: Having a million dollars in the bank is only proof of success if one of your goals is to amass riches. If your goal is to practice acts of charity, then keeping the money for yourself is suddenly contrary to how you would define success. To accomplish your goals, however, you need to know how to set them. You can't simply say, "I want." and expect it to happen. Goal setting is a process that starts with careful consideration of what you want to achieve, and ends with a lot of hard work to actually do it. In between there are some very well defined steps that transcend the specifics of each goal. Knowing these steps will allow you to formulate goals that you can accomplish. Here are our Five Golden Rules of Goal Setting: The Five Golden Rules Rule #1: Set Goals that Motivate You When you set goals for yourself, it is important that they motivate you: This means making sure it is something that's important to you and there is value in achieving it. If you have little interest in the outcome, or it is irrelevant given the larger picture, then the chances of you putting in the work to make it happen are slim. Motivation is key to achieving goals. Set goals that relate to the high priorities in your life. Without this type of focus you can end up with far too many goals, leaving you too little time to devote to each one. Goal achievement requires commitment, so to maximize the likelihood of success, you need to feel a sense of urgency and have an "I must do this" attitude. When you don't have this "must do" factor, you risk putting off what you need to do to make the goal a reality. This in turn leaves you feeling disappointed and frustrated with yourself, both of which are de-motivating. And you can end up in a very destructive "I can't do anything or be successful at anything" frame of mind. Rule #2: Set SMART Goals You have probably heard of "SMART goals" already. But do you always apply the rule? The simple fact is that for any goal to be achieved it must be designed to be SMART. There are many variations on what SMART stands for, but the essence is this – Goals should be:Specific Measurable Attainable Relevant Time Bound Set Specific Goals You goal must be clear and well defined. Vague or generalized goals are not achievable because they don't provide sufficient direction. Remember, you need goals to show you the way. How useful would a map of the United States be if there were only state borders marked on it and you were trying to get from Miami to Los Angeles? Do you even know which state you are starting from let alone which one you're headed to? Make it as easy as you can to get where you want to go by defining precisely where it is you want to end up. Set Measurable Goals Include precise amounts, dates, etc in your goals so you can measure your degree of success. If your goal is simply defined as "To reduce expenses" how will you know when you are successful? In one month's time if you have a 1% reduction or in two year's time when you have a 10% reduction? Without a way to measure your success you miss out on the celebration that comes with knowing you actually achieved something. Set Attainable Goals Make sure that it's possible to achieve the goals you set. If you set a goal that you have no hope of achieving you will only demoralize yourself and erode your confidence. However, resist the urge to set goals that are too easy. Accomplishing a goal that you didn't have to work very hard for can be an anticlimax at best, and can also make you fear setting future goals that carry a risk of nonachievement. By setting realistic yet challenging goals you hit the balance you need. These are the types of goals that require you to "raise the bar" and they bring the greatest personal satisfaction. Set Relevant Goals Goals should be relevant to the direction you want your life and career to take. By keeping goals aligned with this, you'll develop the focus you need to get ahead and do what you want. Set widely scattered and inconsistent goals, and you'll fritter your time - and your life - away. Set Time-Bound Goals You goals must have a deadline. This again, is so that you know when to celebrate your success. When you are working on a deadline, your sense of urgency increases and achievement will come that much quicker. Rule #3: Set Goals in Writing The physical act of writing down a goal makes it real and tangible. You have no excuse for forgetting about it. As you write, use the word "will" instead of "would like to" or "might". For example, "I will reduce my operating expenses by 10% this year." Not, "I would like to reduce my operating expenses by 10% this year." The first goal statement has power and you can "see" yourself reducing expenses, the second lacks passion and gives you an out if you get sidetracked. Post your goals in visible places to remind yourself everyday of what it is you intend to do. Put them on your walls, desk, computer monitor, bathroom mirror or refrigerator as a constant reminder.

To make sure your goal is motivating, write down why it's valuable and important to you. Ask yourself, "If I were to share my goal with others, how would I tell them to convince them it was a worthwhile goal?" You can use this motivating value statement to help you if you start to doubt yourself or lose confidence in your ability to actually make it happen.

Frame your goal statement positively. If you want to improve your retention rates say, "I will hold on to all existing employees for the next quarter" rather than "I will reduce employee turnover." The first one is motivating; the second one still has a get-out clause "allowing" you to succeed even if some employees leave. Tip 2: If you use a To Do List, make yourself a To Do List template that has your goals at the top of it. If you use an Action Program (see Mind Tools' Make Time for Success! course), then your goals should be at the top of your Project Catalog.

Rule #4: Make an Action Plan This step is often missed in the process of goal setting. You get so focused on the outcome that you forget to plan all of the steps that are needed along the way. By writing out the individual steps, and then crossing each one off as you complete it, you'll realize that you are making progress towards your ultimate goal. This is especially important if your goal is big and demanding, or long-term. Read our article on Action Plans for more on how to do this. Rule #5: Stick With It! Remember, goal setting is an ongoing activity not just a means to an end. Build in reminders to keep you on track and remember to review your goals continuously. Your end destination may remain quite similar over the long term but the action plan you set for yourself along the way can change significantly. Make sure the relevance, value, and necessity remain high. Key Points Goal setting is much more than simply saying you want something to happen. Unless you clearly define exactly what you want and understand why you want it the first place, your odds of success are considerably reduced. By following the Five Golden Rules of Goal Setting you can set goals with confidence and enjoy the satisfaction that comes along with knowing you achieved what you set out to do. What will you decide to accomplish today? Backward Goal-Setting Using Backward Planning to Set Goals If your goal is to become an account executive within the next five years, where do you start your planning process? Or if your team needs to redesign the company's organizational structure, where do you begin? In planning, most of us would usually start building our plan from start to finish. What do you have to do first, second, third, and so on? What milestones do you have to reach before you can continue on with the next step in the plan? By what date does each step need to be completed? This is a solid form of Personal Goal Setting that works very well. When combined with the Golden Rules of Goal Setting, you have a motivating formula that can help you actively move yourself forward. A New Approach However, there's another, simple but lesserused method of goal setting that can be equally as powerful. It can show you other ways to achieve the same result, and it can help you deal with the necessary unknowns of goal setting that can so often cause you to give up on your plan entirely. It's called backward planning, backward goalsetting, or backward design, and it's used quite often in education and training. The idea is to start with your ultimate objective, your end goal, and then work backward from there to develop your plan. By starting at the end and looking back, you can mentally prepare yourself for success, map out the specific milestones you need to reach, and identify where in your plan you have to be particularly energetic or creative to achieve the desired results. It's much like a good presentation, when the presenter tells you where he's headed right at the beginning. Then, as the presentation unfolds, it's easy for you to follow the concepts and think critically about what's being said. If you have to figure out the main points as they come, your energy is often used up by just trying to keep up.

The Backward Planning Process Here's how it works:

1. Write down your ultimate goal. What specifically do you want to achieve, and by what date? Example: "By January 1, 2013, I will be the key accounts director for Crunchy Chips International." 2. Then ask yourself what milestone you need to accomplish just before that, in order to achieve your ultimate goal. What specifically do you have to do, and by when, so that you're in a position to reach your final objective? Example: "By September 30, 2011, I will successfully complete the executive training program offered by Crunchy Chips International." 3. Then work backward some more. What do you need to complete before that second-to-last goal? Example: "By March 1, 2011, I will submit my application for the executive training program, outlining my successes as a key accounts manager, and I will be accepted into the program." 4. Work back again. What do you need to do to make sure the previous goal is reached? Example: "By January 1, 2011, I will complete my second year as a key accounts manager with Crunchy Chips International, and I will earn the prestigious Key Accounts Manager of the Year award." 5. Continue to work back, in the same way, until you identify the very first milestone that you need to accomplish. Example: "By January 1, 2010, I will complete my first year as a key accounts manager with Crunchy Chips International, and I will be rewarded for my performance by gaining responsibility for clients purchasing over $10 million per year." "By January 1, 2009, I will be promoted to key accounts manager with Crunchy Chips International, and I will have responsibility for clients purchasing over $1 million per quarter." When you read a backward plan, it doesn't look much different from a traditional forward plan. However, creating a backward plan is VERY different. You need to force yourself to think from a completely new perspective, to help you see things that you might miss if you use a traditional chronological process.

This can also help you avoid spending time on unnecessary or unproductive activities along the way. Furthermore, it highlights points of tension within the plan, showing where you'll need to be particularly creative to make the next step successfully. Key Points On the surface, backward planning doesn't seem much different from traditional goalsetting processes. You start with a basic vision, and then you ask yourself what needs to be done to achieve that vision. You can read your plan from the beginning to the end, or from the end back to the beginning. Backward planning, however, is more than reversing the direction of your traditional plan. It's about adopting a different perspective and, perhaps, identifying different milestones as a result. It's a great supplement to traditional planning, and it gives you a much fuller appreciation for what it may take to achieve success. After all, the more alternatives you have, the better your final plan will likely be.

When you want to achieve something really badly, have you ever tried closing your eyes and imagining yourself "there"? You touch it, feel it and see it clearly. You scan every detail in your mind's eye. This is a powerful and important technique for motivating yourself and building the selfconfidence needed to achieve your goals. Yet when you open your eyes, the vivid image start fades: it takes real concentration to visualize again each time you want some inspiration. What if you could keep hold of that vivid image and refer to it when ever you need a little motivation or reminder of what you are working towards? Treasure mapping is a simple tool to help you do just that. Visualization itself is a very powerful technique. And treasure mapping can be the icing on the visualization cake! It's a very simple but effective idea: Treasure mapping involves creating a physical representation or collage of what you want to achieve. It acts as a constant reminder and representation of your goals. And so it intensifies the effects of visualization, which acts on your subconscious mind to motivate and encourage you towards achieving those goals. Let's say you have the ambition to get fitter and run a marathon: Your "treasure map" could include pictures of runners, people crossing the finishing line, athletes training hard; perhaps it could also include pictures of the foods that you need to eat (and those you need to avoid). If you are a salesman with ambition to beat sales records in your company, your treasure map could include a representation of the sales chart you hope to achieve, pictures of people signing deals with customers, pictures of your product standing proud; perhaps a picture of someone receiving a prize. Using the Tool Your treasure map will represent how you visualize the achievement of your goals and your journey toward that achievement. The first step towards your treasure map is to clarify your goals and then visualize what will happen, or what you will have, once you have achieved the goal. (For further help on clarifying your goals, please refer to Mind Tools article on goal setting.) Once you have are clear about what you want to achieve, write it down in detail and start to visualize your achievement: Ask yourself questions such as: ? What will I see when I have achieved my goal? ? What will I have? What will I be? ? How will I celebrate the achievement? ? How will other people see me and what I have achieved? Now enjoy collecting images that represent this visualization and arrange the images on paper as a collage. These image of the ultimate achievement go in the most prominent position of you treasure map – at the top or in the middle. The next step is to visualize the journey towards achieving the goals. What will you have to do? What will you have to stop doing to achieve your goals? There may be important milestones or necessary sacrifices to achieving your goals. Visualize these too, and find images that represent them. Now arrange these on the collage too. Now paste the pictures of your goals, your journey towards them, and sacrifices on your collage. Make sure you arrange them in a way that helps imprint upon you the desire to achieve your goals.

Hang your chart in a prominent place so that you see it daily: There it will help motivate and inspire you towards achieving your goals. Key Points Treasure mapping helps bring you goals to life and gives you a clear image of what you want to achieve and how you will achieve it. First clarify you goals and what you need to do to achieve them. Then visualize these. Choose images to represent how you see your achievement and make a collage; and use this as a constant reminder to keep motivating and inspiring your achievements.

Are you busy making your New Year Resolutions. or have you resolved never to make a New Year's resolution ever again.? If the latter, you're not alone. So many people get demoralized when, year after year, they make resolutions that they keep for only a few weeks or maybe even just a few days. Why is this? After all, we all have the best intentions and the timing (new year, new start) couldn't be better. The problem may lie in the fact that we place a huge amount of pressure on ourselves. During the last week of December and the first week of January, all you hear is, "What're your New Year's resolutions?" "What are you going to work on this year?" And the focus is on the "what" not the "how." When you are more concerned with the goal you set than on the specifics of how you are going to accomplish it, or even whether it is realistic and achievable, you can set yourself up for failure. So if you resolve to set successful New Year resolutions, read on. Let's focus on how, this year, you can set yourself up for a year of achievement! New Year Resolution Mistakes There are two common mistakes that people tend to make before they even start to make their New Year resolutions: They think about what they "should" do, rather than what they really want to do. And worse they think in about what they should stop doing, rather than what they actually want to achieve. "What should I do this year?" "What should I stop doing?", "What do other people suggest I should work on?" To be successful at any change, you need to really want it. Unless you take time to consider what it is you really want you (rather than what you should do or should stop doing) you will invariably end up making a resolution to which you are not entirely committed. Without commitment, you aren't motivated and after the first setbacks or obstacles you will quit. So the first rule of New Year Resolutions is to only make ones that you are committed to - Don't make a resolution simply because it is "the thing to do", or because someone has told you that you should. The irony of it is that New Year's resolutions have the potential to be very powerful because they are such a well recognized practice. Everyone knows that everyone else is setting resolutions. And what a great mutual support network that can provide! This external motivation and support, along with your internal motivation - the desire to succeed - is what can make the difference between success and failure. Eight Rules for New Year's Resolutions Our Eight Rules for New Year's Resolutions will help set you up for success right from the start. Inevitably you will come up against challenges and road blocks along the way; however by planning ahead and following these rules, you will be better placed to negotiate these easily, rather than stumble and quit.

Rule 1: Commit to Your Resolution Successful resolutions start with a strong commitment to make a change. To succeed, you must believe that you can accomplish what you set out to and that belief is bolstered by the unwavering support you give yourself. ? Choose resolutions that you really want to achieve - and make them positive; ? Announce your resolution to everyone around you - they will help hold you accountable; ? Develop a ceremony to mark the beginning of your commitment - this makes it more "real" and special for you; ? Don't leave your choice of resolution to the last minute - take time to think about your goals. If you don't, you risk reacting to your current environment and missing the big picture; ? Questions to ask yourself to determine if you can take ownership of your resolution include: o Is this resolution my idea or someone else's? o Does this resolution motivate and invigorate me? o Is this resolution sit comfortably with other factors in my life such as my values and long-term plans? ? Remember that there's no reason why your New Year's resolution should take all year to achieve. Rule 2: Be Realistic The key to achieving goals is continued motivation. If you set the bar too high, you risk failing. Consistently failing at something is profoundly de-motivating (It's no wonder that after a few dismal attempts some people abandon the idea of New Year's resolutions altogether!) ? Consider carefully before setting the same resolution you set last year. If it didn't work then, you need to make sure there is good reason to believe you can achieve it this year? What has changed? Do you have more commitment to make it work? (Be careful, or else you will end up with a repeat performance, and another failed resolution). ? Aim lower, rather than too high - aim for something that is challenging but that you have a good chance of accomplishing. If there is any doubt, err on the side of caution and expand your goal later if you still want to keep improving. ? Don't bite off more than you can chew. There is no reason to set more than one or two resolutions. Anymore than that and you divide your focus and energy and lessen your chances of success in any area. Rule 3: Write It Down A simple but powerful technique for making your goal real is to put your resolution into writing. There is something inside us that creates more commitment and drive when we take the time to do this. Consider writing it down on pieces of card and keeping it where you'll see it often – on your desk, the fridge, in your wallet. Rule 4: Make a Plan This is where so many resolutions fall down. Articulating what you want to achieve is one thing; deciding how to do it is quite another. Don't miss out this step! ? Start by envisioning where you want to be. ? Then work back along your path to where you are today.

Imagery is a powerful technique to help you own and commit to your goals or resolutions. Try picturing yourself having attained your goal. How do you feel? How do you look? Where you are, what you're doing? How do others react to you? By visualizing yourself in the position you desire, you can bolster your belief that you can do it and strengthen your motivation.

Write down all the milestones you note in between. ? Decide what you will do to accomplish each of these milestones. You need to know each step and have a plan for what comes next. Rule 5: Be Flexible Not everything will work out precisely the way you planned. If you are too rigid in your approach to resolutions the first minor obstacle can throw you off your course completely. ? When creating your plan try to predict some challenges you will face - make a contingency for the ones that have the highest probability and mentally prepare yourself for the others. ? Realize that your resolution itself might change along the way as well. That's not failure, it's reality. As your life changes so will your goals, dreams, and desires. Remember Rule 1 (Commit to Your Resolution): If you need to make changes to the goal so you continue to care about it, do so. Rule 6: Use a System of Reminders It's hard to keep focused on your plan when you have many other commitments, responsibilities, and obligations. The best way to stay on top of your resolution is to develop a formal reminder system. ? Have your written down resolutions visible as many times of the day as possible. Leave reminders at work, at home, in the car, on your calendar, in your briefcase, etc. ? Make sure the planned actions are on your to-do list (perhaps have a special section for them at the top). ? Set up reminders in your desktop calendar or subscribe to an email reminder service. ? Be as creative as you can to keep being reminded, and so make sure your goals stay in the front of your mind. Rule 7: Track Your Progress You won't know how well you are doing unless you keep track of your progress. This is why your detailed plan is so important. You need to know when each milestone in accomplished. The excitement around the little successes will keep you motivated and keep you pushing forwards. ? Use a journal and make an entry regarding your progress regularly. ? Note when you felt particularly pleased with your efforts. ? Note when you felt down or felt like quitting - over time, look for common themes and decide if there is an underlying issue that needs to be addressed. ? Record challenges you faced as well as things that went better than planned. ? Look back at your entries on a regular basis and use your past experiences to shape your attitude as you move forward. ? Ask a friend or family member to call you on pre-defined occasions to discuss your progress. Rule 8: Reward Yourself Although knowledge of a job well done can be reward enough, we all enjoy a little treat from time to time. Even the most committed person needs a boost and sometimes that is best accomplished through an external reward. When you are developing your plan, make a note of a few milestones where you will reward yourself once they are achieved. But spread them out – you want to make sure the rewards remain special and are not too easy to get.

There is no fixed rule saying that a resolution must be set in January. If your circumstances say it is better to wait until March, then do so.

Resolutions and goal setting are a year round activity. Don't get too caught up in the New Year frenzy!

New Year's resolutions can be a pain or a pleasure. The choice is yours. If it's a pain, you may resolve never to make a resolution again. So resolve to make it a pleasure! The starting point is to focus on something that you really want and are ready to give your commitment to. Do this and you'll be in a great position to stay motivated and be successful! As you plan your New Year resolutions, apply the Eight Rules to set yourself up for success.

CHAPTER EIGHT

Patient mindset.

Patient mindset matters in healing and deserves more study, experts say share

Researchers encourage more health care providers to place emphasis on the importance of people's mindsets and social context in healing.

A growing body of research has shown that people's mindsets can measurably affect physical healing.

Social context, including patients' relationships with their doctors, as well as patients' expectations about healing can drive these placebo responses.

Despite this research, the benefits of these psychological and social forces still receive much less attention than drug and device treatments.

In a report published online Feb. 15 in The BMJ, researchers at Stanford call for more health care providers to place emphasis on the importance of individual mindsets and social context in healing.

Alia Crum, PhD, assistant professor of psychology, is the lead author of the report. The senior author is Abraham Verghese, MD, professor of medicine.

Crum and her co-authors urge researchers to develop more studies that measure the physical effects of these psychosocial elements to understand and quantify patients' subjective experiences of expectations, connection and trust.

"We have long been mystified by the placebo effect," Crum said. "But the placebo effect isn't some mysterious response to a sugar pill. It is the robust and measurable effect of three components: the body's natural ability to heal, the patient mindset and the social context. When we start to see the placebo effect for what it really is, we can stop discounting it as medically superfluous and can work to deliberately harness its underlying components to improve health care."

Power of mindset

A health care provider's bedside manner is important, and what patients think and expect about treatments can influence health outcomes, Crum said.

But the health care and education systems in the United States generally do not emphasize psychosocial training. As a result, new doctors and health care workers take few courses on how to effectively form meaningful relationships with patients and how best to help them adopt useful mindsets.

Crum and her colleagues argue that the health care and education systems need to prioritize the role of psychological and social forces in healing.

For example, medical schools should develop more training that helps students and residents use their personal strengths to connect with patients and learn the best ways to harness social context and patient mindset.

"It should be about designing a formal curriculum for medical school that weaves all of this throughout the training," said Kari Leibowitz, a graduate student and co-author of the paper. "So it's not just mentioned in one or two classes or taught for one semester and then forgotten about."

The authors also call for a reform of standard randomized trials in the health care system. When examining the effects of a new drug, researchers should include, in addition to placebos, natural conditions, which don't use placebos, alongside conditions that include altered social context and mindset. This, Crum said, will help researchers understand how beliefs, labels and context can help magnify or reduce the effects of the drug and treatment.

These reforms, however, would require additional research that builds more scientific evidence for the importance of the effects of social context and mindsets, they said.

"Taking time and energy to develop provider-patient relationships is crucial, and we know that it makes a difference," Leibowitz said. "But you have to be able to justify why structural changes, like increasing the length of time spent with a patient to build trusting relationships and shape adaptive mindsets, actually saves all of us money."

Verghese, who is also director of the Stanford interdisciplinary center Presence, which champions the patient experience in medicine, has been teaching the value of connection and bedside manner for years.

"The wise and seasoned physician does much of this intuitively," said Verghese, who holds the Linda R. Meier and Joan F. Lane Provostial Professorship. "What is missing is the science behind it and the structure to help physicians understand these psychological and social forces so they can deliberately leverage them in health care."

The placebo effect

Over the past 30 years, neurobiological research has shown that the placebo effect, which stems in part from an individual's mindset or expectation to heal, triggers distinct brain areas associated with anxiety and pain that activate physiological effects that lead to healing outcomes.

Mindsets can also lead to negative, or "nocebo," effects. For example, patients have been shown to have a heightened pain response after being informed that an injection will hurt. Those who were told about possible negative side effects of a medication had an increased presence of those effects.

Crum has produced research suggesting that people's mindsets also influence the benefits they get from certain behaviors. For example, she co-authored a 2011 study showing that the physical effects of food depend on how caloric or indulgent it is in a person's mind. A study she co-authored two years later demonstrated that viewing stress as a helpful part of life, rather than as harmful, is associated with better health, emotional well-being and productivity at work.

Crum said she intends to continue to contribute research on the components that make up placebo effects, such as people's mindsets. She said several studies are in progress, on which Crum's Mind and Body Lab has partnered with Presence.

But more work remains to be done, Crum said.

"We know that psychological and social forces are at work in health in healing, for better or for worse," Crum said. "But we need to develop more rigorous research to measure their physiological effects. It is time we start taking these forces more seriously in both the science and practice of medicine."

CHAPTER NINE

Courageous mindset.

One stellar example for showing a courageous mindset is author, screenwriter, and producer, JK Rowling. Her story of perseverance and fearlessness in the face of poverty, divorce, raising a child as a single parent, and losing her mother did not stop her from writing the first Harry Potter novel. Even after publishing several books, Rowling continues to be challenged by bad press and other business issues which she faces head on without fear.

To have a courageous mindset, it is important to establish your priorities and re-confirm your objectives and goals. Try not to think of the end result and instead, focus on your goals and the process. Develop identity-based habits. Identity-based habits are habits that reflect who you are. It is founded on your self-belief so if you do not have any confidence as a leader, your actions will show this weakness. You have to believe that you can achieve great things. You can do this by:

1. Make a decision on the kind of leader you want to be.
2. Find a source of inspiration.
3. Celebrate small wins.

As implied by these 3 steps, a courageous mindset cannot be developed instantly. Plus, this kind of mindset is constantly evolving because as a leader, you should not settle for small wins or a big single win. The ultimate aspiration is sustainable and long-term leadership.

Change will take time.

Trust yourself.

Believe in what you can do; in what you know but strive to keep improving. Accept that you will face adversity. Once it comes, take it slowly and avoid making rushed decisions. If necessary, talk to someone whose opinions you trust and respect. Anything you decide to do, stay grounded by balancing your beliefs and company policies.

Learn to Adapt to This VUCA Environment we all live in

VUCA or volatile, uncertain, complex and ambiguous environment is a military term that first came out in the early 1990s after the Cold War ended. All leaders have to deal with situations that are multipolar which make it difficult to predict outcomes. VUCA has led to mindsets that have collapsed under pressure. Fortunately, in spite of what experts are saying to scare you about today's business environment, VUCA is not an impossible situation. There are solutions.

1) Step out of your comfort zone. Try to see situations from different perspectives. Use your team to come up with ideas and suggestions that would help you overcome adversity.
2) Encourage feedback from your staff and ask open-ended questions for high-quality analytics.
3) Stay transparent so there is no room for doubt among your team members
4) Stick to company policies
5) Be consistent with your actions and words
6) Practice flexibility in your strategies so you can easily adapt to abrupt changes

In summary, a courageous mindset is a willingness to adapt to changes. It is resilience against what may seem like an unstoppable force with the use of creativity, intelligence, and courage. It allows us to stop playing safe so we can enjoy the rewards of true leadership and enduring success.

If you would like to some help in developing further your courageous mindset, contact me and arrange a free initial call to see how I might help you.

Courage: the most important of all the virtues because without courage, you can't practice any other virtue consistently. – Maya Angelou

The Courageous Mindset is a coaching model created for women in transition. It highlights the crucial role of courage in the process of personal growth and change. The model illustrates the open cycle we go through in order to move into action on things that frighten us. It shows how clarity leads to more successful mindsets which leads to more courageous action, which leads to more clarity, and on and on.

Courage is an underrepresented component to success. You can be clear about who you are and what you want. You can have your highest values well-defined and a list of goals to go with them. You can have self-awareness, a great plan and tons of focus. You might even have lots of confidence and be totally prepared. But if your goal is to bust out of the same old cycle, thrive in the face of change, or take on a big personal or professional goal, you will be pushing yourself beyond your comfort zone to get there. And when we push beyond the comfort zone, there will be fear. Where there is fear, success requires courage.

Sheryl Sandberg, COO at Facebook and author of Lean In says in her 2010 Ted Talk that women are not making it to the top in any profession worldwide and that since 2002 the numbers of women in high level jobs has been dropping. She believes women need to stay in the workforce and offers 3 things that need to happen to fix the problem. She says women need to come to the table, make their partners real partners (share responsibilities equitably in home life) and not leave before they leave (making career sacrifices before a partner or baby are even in the picture). In these three directives, Sandberg tells women leaders what they need to do, but she doesn't tell them how to get there. She doesn't address the hurdles many women face in pushing their comfort zone beyond the gender barriers they've grown up with. She doesn't address the fear that women have about starting to act in a different way, starting to step up, be heard and "lean in." I believe they can get there by practicing courage.

I created The Courageous Mindset coaching model because I believe courage is the missing link when it comes to women finally appearing in equal numbers in leadership roles in every level of personal and professional life – at home or work, locally or worldwide. There are opportunities for practicing leadership and courage every day of our lives and taking these opportunities makes a big difference in how we see ourselves, how others see us (including our children) and what we are capable of in the future. I created this model and my coaching practice to help women find within themselves what they need to "lean in" to their entire lives.

The three main tenets of The Courageous Mindset are clarity, mindset and courage. Below is an explanation of each tenet, how each one affects the quality of our lives and how the coach-client discussion space creates an environment that encourages clients to find within themselves the kinds of clarity, mindsets and courage that support them in setting and accomplishing life goals.

Clarity

Clarity is power. The more clear you are about what you want the more likely you are to achieve it.- Bill Cox

What is Clarity?

When we think of clarity, we think of being able to see further and more distinctly. Clarity helps us understand who we are in the landscape, where we've been, and where we want to go. With clarity, we can see the hills and valleys, the distant peaks, even the clouds that might be blocking the sun, and we can channel our energy accordingly. In this way, clarity matters a great deal in setting and working towards goals, but like with any distant view, we have to do a little climbing to achieve it.

How does clarity affect the quality of your life?

Lack of clarity causes us to spin our wheels, be stagnant, scatter our energy, move in a direction but not move toward our goal. Sometimes it means putting all our efforts into someone else's goals but not our own.

Having clarity means we know ourselves so we can act in line with who we are, our roles and values – not someone else's. With clarity, our energy is focused on the things that give us the most meaning, fulfillment and happiness. As a result, we can give more of our best selves to personal and work life, our important relationships, our passions, our endeavors and the world. This is what it means to live authentically.

Clarity also makes it possible for us to know others so that we can understand their motivations and intentions in order to engage with them in a productive way. It requires reflecting on interpersonal experiences, investigating assumptions, and being open to the kinds of information that they may be providing, intentionally or not.

Clarity is power because it occurs at moments when experience and knowledge come together to reveal new truths, and these truths can give focus and energy to the journey through life transitions.

In coaching, clients gain clarity on the areas of life that matter most so they can set meaningful goals. The coach facilitates this process by asking open questions that help the client articulate as honestly as possible her relationship to her life circumstances and goals. The following are some important areas where the coach-client conversations will focus.

What are your Strengths?

Many people, particularly women, feel social pressure to downplay strengths. However, in coaching clients are encouraged to talk frankly about their talents, skills, and abilities. It is a waste of time and energy to worry about being boastful or to downplay competence. Recognizing and marshaling strengths is essential to success for two reasons: first, it feeds healthy self-confidence; and second, it gives much needed energy for the journey.

What are your life roles?

Society offers people many roles, and sometimes we accept these roles without questioning them. Take being a parent for example. Most cultures have strong expectations for how women should mother and men should father. It may be frowned upon to consider other ways of doing it that might threaten the norm. In coaching, clients investigate these roles in light of the changing circumstances and opportunities of modern life. They can then identify roles they are comfortable with and that are in line with their values.

What are your values?

As with life roles, people often take on the values of others. These received frameworks for interpreting information and making decisions may come from families, educational institutions, organizations, churches, or the workplace. These values may serve them well; however, there are times when certain patterns of thinking can be detrimental to achieving one's potential. In coaching, clients examine their values with a deliberate eye towards culling the ones that do not serve their best interests and cultivating the ones that they truly believe will help themselves and their community.

What are your goals?

Sometimes, clients come to coaching knowing they need change but are not sure about the exact goal. Other times they come with a specific goal and find that the process of coaching and gaining clarity causes them to question, change, or adjust the goal. This recursive process is normal. In coaching, clients get clear on a goal before moving forward. When this alignment happens, the goal is crystalized and lights the path forward.

With clarity of self, roles, values and goals, clients build a solid foundation to support them as they move forward into developing a mindset that will lead them to success and fulfillment.

Mindset

Our life always expresses the result of our dominant thoughts. – Soren Kierkegaard

What is mindset?

The Oxford dictionary says mindset is a "fixed mental attitude or disposition that predetermines a person's responses to and interpretations of situations."

Basically, it's our thinking patterns. Most of us accept that our attitude affects what we experience. It's the difference between having a good day or a bad day. But can we take this a step further and say that our mindset actually creates our reality? The answer is yes. This is what Kierkegaard is saying in the quote above. There are practical scientific and psychological reasons to explain why.

Put simply, mindset is the lens through which we personally view the world. It's a collection of our dominant beliefs and thoughts and we wear it like a pair of glasses with a unique pair of lenses – made by me for me. The glasses color everything we see and they let certain information in and keep other information out. In this way, they affect what is possible in life.

Carol Dwek, psychologist and author of the book Mindset, says people have fixed mindsets and growth mindsets. For people in a fixed mindset, past experiences prove who we are and what we are good or bad at. We are either smart or not smart, a good athlete or a bad athlete. A bad or good grade or making the team or not proves these things. The fixed mindset says you are who you are, and there's nothing you can do about it.

For people in a growth mindset, however, past performance simply indicates past effort and training or the lack of it. There is always the possibility for change, learning, and growth. A poor grade means something needs to change (more study maybe). A great grade, getting picked for a team, or having your artwork selected means you worked hard and it paid off. The growth mindset is all about being optimistic because we believe our decisions and actions have a powerful affect on the outcome.

According to Dwek, "In a fixed mindset students believe their basic abilities, their intelligence, their talents, are just fixed traits. They have a certain amount and that's that, and then their goal becomes to look smart all the time and never look dumb. In a growth mindset students understand that their talents and abilities can be developed through effort, good teaching and persistence. They don't necessarily think everyone's the same or anyone can be Einstein, but they believe everyone can get smarter if they work at it."

How does mindset affect quality of life?

People with a fixed mindset has fewer opportunities because they see fewer opportunities, whereas, a person with a growth mindset sees more and therefore has more. Seeing fewer opportunities in general means fewer chances for happiness and fulfillment in all aspects of life. But what is happiness and wellbeing? Martin Seligman, psychologist, author and father of the Positive Psychology movement created the Well-Being Theory to define it.

Well-being has five measurable elements (PERMA) that count toward it.

Positive Emotion (Of which happiness and life satisfaction are all aspects)

Engagement

Relationships

Meaning and purpose

Accomplishment

No one element defines well-being, but each contributes to it.

If we combine Dwek's theory of the fixed and growth mindset with each component of Seligman's Well-Being Theory, we can easily see how mindset limits or expands the possibilities of our life. Our mindset basically determines how happy and fulfilled we can be.

It's very easy to make judgments about who is courageous and who is not by looking at their particular circumstance. However, for courage to be present – by definition – there is also fear. Whether fear is present for someone is a very personal thing. What you might be able to do with little or no fear, may cause someone else to be terrified. The important thing to recognize is that whenever one acts in spite of the fear, it's an act of courage.

In fact, most courageous people are not born that way. They are made. Firefighters, for example, have an entire training process in which they extensively and regularly practice skills and courage before they are required to act at a real emergency fire. They are constantly assessing strengths and gaps, honing their skills, adding new ones, and keeping themselves, their minds, bodies and equipment fit for the job. Eventually, when the real life situation calls for it, they are prepared and use their best skills and tools to act. Fire men and women and other people doing similar jobs are on a constant cycle of assess-learn-prepare-plan-practice-act-repeat. This courage inducing process is one we can all adopt.

It is important to note here that confidence is different from courage. It is a feeling of self-assurance from appreciating your own abilities and qualities (Oxford). Confidence may or may not be present when courageous action occurs but it makes sense that the more confidence you have about something the less fear you may be dealing with when it comes time for action.

10 Elements of Courage

People with courage possess ten shared characteristics. They should remain as guideposts in your journey through life:

Self-confidence. Courageous people believe in themselves. They know who they are and what they stand for. They have strong values, recognize their personal capabilities, and are confident in meeting the challenges that lie before them. Courageous people are passionate and purposeful. You can sense courageous people when they walk into a room — they have a bounce in their step, maintain a positive outlook, and are comfortable in their own skin.

Conviction. You always know where courageous people stand. They're passionate about their beliefs and values and have consistent and predictable behavior. They don't blindly follow the crowd, waffle in the face of adversity, or change their opinion unless the change is supported by a strong, factual case.

Integrity. Courageous people know the difference between right and wrong. They don't just talk about honor; they live it every day by following the letter, as well as the spirit, of the law. They are trustworthy, objective, fair, and tolerant, and they stand up against injustice — backing their words with action.

Leadership. Courageous people aren't deterred by adversity or afraid of what people may think of them. Courageous leaders motivate people with personal charisma, expertise, integrity, and respect rather than by using their position or authority as a crutch. Courageous people are tough, but fair. While they may ask others to achieve the "impossible," they ask of others only what they're willing to do themselves.

Compassion. Courageous people put other people's needs ahead of their own. They know that the Captain must go down with the ship and that being selfless helps to gain the respect of friends and colleagues.

Objectivity. Courageous people understand the importance of trust, honesty, and full disclosure while confronting people who hide behind untruths. They believe that people are willing to make tough decisions if the options are presented to them in an open, honest, and objective manner. They also believe that people should admit their mistakes, learn from them, and move on rather than waste precious time playing politics.

Strength in Adversity. Courageous people aren't afraid of swimming against the tide or challenging the status quo. They stare adversity in the eye — running toward the problem rather than away from it. They know that saying "no" to one idea may enable them to say "yes" to another, and that old ways of doing things shouldn't stand in the way of a better solution.

Change Masters. Courageous people step outside their comfort zone to meet the challenges that lie ahead. They know that change is part of life and that some of the greatest advances have been realized by embracing change.

Embrace the Unknown. Courageous people follow their intuition. If information required to make a good decision isn't available, they follow their instincts.

Action. Courageous people put their money where their mouth is. They know that it's not enough to talk about doing something — instead, they act.

15 Everyday Acts Of Courage

There are so many different types and ways to be courageous. My favourite story is one of a young lady who was battling severe anxiety and depression due to bullying at school. She left school at 14 and spent time in and out of hospital for three years. One evening it took a lot of courage to come to her mum's book launch with a room filled with people. She seemed to change that evening which made her mum's heart sing. On the way home she told her mum she wanted to find the courage to speak at schools around her journey to help others. A few months later her daughter's dream came true and she spoke in front 300 students about her journey with three key messages around kindness, compassion and non-judgement. There was not a dry eye in the room. Her courage changed her life and that of others too. That young girl is my daughter.

Here are my everyday acts of courage and leadership to practice and celebrate:

1. Saying sorry.

It takes courage to admit when you are wrong. It's a bold act to admit when you make a mistake. Saying sorry takes you out of your comfort zone and enhances your relationships. That's big. Do it!

2. Be yourself and own it.

Don't imitate anyone. Take off your mask. Allow yourself to become vulnerable. Share your flaws with others. See perfection in your imperfections. Who you are is a gift to the world. Allow yourself to shine.

3. Take responsibility and accountability.

You are where you are in life because of the choices you make. If you don't like what you see, change it. Reflection and choices are the keys and I often ask myself – I am living and leading a life I truly want? Responsibility brings freedom.

4. Keep your commitments and make goals.

Write down everything you say you are going to do and want to achieve. Write down the promises you make to others and what you want to achieve in your life. When you keep your promises, you build self-respect. Others respect you as well.

5. Have a voice and say no.

Speak up. Make a difference. Share your feelings when you witness an injustice. Practice sharing your opinion. Don't allow someone to take advantage of you. Learn to say, "no." Refuse to hold back when your gut says to move forward.

"The most courageous act is still to think for yourself. Aloud."

Coco Chanel

6. Let go and forgive.

Stop wallowing over what could have been. Forgive yourself. Forgive everyone. What happened is over unless you keep it alive by reliving it in your mind. When we know better, we do better. It takes courage to move on.

7. Grow and learn.

Learn something new. Step into the unknown. Change the way you do things. It doesn't matter if you get it the first time. Try again. Give yourself permission to learn. Seize the opportunity. Growth brings new opportunities.

8. Listen and be present.

Listen to people who disagree with you. Listen to family members who think you are wrong. Listen to the elderly person in the coffee shop. Listen when you only want to speak and give advice. Listen and thank the other person for sharing.

9. Help others.

Help someone who doesn't help you. Help others when you don't have the time. Help someone who can't pay you back. Help someone when you are the one needing help. Learn to be of service. That's why we're here.

10. Courage is Love.

Be kind to each other. Be truthful. Accept differences. Spend time together. Act like a loving person. You can love difficult people as well. Forgive them and wish them the best. Let them go with love.

11. Practice gratitude.

Count your blessings. Tell the people in your life "thank you." Be grateful for the people you love and for the people who love you. Focus on what you are grateful for.

12. Choose happiness.

Make a decision that you will think happy thoughts, speak kind words, and spend time doing things that bring you joy. Have a good attitude. See the glass half full. Look at the bright side. Expect the best. Choose to focus on what's good.

13. Learn from your mistakes.

Reflect on what went wrong and what you could have done better. Look for your lesson. Choose to grow forward. Be compassionate. Make a new plan. Refuse to give up.

In general, we experience two types of fear: the fear that indicates we're in physical danger (for example, when we're standing in the middle of a busy road), and the fear that indicates our ego is in danger (e.g. fear of public speaking).

In modern society, there are very few situations in which we are in physical danger, so most of the fear we feel has more to do with threats to our ego and self-concept than threats that could cause us physical harm. However, these two types of fear feel very similar, and provoke the same primal fight or flight response in our body.

Boosting our courage isn't about eradicating our fear; it's such a primal, instinctive response that this isn't a realistic goal. Instead, it's about learning how to respond to our fear in a healthy way. Here are seven effective ways you can start boosting your courage today:

1. Remind yourself that fear isn't always helpful.

Fear is helpful in situations where we have control and can take steps to minimize the risk of our disaster scenario coming true. For example, if we're still standing in the middle of that busy road I mentioned above, fear is a good indicator to start moving. Equally, if we're facing an upcoming public speaking gig, our fear might indicate that we need a little more practice.

In some situations, however, fear can do more harm than good. If we respond to every fear-inducing situation like we're in mortal danger, we're going to end up missing out on valuable opportunities to live fully and enjoy growth and new experiences. A helpful, courage-boosting question to ask yourself when deciding how to respond to a situation is: "Am I avoiding pain, or seeking growth?"

2. Expand your comfort zone gradually.

Boosting your courage isn't something that happens overnight. It's a day-by-day process and you're more likely to experience success in this area if you focus on expanding your comfort zone one step at a time.

For example, if you notice that you feel fear around talking to new people, start small by asking someone for directions or striking up a short conversation with people you encounter in your day-to-day life but are unlikely to see again (shop assistants, checkout staff, people waiting in line, and so on). Once you feel more comfortable doing that, start working your way up to longer conversations with people you are likely to see infrequently (new work colleagues, friends of friends), then people you're likely to see on a regular basis, and so on.

3. Remember to breathe.

Our physical state has a huge impact on our emotional state. Try slouching over and drooping your mouth into a frown for 10 seconds, then sitting up straight with a dazzling smile for another 10—did you notice a difference in how you felt?

If we want to boost our courage in a particular situation, one of the most effective ways of doing this is to slow down our breathing. When we're feeling fearful, our breathing unconsciously becomes faster and shallower. Taking a few deep breaths sends the signal to our minds that everything is OK and helps us relax.

4. Take a step back and get objective.

Usually, the fear we feel isn't so much about the worst case scenario we're thinking of—it's about how we would feel if that scenario comes to pass.

Using the public speaking example, let's imagine the worst case scenario is that you forget what you wanted to say. Even if the audience ended up booing you off the stage, all that would happen on a factual level afterwards is that you go home and learn from the experience for next time. How you feel, on the other hand, might include embarrassed, ashamed, hopeless, and a host of other uncomfortable feelings. The next time you're faced with a public speaking opportunity, it will be the feelings you remember and fear more than what actually happened.

To boost your courage, try to stay objective and focus on the facts of the matter. Pay attention to what actually happened, rather than the meaning you're attaching to it.

5. Think of how you'd view a friend in the same situation.

One of the biggest challenges to our courage is the fact that we tend to be harsher with ourselves than we are with other people.

The next time you're faced with an opportunity to expand your comfort zone, ask yourself how you would perceive your best friend in the same situation. Would you focus on the potential pitfalls, or would you admire them for taking the risk?

Thinking about how we'd view other people in the same situation can help reset any stories we're telling ourselves and engender more self-trust and courage.

6. Ask, "Who do I need to become?" instead of, "What do I need to do?"

When it comes to stretching our comfort zone and committing acts of courage, we often focus on what we need to do. The real shift that needs to take place, however, revolves around who we need to become.

For example, if you decided you wanted to get active and train for a triathlon by the end of the year, information that will tell you what to do to get there is readily available. What will decide whether or not you have the courage to actually go out and do it, however, is thinking about who you need to become in order to be someone who does that.

What qualities would a courageous future version of yourself have? How would they start each day? What new habits would they develop? What old habits would they change?

7. Take action.

When we're feeling low on courage, it's tempting to sit and think about how we're going to find the motivation we're looking for, to read articles online (present company excepted, of course), talk about it—anything but actually do the thing we're afraid of doing.

If you're waiting to feel more courageous before taking action, you're going to be waiting a long time. In reality, the longer you wait before taking action, the less courageous you'll feel. The only thing that will help you feel more courageous is taking action, stepping outside your comfort zone, and sending yourself the message that you are a courageous person.

14. Embrace the small things.

Take time to love the small stuff. The taste of a glass of cold water, the different shades of red, a child's laugh or an elderly person's worn hands. Enjoy the sunrise and walk in the park. Enjoy...

15. Love Yourself. Accept your imperfections. Be your own best friend. Show yourself compassion, understanding and respect. This is the most courageous act of all.

Dear You,

People talk about finding courage.

But really, you're not "finding courage." You're practicing courage, creating it as a daily and consistent practice of walking into the fire of your fear and emerging as a braver, even more courageous self.

Important: this is not just semantics!

When you walk with the mindset that you're finding courage , this carries the implicit assumption that spades of courage are out there, outside of you, for you to find.

This very mindset keeps people on the self-help treadmill of trying to look for something outside themselves, and it buys right into the idea of being fearless (fearless is really the new perfectionism).

By contrast, when you are practicing courage, you're present, attentive, and embodied. You're looking at your life and asking yourself where you want to go, next, and what integrity requires, and what your heart's longing is, and what fear is saying NOT to do. Then, you're stepping into the heart of that, even though the fear is still there.

Finding courage is about something outside yourself.

Practicing courage is about going within.

CHAPTER TEN

Focused mindset.

The more focused you are on success the more likely you are to experience it. If only it was that simple, however having a success focused mindset will help you achieve more success. If you're not naturally predispositioned to think in terms of success, how can you develop a success focused mindset?

Developing a success focused mindset starts with developing three aspects of yourself: the mind, body, and spirit. If you can focus on all three of these, having a success focused mindset will become second nature.

The Mind

The mind is the part of you that makes you who you are, it enables you to reason and perceives the world around you. By taking care of your mind and training it, you'll be able to think more positively and focus on success.

The Body

Your body is important because while your mind controls your body if your body is not healthy no amount of mind control is going to help. Keeping your body healthy as well as your mind allows your mind to focus on success.

Spirit

The spirit is what you make of it. Think of your spirit as the part of you that either feels at peace or does not feel at peace. If your spirit is distracted it shows up in your mind as bad thoughts. The trick to developing a success focused mindset is to experience success. Start by trying new things that help you feel successful.

Evaluate

The ability to look honestly at any situation and evaluate it without emotion is an essential part of turning your mind around to successful thoughts instead of thoughts of failure.

Focus

Many times we are put under pressure we tend to have some go-to attitudes and emotions that we feel. Adversity is a necessary component in life. Without trials and tribulations, what good is success?

It is important when trying to become success focused on maintaining your focus on positive affirmations and thoughts. Turn each negative thought into a positive, flip it around in your mind, and move forward. Sometimes you only need a little modification in something to turn a sure failure into an outright success.

Attention is the most precious resource that we can leverage to actually get things done. The ability to focus and for a longer period of time on one activity is undoubtedly essential to every person who wishes to attract abundance and results.

Our brain is a very complex mechanism that often works without our awareness. Our subconscious mind, the deep place where all our memories, feelings, and neuro-associations are stored can be our best friend or our worst enemy.

No matter what goals, profession, or work you are currently pursuing, a disciplined mind is critical for your success. For that reason, in today's post, I'm sharing 10 effective ways to train your brain to stay focused and productive. Pay attention and apply!

1. Plan and Visualize a Few Critical Tasks Each Day

Our thoughts shape our reality. Why? Because our thoughts generate feelings, feelings lead to action, and action leads to results.

As a part of your morning routine, establish one to three critical tasks that must be done throughout the day. Don't just think of them superficially. Visualize them and simulate the feelings you'll get after finishing each task. If you truly think about your day's success, your subconscious will do everything it can to help you turn thoughts into reality.

2. Find Your Peak Hours

Some people perform better during the day, while others do great during the night. To find your most productive hours – the "peak hours" – you should actively measure your productivity during various hours of the day.

Pay attention to your energy, thought patterns, distractions, motivation, and moods while experimenting different work hours. Make sure you allow at least a week to establish these peak hours. So, if you try to get your most important tasks done from 8 AM to 10 AM, experiment it for a week. Next week, focus your attention on critical tasks starting from 10 AM and ending at 12 PM.

3. Avoid Multitasking

Multitasking has been proven to reduce our cognitive abilities due to the fact that the brain can only fully focus on one task at a time. Even though multitasking can be beneficial in various situations, you should avoid it as much as you can whenever you deal with important tasks. Give your full attention to the task at hand to improve the quality and speed of work!

4. Treat Your Mind Like a Muscle

What do you do when you want to build muscles? You exercise. Not just once, but regularly. Training your brain to stay focused is a matter of practice. Every time you experience distracting thoughts, you have to acknowledge them for what they are – time and attention killers.

Whenever you feel like you "must stop working", you should push it a little further. If you have big trouble focusing right now, you shouldn't try to work for 60 minutes straight. Build your levels of focus gradually. First two weeks, try focusing for 20 minutes, take a 5-minute break, then go again. In two months, you should be able to stay focused for 60 minutes and get a lot of things done!

5. Build Willpower and Discipline

Very few of us are making real decisions. A decision is a deal with your mind that no matter what happens, your decision sticks. Therefore, when you say, "I should exercise", you should immediately replace the "should" with "must". Otherwise, your brain won't take your intent seriously and it won't "care" to help.

Willpower and self-discipline are two related traits that should be developed at the same time. Your willpower is the fuel of your actions. Your discipline is your ability to go past intrusive thoughts, comfort zone, and laziness.

Here's what few people tell you: these skills require consistent practice, building them is not easy, and giving up is not an option.

6. Acknowledge Your Need to Avoid Pain and to Gain Pleasure

When we do something, we do it because we seek pleasure or because we want to avoid pain. Think about it – when students must do their homework, they procrastinate because their subconscious minds signal incoming pain. When the deadline is close, they'll take action in order to avoid the pain of receiving a bad grade.

Take this example and synchronize it with your life. Every time you want to focus on a task, acknowledge your immediate response. Are you trying to avoid pain? Or you're looking for pleasure? When you become the observer, you'll be able to be in charge.

7. Avoid Distractions

You can't train your brain to stay focused unless you ensure that your external environment also lacks distractions. Your phone, for example, should never disturb your attention. Turn off the notifications, say "NO" whenever someone interrupts you, and be committed to cut off every possible distraction around you.

8. Leverage the Power of Habits

If you build empowering habits, you'll no longer have to use your motivation and willpower to become focused. Your mind will recognize the pattern and will make your job easier. For example – when you wash your teeth and face in the morning, you're doing automatically without using any significant amounts of focus, energy, and motivation. Building productive habits is like teaching your brain how to behave at different yet specific times.

9. Practice Mindfulness

Mindfulness implies self-awareness. Practicing mindfulness is nothing more than focusing your entire attention on the present moment. Your present thoughts and feelings, the environment that surrounds you, your breath, your heartbeat...you choose. It doesn't matter what you focus on – as long as you're "here", "now", your mind is present.

You can practice mindfulness in various situations: while reading, working, studying, washing dishes, walking in the park, and so on. When your focus is prioritized on what's happening now, you'll perform better in most of the situations.

10. Become Sovereign

Sovereignty is the practice of aligning your thoughts, emotions, and actions. Most people lack sovereignty, which means that their emotions aren't in harmony with their thoughts, neither with their actions.

For example, if you want to read a book today but you instantly feel that this is going to be boring, you'll never actually read that book. However, if you think of something and you get positive feelings as a reaction, taking action won't be that difficult.

If you're aware of this, you can easily implement it. As a result, staying focused on your responsibilities and work will become a piece of cake.

Takeaways

Improving your mind is everything. Until you let yourself be carried by your thoughts, immediate pleasures, fear, and pain, you will experience exactly what you "cultivate". As they say, you reap what you sow.

This refers to the universal cause-and-effect principle, which suggests that every thought and feeling you experience and every action you take will generate an effect. Good or bad, that's totally up to you.

Learning how to stay focused through the ups and downs of each day is critical to your achieving success. Why?

Because distraction is all around you.

Lurking behind every corner is a time-waster waiting for you to give in. To ruin an otherwise productive day and derail your progress. But you don't want that! You want focus.

Because focus leads to achievement and achievement leads to success. And I don't know about you, but that sounds good to me.

What does it mean to stay focused?

To stay focused means to simply persist with the task at hand. To continue to work towards whatever it is that you need to do and ensure that you stay concentrated on that one activity.

It isn't multitasking. It isn't daydreaming. It's focusing in on the task at hand and putting in the work to get it done.

Now, staying focused is an easy concept to explain, but is it easy to do? It can be with practice.

I've always found that the more deliberate I was about my focus, the stronger it was. Meaning that the times where I never considered my focus levels were times that I was completely distracted.

But, when I actually put in the effort to improve my focus, I found that I was able to hone in on my work that much more.

Which is great news for you!

Because by being here, by taking the initiative to enhance and learn how to stay focused, you are being deliberate in your methodology and are well on your way to better concentration.

It's all connected

Focus is a powerful thing. Sure, it's great for getting a task done in the moment, but it's so much more important than that.

Because what focus actually allows you to do is something much bigger – it allows you to make progress.

Yes, progress.

Progress in your work, on your goals, with your fitness. Focus, properly aimed, is a strong tool in your tool belt. See it like this – the stronger your focus, the more you can get done and make real progress.

The more you progress, the more you will achieve, and the more you achieve, the sooner you will be able to achieve your goals and create your ideal life.

It's all connected. And focus is at the heart of it all.

So be sure to use the following tips to help you increase your focus each day. Remind yourself how important it is to stay locked in on the task at hand and use them to your advantage to move forward faster and better than ever before.

Whenever you need to focus

We're just about there. Just about ready to start exploring the tips for how to stay focused and productive each day. But there's one last thing I want to touch on – when to apply these tips.

Because you can't simply read these tips and move about your day.

You need to actually apply them. To use them in your daily life and experiment with what works best for you.

With that in mind, use these tips whenever you need to focus. Whenever you have a task that needs to get done, whenever you have a plan that you want to make, whenever you want to make progress forward in some way, shape, or form.

That's when it's time to focus.

How To Stay Focused: 7 Tips For Solid Focus And Productivity

As I mentioned above, use the following tips to help you stay focused and productive each day. See each tip as an experiment.

Whenever you need to buckle down and concentrate, choose 1 from the list below and see if it helps.

If it does, keep using it in the future.

If it doesn't, try 1 of the other tips until you find a good fit.

Choose 1, try it out, see what works. Continue to run trial and error with the various tactics to discover what works best for you. Everyone is different and what works for everyone is different, but by being here and by taking the time to learn and grow, you're certainly heading in the right direction.

With that, it's now time to explore the list of ways to solidify your focus and productivity.

1. How to stay focused – Track your time

You may think you know how much time you spend on various tasks throughout the day.

You're probably wrong.

That's nothing against you. It's just that unless you actually track your time, you'll never truly know where it goes. In fact, some studies suggest that only a small percentage of individuals can precisely gauge their time.

That's crazy!

Don't work in the dark. Instead, harness your productivity by recognizing where your time goes each day. How can you do that?

By tracking it.

Meaning that for a couple of days try jotting down exactly what you do and when. For example:

Work on report: 8:15-9:15

Check Instagram: 9:15-9:22

Send client emails: 9:22-10:10

And so on and so forth all day. Then after a day or 2, look back at your list of tracked time. You'll be surprised by where your time actually went.

When I first did this, I was blown away by where my time was going. But by going through this activity, I was able to better understand my time and was therefore able to more deliberately act on it.

Doing so allowed me to increase my focus and work on the things that actually mattered. It helped me turn each day into a productive day where I could better concentrate and work on things that were truly important.

And it can do the same for you.

So grab some paper or start a new note on your phone and try tracking your time for the next day or 2.

2. Take consistent breaks

It may sound counter-intuitive, but taking planned breaks can really help improve your focus.

Short breaks, even if only for a few minutes, will allow you to maintain a consistent level of execution. Taking them will allow you to rest, recover, and reset so that you can get back to your work with renewed energy and concentration.

What happens if you don't take breaks? Well, you've probably experienced it before – decreased effectiveness, feeling cloudy, burnt out, tired.

No good.

Be sure to take breaks, then, so that you can recharge and resume your work with better clarity and determination.

This is one of my favorite (and easiest to follow) tips for how to stay focused and motivated in the long term. Breaks are a simple thing that you can start doing to give yourself the jolt of focus you need.

And if you're feeling a little sluggish, here are some strategies to help you get motivated.

3. How to stay focused – Work towards your goals

Goal setting isn't something you would normally think of when trying to stay focused, but hear me out. When you set a goal for yourself, you are giving a direction to your time.

You're saying, "This is where I want to go."

You are giving purpose and clarity to your time and are taking active steps to achieve or do something of value. And then while putting in the work, you know where to go and what to do along the way with your goal acting as the guide.

In other words, by going through the goal setting process, you will be able to better focus in the moment through the clarity and direction that the goal provides.

You'll understand what needs to get done and then you'll be able to put in the work and make progress forward because of the goal you set for yourself.

Goal setting gives you the clarity you need to be effective with your time. It allows you to concentrate on what's in front of you because you're working on the things that actually need to get done.

So when it comes down to staying focused, make sure to set some goals for yourself. To help, I recommend my post on how to set goals or if you want something more detailed, my goal success course.

Oh and by the way, if you're wondering how to stay focused on your goals specifically, well that's a whole other discussion.

4. Have a plan for your time

One of the best ways to help you stay focused is by having a plan for your time. Creating a plan for your time each day will ensure that you:

Know what needs to be worked on

Work on things that actually matter

Make progress in a positive direction

And are productive with your time each day

It's a way that you can better harness your time for maximum effectiveness. In fact, this is one of my favorite tips for how to stay focused on a task because of how valuable it is.

Create a plan for your time and watch how much more productive and better focused you will be.

5. How to stay focused – Turn off your notifications

When it comes to how to stay focused while studying or how to stay focused at work, this tip is mandatory.

Turn off your notifications!

It is such a simple thing to do, but for some reason no one does it. But, notifications are incredibly distracting.

Just look around.

If you're sitting by someone, watch them for a mere 30 seconds. More than likely some new thing is going to pop up in front of them, completely distracting and derailing their focus.

If they give in and check the notification, they'll be distracted, lose their focus, and then have to spend time trying to remember where they left off.

Or almost worse, if they don't check the notification they'll still be doing their work, but will be wondering the entire time about that notification and what amazing promise of entertainment it possesses.

It's a lose-lose.

So don't even play that game by turning off your notifications. You can:

Mute group texts

Turn off new-email pop-ups

Disable social media notifications

And silence your chats (Slack, Skype, G-Chat) too

There is so much noise coming at you all the time. Do yourself a favor and limit some of that noise so that you can focus on the things that actually matter.

Because when it comes down to how to be productive AND how to stay focused throughout the day, turning off notifications is a must.

6. Listen to the right music

Another easy tip for staying focused throughout the day is to play some music. But, not just any music.

You want music that will help you concentrate.

Generally that means music with a steady, uplifting rhythm and little to no words. In turn, that will provide something pleasant to listen to without being distracting.

You can't focus on your task and sing your favorite song at the same time. At least, not well. So listen to music geared towards helping you focus and watch how your concentration levels improve because of it.

If you're looking for something good to listen to, I recommend this music for productivity.

7. How to stay focused – Get organized

Finally, when learning how to stay focused during the day, the final tip for this list is to get organized. What does it mean to get organized?

It means that you'll want to clean up the space around you – both internally and externally. Organize your immediate environment so that you can focus on what's in front of you.

Externally that means cleaning up those distracting piles of clutter around you. Or tidying up your desk. Or putting in headphones to block out loud co-workers.

Internally that means having a plan for random thoughts that you come across. Have a strategy for where to put them, how to handle them, and when to acknowledge them.

There's a lot to do when it comes to getting organized, but doing so will allow you to reduce the distractions around you; giving you better focus on what needs to get done.

This is one of those time management skills that not a lot of people take the time to develop, but once you have an organizational plan in place, you will be able to focus that much more.

Use the tips above to help you stay focused each and every day. Pick 1 and try it out. If it helps you get more done and better concentrate, keep using it. If it doesn't, try out 1 of the other tips.

Your focus-strategy may take some time to develop, but the results you gain will be well worth it.

Because again, the better you can focus, the more you can get done, and the sooner you can achieve your goals and ideal life. So put in the time and continue to work towards better focus.

Focus in terms of definition, seems simple but many people find it a very difficult concept to achieve or practise. You can accomplish a few things in this world without a large degree of focus.

What makes it difficult for humans to maintain focus for a while or a long time? Humans find it difficult to maintain a focus for a while or a long time because there are many distractions and activities that cause us to lose focus. By spending more time in nature, not only helps to regenerate your system but has many important lessons to teach us all. For example, an eagle can combine focus and force that leads it to capture its prey successfully. Lions barely use 20% of their energy to get 80% of their meals.

Why is focus or becoming a focused person challenging? It is important to talk about traits of a focused person and associated benefits. It is no longer a secret that having focus has led to many ingenious and innovative products being created to benefit individual or collective minds. Here are the 13 traits of a focused person:

1. They do not participate in small talk. You will not engage them in pretentious, small talk and unnecessary social hook-ups. Eleanor Roosevelt once said, "Great minds discuss ideas; average minds discuss events; small minds discuss people."

2. They do one thing at a time. I have a friend that claimed that they could multi-task but when he is involved in other things, he kept repeating himself because his attention was divided in many directions. The focused person always strives to do the difficult thing first from their list of priorities. As a result, they are highly productive.

3. They do not postpone decision or action. They hardly procrastinate, what needs to be done today, they do not postpone it until tomorrow.

4. They have a mature emotional regulation. When people give feedback or distract them from the work which is at hand.

5. They do not take things personally. They manage their mind, rather than let their mind manage them.

6. They keep a small and able group of people. A small group of trusted friends and family and as a result, they do not seek validations.

7. They avoid toxic people or environment. As they would drain their resources or life.

8. They live in the moment and are realistic. The past has no hold on their life and future does not exist either. They are in touch with their body, mind and soul.

9. They are very diligent. They are not impulsive when making decisions.

10. They are not involved in other people's business. If it does not involve them, they will respect your privacy.

11. They are realistic optimists. They avoid illusion or escapism to run away from reality.

12. They have strong boundaries. These are with themselves and others.

13. They know when to end a project or relationship without being overly sentimental about it. It takes lot of focus to keep going when tough times arrive. They do not quit if it is a worthwhile goal to pursue or complete.

Many extraordinary people who have remarkable traits, which they have developed or acquired through either nurture or nature. Meanwhile, being focused is a very difficult and challenging habit to have and develop. Part of being focused is to live consciously, to be aware what is taking place around you with regards to your body, feelings and mind. Meditation is known to be a powerful tool to raise awareness of this, but it is not for everyone. Discipline yourself to commit yourself to one thing at a time, more practise of this will increase your ability to focus.

CHAPTER ELEVEN

Positive mindset.

Is your glass half-empty or half-full? How you answer this age-old question about positive thinking may reflect your outlook on life, your attitude toward yourself, and whether you're optimistic or pessimistic — and it may even affect your health.

Indeed, some studies show that personality traits such as optimism and pessimism can affect many areas of your health and well-being. The positive thinking that usually comes with optimism is a key part of effective stress management. And effective stress management is associated with many health benefits. If you tend to be pessimistic, don't despair — you can learn positive thinking skills.

Understanding positive thinking and self-talk

Positive thinking doesn't mean that you keep your head in the sand and ignore life's less pleasant situations. Positive thinking just means that you approach unpleasantness in a more positive and productive way. You think the best is going to happen, not the worst.

Positive thinking often starts with self-talk. Self-talk is the endless stream of unspoken thoughts that run through your head. These automatic thoughts can be positive or negative. Some of your self-talk comes from logic and reason. Other self-talk may arise from misconceptions that you create because of lack of information.

If the thoughts that run through your head are mostly negative, your outlook on life is more likely pessimistic. If your thoughts are mostly positive, you're likely an optimist — someone who practices positive thinking.

The health benefits of positive thinking

Researchers continue to explore the effects of positive thinking and optimism on health. Health benefits that positive thinking may provide include:

Increased life span

Lower rates of depression

Lower levels of distress

Greater resistance to the common cold

Better psychological and physical well-being

Better cardiovascular health and reduced risk of death from cardiovascular disease

Better coping skills during hardships and times of stress

It's unclear why people who engage in positive thinking experience these health benefits. One theory is that having a positive outlook enables you to cope better with stressful situations, which reduces the harmful health effects of stress on your body.

It's also thought that positive and optimistic people tend to live healthier lifestyles — they get more physical activity, follow a healthier diet, and don't smoke or drink alcohol in excess.

Identifying negative thinking

Not sure if your self-talk is positive or negative? Some common forms of negative self-talk include:

Filtering. You magnify the negative aspects of a situation and filter out all of the positive ones. For example, you had a great day at work. You completed your tasks ahead of time and were complimented for doing a speedy and thorough job. That evening, you focus only on your plan to do even more tasks and forget about the compliments you received.

Personalizing. When something bad occurs, you automatically blame yourself. For example, you hear that an evening out with friends is canceled, and you assume that the change in plans is because no one wanted to be around you.

Catastrophizing. You automatically anticipate the worst. The drive-through coffee shop gets your order wrong and you automatically think that the rest of your day will be a disaster.

Polarizing. You see things only as either good or bad. There is no middle ground. You feel that you have to be perfect or you're a total failure.

Focusing on positive thinking

You can learn to turn negative thinking into positive thinking. The process is simple, but it does take time and practice — you're creating a new habit, after all. Here are some ways to think and behave in a more positive and optimistic way:

Identify areas to change. If you want to become more optimistic and engage in more positive thinking, first identify areas of your life that you usually think negatively about, whether it's work, your daily commute or a relationship. You can start small by focusing on one area to approach in a more positive way.

Check yourself. Periodically during the day, stop and evaluate what you're thinking. If you find that your thoughts are mainly negative, try to find a way to put a positive spin on them.

Be open to humor. Give yourself permission to smile or laugh, especially during difficult times. Seek humor in everyday happenings. When you can laugh at life, you feel less stressed.

Follow a healthy lifestyle. Aim to exercise for about 30 minutes on most days of the week. You can also break it up into 10-minute chunks of time during the day. Exercise can positively affect mood and reduce stress. Follow a healthy diet to fuel your mind and body. And learn techniques to manage stress.

Surround yourself with positive people. Make sure those in your life are positive, supportive people you can depend on to give helpful advice and feedback. Negative people may increase your stress level and make you doubt your ability to manage stress in healthy ways.

Practice positive self-talk. Start by following one simple rule: Don't say anything to yourself that you wouldn't say to anyone else. Be gentle and encouraging with yourself. If a negative thought enters your mind, evaluate it rationally and respond with affirmations of what is good about you. Think about things you're thankful for in your life.

If you tend to have a negative outlook, don't expect to become an optimist overnight. But with practice, eventually your self-talk will contain less self-criticism and more self-acceptance. You may also become less critical of the world around you.

When your state of mind is generally optimistic, you're better able to handle everyday stress in a more constructive way. That ability may contribute to the widely observed health benefits of positive thinking

I know, I know. You're probably thinking it's impossible to be positive every day. However, extenuating circumstances aside, it's quite possible to start your day with a positive mindset. When things go wrong, there's always a silver lining to keep you above water, even if you're swimming against the current.

There are many ways you can maintain a sunny disposition in even the worst of situations. Be sure to:

1. Make a plan

Things won't always go according to this plan, but if you set out a list of goals you want to accomplish by the end of the day (or week), you'll always have something to strive for. By making a to-do list, you ensure that each day you experience will be at least a little different than the one before it. Plus, when you check off that last item every day, you'll go to bed knowing you did much more than simply go to work, come home, and watch TV.

2. Have a routine

Although you appreciate variety, there are some things you should do every day. Take some time to stretch and exercise, even if it means taking the stairs instead of the elevator. Use quiet mornings to spend a few moments in deep thought, or the time right before bed to reflect on what you accomplished throughout the day. If you have a hobby, set aside a specific block of time to work on it every day. Once you get into a routine, you'll have specific things to look forward to.

3. Appreciate the small stuff

How do you feel when you spill coffee on yourself, first thing in the morning? Or hit every red light on the way to work? Do you think "Ugh, this happens to me every time"?

Obviously, this is an overreaction. You simply don't make a big deal about all the times you avoid spilling coffee on yourself. And there have definitely been times you've hit every green light on the way to work that you didn't jump up and down about. It's an odd phenomenon that spilling coffee on yourself is enough to start your day off badly, but not spilling coffee on yourself isn't enough to make your day absolutely incredible.

Maybe it's time we start celebrating these victories all the time, like that football player in the commercial: "Woo!!! 44, that's me!" (C'mon, you know the one...)

4. Smile

It sounds cheesy, but starting your morning off with a smile can set the ball rolling toward an incredibly positive day. Keep that smile on your face as you walk past people on the street and in the office. Not only will it subconsciously keep you in a great mood, but it may also have a contagious effect.

Especially on Mondays, when many people are feeling pretty crabby, try to be the catalyst that lightens up everyone else's day.

5. Use positive vocabulary

A few weeks ago, a colleague of mine asked how I was doing. I replied, as a courtesy, "Not too bad!" (with a smile on my face). He responded with, "Not bad? I want to hear 'ecstatic', 'incredible', 'amazing!'"

There's a big difference between "not bad" and "amazing". The former makes it seem like you're amazed that you're not feeling atrocious, whereas the latter is bursting with excitement. Express yourself with vivacious vocabulary (and that cheesy smile) to spread positivity throughout your life.

6. Spend time with positive people

Nobody likes a "Debbie Downer." If you find yourself surrounded by people who thrive on being unhappy, ditch them immediately. Obviously, your friends will have their ups and downs. But if they are constantly trying to bring you down with them, you need to take control of the situation before you lose your sunny disposition.

Find people who exhibit the same excitement for life that you have, and you'll never experience a dull moment.

7. Do something nice for others

Being positive isn't all about yourself. Spread the love around! You could pick up your wife's favorite flowers on the way home from work, or volunteer at a soup kitchen during your free time. You'd be surprised how good it feels to help others out and make their lives just a bit easier. If we all took time to pay it forward, we could set off a chain reaction of good deeds that spread throughout the entire world.

8. Control your own destiny

No one can force you to be positive; you have to make it so. It might take work, but the rewards are definitely worth the effort. Don't just sit back and hope to get promoted; put yourself out there and make sure your boss sees how hard you've been working. Don't wait for your future husband to sweep you off your feet; go out there and find him.

Your dreams will never become a reality unless you decide to go for it.

9. Don't beat yourself up

Everyone has bad days, and everyone makes mistakes. Don't waste precious time kicking yourself for some bonehead decision you made. Instead, use what you learned to help yourself improve the next time a similar situation arises. If you went for a job interview and didn't get a call back, think about how you could have presented yourself a little better. Then, view that lesson learned as ammo for your next interview.

Life is a learning process. If you're not learning, you're wasting your time.

10. Do something different

Getting caught up in the daily grind can make you bored and complacent. Try to do something new every single day. It could be something simple like using your GPS to find a different way home. Or something more drastic like picking up that musical instrument you've always wanted to learn. Learn to cook a new meal. Take that book off your shelf that you've been dying to get into. Take your family out for an impromptu ice cream date.

There are infinite experiences to have on this Earth, and only one life to experience them all in. So what are you waiting for? Don't waste a minute!

Across the globe, the term 'the power of positive thinking' is well known. Some may find it to be too cliche, but those who have learned to truly embrace it can surely tell you that it works wonders! Regardless of our circumstances and situations, we are all capable of being positive. It's all just a matter of believing that we can be, and putting that into practice. Here's how to stay positive and keep your happy on, no matter what comes your way!

Here's How To Stay Positive

Life is constantly throwing unexpected challenges at us — so here's how to stay positive no matter what.

1. Change Your Perspective

Being positive starts with changing your perspective on how you see things. If you believe something is negative, then it probably will be (and vice versa). Challenge that negativity by embracing the mindset of a fixer and a doer. If there's a will, there's a way! That's truly how to stay positive.

2. Take A Step Back

Take a deep breath, and take a step (or two) back. Let go of your negative energy, let go of the anger and resentment, and focus on improving and finding a positive. There's always a light at the end of the tunnel, you just have to find it.

3. Be Mindful

To stay positive means being self aware and in touch with your feelings. Don't let fear take over and have you convinced that things won't work out for the best. Accept the criticism that comes your way, and know that most things in life aren't personal.

4. Create A Positive Environment

Create a positive environment for yourself. Surround yourself with positive people that bring you up, support you, and want only the best for you. Avoid bringing yourself into situations that don't add anything to your happiness — they are a waste of your precious time.

5. Take It Slow

Take things slow, and don't be so hard on yourself. Learning to stay positive is a process. Trust that your patience and optimism will pay off, and that good things will come your way when the time is right if you allow them to.

6. Bring Positivity To Others

When it comes to how to stay positive, it starts by bringing positivity to others! Be generous with others, be respectful, be open-minded, and all of that good energy will surely make its way back to you.

7. A Healthy Body Makes A Healthy Mind

The body-mind connection is absolutely undeniable, and is key when it comes to happiness. In order to bring more positivity into your life, working out on a regular basis, eating a balanced diet, meditating, and getting sufficient amounts of sleep (at least 7 hours) are all great ways to make for a healthy body and mind.

8. Practice Being Grateful

Being grateful for what we have can help us see how many amazing things we have in our lives, and help us focus on the good. Being stuck on our problems and what we don't have will never get us anywhere. Keep a journal or a diary to express your daily gratitude, even for the smallest things.

9. Enjoy Nature

Nature is a great way to stay positive and bring more happiness into your life. If you're feeling down, treating yourself to some quiet time outdoors is always a good idea. It's been found that we react better in natural spaces, and that spending time in nature can both reduce stress and increase creativity. One study conducted in Finland found that urban dwellers who walked through nature for even just twenty minutes daily were less stressed compared to those who walked through the city.

10. Reduce Materialism & Ideals

Our modern society puts all kinds of ideas into our heads — that we have to be a certain way and have certain luxurious, material things in order to be a worthy person. But before social media and television, we never needed such things to self-justify. Get rid of these ideals, and focus on the reality, not what you think you should be.

11. Listen To Music

Music is always a wonderful way to bring more positivity into your life! There are endless feel-good songs and playlists out there that can surely get you singing and dancing, forgetting what you were even upset about in the first place. In fact, it's actually a scientific fact that listening to music releases dopamine, the feel-good chemical in your brain.

12. Smile!

When you're happy, you smile. But believe it or not, when you smile, it also makes you happy. Practice smiling even when you don't feel like it. Look at yourself in the mirror, and show yourself what a beautiful, big smile you have. Smiling is key when it comes to how to stay positive in a negative environment.

13. Follow Your Passion

Do what you love! When it comes to being positive, you have to surround yourself with things and people that make you feel good. For example, if creative writing is your passion, then do that! Even if it's not your current job, make sure to find the time for the things that bring you joy.

14. Join A Support Group

Being alone can be hard. Having a support group to share your feelings with can be highly beneficial in learning new techniques on how to stay positive no matter what.

How Does Staying Positive Benefit You?

There's no doubt about it that being positive can benefit every aspect of your life.

Being positive has been found to improve health and increase longevity. In fact, it's been found that those with a positive attitude can add as much as 10 years to their lives!

Being positive has also been found to help with career advancement, team building, financial success, and even with athletic performance for those that have emotions such as gratitude and appreciation.

When it comes to relationships, positive people tend to have more friends, which is key to happiness and living a long life. Couples with a more positive-to-negative ratio of interactions are also found to last longer.

How To Stay Positive At Work

It can be a challenge to figure out how to stay positive at work, with constant stress around you and perhaps co-workers that don't always see eye to eye with you.

In order to stay positive at work, it's important to change the way you think of your job:

Spread appreciation, gratitude, and good vibes throughout the office, no matter what comes your way.

When something ticks you off, stop for a minute and think before you speak. Our instant reactions tend to not be the most positive.

Listen to others, be open-minded, and be on top of your tasks to avoid being overloaded.

How To Stay Positive During Job Search

While our jobs can be seriously frustrating, not having one at all is even more frustrating. It's hard to keep your head up during a job search that feels like it has no end date.

Here's how to stay positive during job search:

Don't keep those feelings bottled up inside, and don't be afraid to share them with your friends and family — they will be happy to support you through this difficult time.

Be realistic with yourself, and don't expect things to happen overnight. Finding a good job is a process, but with patience, something good will come along before you know it.

Try to create a routine for yourself so that you still feel productive and motivated to wake up every morning as you continue your job search.

A Friendly Reminder To Not Give Up!

It can be hard to constantly stay positive, but it's important to keep your head up and always trust that everything will be ok. When it comes to how to stay positive, the secret lies in the power of positive thinking. While our life circumstances might not always be in our hands, the way we think sure is!

CHAPTER TWELVE

Learning mindset.

Changing the way you think can change the way you learn. Because of this, having a growth mindset might be one of the most important parts of education.

Imagine if you could do anything, just because you believe you can. That's essentially a growth mindset – knowing your talents can be developed can help you achieve more in education and life.

Carol Dweck, a Stanford psychology professor, pioneered research that revealed that underlying beliefs about intelligence can have a dramatic impact on education.

Studies by Dweck showed that individuals who believe talents can be learned achieve more than those who believe talents are innate qualities. This led her to coin the phrase "growth mindset".

The growth mindset is based on the idea that intelligence is malleable and that when you change your mindset to a growth perspective, you can achieve more.

The idea of pliable intelligence ties in with neural development. Studies on brain plasticity have shown how connections between neurons can change with experience. When you practise something, neural networks develop new connections and strengthen existing ones.

So, when you practise a new skill or learn something new, you are stimulating neural growth. Through the process of learning, you can actually change the structure of your brain, developing and rewiring it to engage in more positive ways of doing things.

A fixed mindset is based on the assumption that our intelligence, creativity, and skills are fixed traits that we can't change.

As such, when people with a fixed mindset make a mistake, they believe it reflects weaknesses that are impossible to change. People with this mindset prioritise documenting talent, as they are concerned with appearing intelligent, instead of working to improve personal qualities.

This view also dictates that talent is a quality a person is born with and is the main factor in success, meaning effort isn't necessary to succeed.

The key difference between a fixed and a growth mindset is that people with a growth mindset believe qualities such as intelligence, personality or character can be cultivated through effort. Through application and experience, anyone can grow and learn.

HAVING A GROWTH MINDSET IN THE CLASSROOM

Believing you can learn anything you put your mind to is crucial in education. Cultivating this growth mindset often starts with teachers and the way they respond to students' work.

Praising students for hard work, rather than intelligence, will help to foster confidence that anything can be learned with the right amount of effort. When students worry less about looking intelligent and put more energy into learning, they'll achieve more overall.

Conversely, Dweck's research found that when teacher's praise children for being smart, they encourage a fixed mindset, which discourages students from taking on challenges.

Many students can be afraid to admit they need to work at a task, out of fear they'll look unintelligent. In fact, psychology researchers have found that a fixed mindset is associated with more mental health challenges in adolescents.

Teenagers with a fixed mindset were 58% more likely to have symptoms of anxiety, depression, or aggression than their peers with a growth mindset.

However, putting effort into learning doesn't mean a student isn't naturally smart. Putting in effort should be viewed as the reason students enjoy academic success, rather than a reason to be embarrassed.

When a growth mindset for students is adopted in the classroom, learning potential is limitless.

HOW TO DEVELOP A GROWTH MINDSET

To develop a growth mindset while learning something new, view challenges as opportunities and mistakes as lessons learned, rather than failures.

One of the best ways to remind yourself to persevere and resist giving up after you have a setback is to use the word "yet".

For example, you might not know how to speak Spanish yet.

You might not know how to teach others yet.

You might not know how to lead a team yet.

You might not know how to carry out biological surveys yet.

But, with the right attitude and determination to learn, you'll be able to do all of these things while learning more about local and global issues and improving your employability at the same time.

APPLYING A GROWTH MINDSET TO FOR-GOOD WORK

The growth mindset is an important part of GVI's commitment to growth and development, both in terms of training individuals and working towards the United Nations Sustainable Development Goals (UN SDGs).

The UN SDGs require persistent growth, and a willingness to change how you approach them. We adapt how we work to ensure we are responding to current best practices, a mentality that is reflected in our Badge of Ethics. Our badge represents our journey of consistent development and growth through reflection.

We also apply the growth mindset to our training for participants. Our programs can present a range of challenges, so we encourage you to approach them with an open mind. We'll provide you with comprehensive training for all of the skills you'll need, and a growth mindset will help make sure you get the most out of this learning process.

Participating with GVI is an excellent way to exercise your growth mindset and apply this perspective to new learning opportunities. Explore our range of service-learning and sustainable development programs to find out more about the skills you can learn, while making an impact in the world.

Children who understand that the brain can get smarter—who have a growth mindset—do better in school because they have an empowering perspective on learning. They focus on improvement and see effort as a way to build their abilities. They see failure as a natural part of the learning process. In contrast, students who have a fixed mindset—those who believe that intelligence is fixed—tend to focus on judgment. They're more concerned with proving that they are smart or hiding that they're not. And that means they tend to avoid situations in which they might fail or might have to work hard.

Many studies show that children who have a growth mindset respond differently in challenging situations and do better in school over time.

In another study, researchers were interested in the kind of feedback people would seek out after they struggled. Researchers gave participants a difficult test and then told the participants that they hadn't done well on the test. Then, they gave them a choice: Did they want to look at the tests of people who had done worse than them or the tests of people who had done better? People with a growth mindset chose to learn from people who had done better than them. But people with a fixed mindset seemed more interested in making themselves feel better. They looked at the tests of people who had done worse.

How people maintain and repair their self-esteem has been a topic of widespread interest. In this article, the authors ask, What determines whether people will use direct, remedial actions, or defensive actions? In three studies, they tested the hypothesis that a belief in fixed intelligence (entity theory) would produce defensiveness, whereas a belief in improvable intelligence (incremental theory) would foster remediation. In each study, participants assigned to the entity condition opted for defensive self-esteem repair (downward comparison in Studies 1 and 3; a tutorial on already mastered material in Study 2), but those in the incremental condition opted for self-improvement (upward comparison in Studies 1 and 3; a tutorial on unmastered material in Study 2). Experiment 3 also linked these strategies to self-esteem repair; remedial strategies were the most effective in recovering lost self-esteem for those in the incremental condition, whereas defensive strategies were most effective for those in the entity condition.

Growth mindset leads to better math grades

A study with middle school students looked at the impact of fixed versus growth mindsets on achievement in math—a subject that many students find challenging. Students with a growth mindset earned higher math grades over time compared to students with a fixed mindset.

Growth mindset and advanced class placement

Mindsets have also been shown to predict who takes more advanced courses. In a study with middle school students, those with a growth mindset were more likely to be placed into advanced math over time.

Mangels: Mindset affects learning from mistakes

A growth mindset focuses students on learning, rather than simply performing well. You can see this when you look inside the brain. In one study, scientists brought people into the lab. They put an EEG cap on their heads to measure how active their brains were. While scientists were measuring brain activation, they asked participants a trivia question. Participants gave their answer, and then the scientists told them if they were right or wrong. In other words, they were given performance feedback.

The scientists found that the participants with a growth mindset and with a fixed mindset both had active brains when they were told whether they were right or wrong. So all participants paid attention to the performance feedback. What's interesting is what happened next. Participants were told the correct answer. And again, the scientists looked at how active the participants' brains were. The brains of people with a growth mindset were significantly more active than the brains of people with a fixed mindset. People with a fixed mindset were tuning out after they found out if they were right or wrong; they weren't interested in learning the correct answer. At the end of the study, the scientists gave participants a pop quiz with the same trivia questions. Not surprisingly, the people with a growth mindset did better.

Learning mindsets are a set of beliefs that are linked to increased academic performance in students. There are three main learning mindsets we commonly reference: growth mindset, belonging, and purpose & relevance. Each has its own unique characteristics and is based on years of research.

When I was a young researcher, just starting out, something happened that changed my life. I was obsessed with understanding how people cope with failures, and I decided to study it by watching how students grapple with hard problems. So I brought children one at a time to a room in their school, made them comfortable, and then gave them a series of puzzles to solve. The first ones were fairly easy, but the next ones were hard. As the students grunted, perspired, and toiled, I watched their strategies and probed what they were thinking and feeling. I expected differences among children in how they coped with the difficulty, but I saw something I never expected. Confronted with the hard puzzles, one tenyear-old boy pulled up his chair, rubbed his hands together, smacked his lips, and cried out, "I love a challenge!" Another, sweating away on these puzzles, looked up with a pleased expression and said with authority, "You know, I was hoping this would be informative!" What's wrong with them? I wondered. I always thought you coped with failure or you didn't cope with failure. I never thought anyone loved failure. Were these alien children or were they on to something? Everyone has a role model, someone who pointed the way at a critical moment in their lives. These children were my role models. They obviously knew something I didn't and I was determined to figure it out––to understand the kind of mindset that could turn a failure into a gift. What did they know? They knew that human qualities, such as intellectual skills, could be cultivated. And that's what they were doing––getting smarter. Not only weren't they discouraged by failure, they didn't even think they were failing. They thought they were learning. I, on the other hand, thought human qualities were carved in stone. You were smart or you weren't, and failure meant you weren't. It was that simple. If you could arrange successes and avoid failures (at all costs), you could stay smart. Struggles, mistakes, perseverance were just no part of this picture. Whether human qualities are things that can be cultivated or things that are carved in stone is an old issue. What these beliefs mean for you is a new one: What are the consequences of thinking that your intelligence or personality is something you can develop, as opposed to something that is a fixed, deep-seated trait? Let's first look in on the age-old, fiercely waged debate about human nature and then return to the question of what these beliefs mean for you.

Since the dawn of time, people have thought differently, acted differently, and fared differently from each other. It was guaranteed that someone would ask the question of why people differed––why some people are smarter or more moral––and whether there was something that made them permanently different. Experts lined up on both sides. Some claimed that there was a strong physical basis for these differences, making them unavoidable and unalterable. Through the ages, these alleged physical differences have included bumps on the skull (phrenology), the size and shape of the skull (craniology), and, today, genes. Others pointed to the strong differences in people's backgrounds, experiences, training, or ways of learning. It may surprise you to know that a big champion of this view was Alfred Binet, the inventor of the IQ test. Wasn't the IQ test meant to summarize children's unchangeable intelligent? In fact, no. Binet, a Frenchman working in Paris in the early twentieth century, designed this test to identify children who were not profiting from the Paris public schools, so that new educational programs could be designed to get them back on track. Without denying individual differences in children's intellects, he believed that education and practice could bring about fundamental changes in intelligence. Here is a quote from one of his major books, Modern Ideas About Children, in which he summarizes his work with hundreds of children with learning difficulties: A few modern philosophers... assert that an individual's intelligence is a fixed quantity, a quantity which cannot be increased. We must protest and react against this brutal pessimism... . With practice, training, and above all, method, we manage to increase our attention, our memory, our judgment and literally to become more intelligent than we were before. Who's right? Today most experts agree that it's not either–or. I t's not nature or nurture, genes or environment. From conception on, there's a constant give-and-take between the two. In fact, as Gilbert Gottlieb, an eminent neuroscientist, put it, not only do genes and environment cooperate as we develop, but genes require input from the environment to work properly. At the same time, scientists are learning that people have more capacity for lifelong learning and brain development than they ever thought. Of course, each person has a unique genetic endowment. People may start with different temperaments and different aptitudes, but it is clear that experience, training, and personal effort take them the rest of the way. Robert Sternberg, the present-day guru of intelligence, writes that the major factor in whether people achieve expertise "is not some fixed prior ability, but purposeful engagement." Or, as his forerunner Binet recognized, it's not always the people who start out the smartest who end up the smartest. WHAT DOES ALL THIS MEAN FOR YOU? THE TWO MINDSETS It's one thing to have pundits spouting their opinions about scientific issues. It's another thing to understand how these views apply to you. For thirty years, my research has shown that the view you adopt for yourself profoundly affects the way you lead your life. It can determine whether you become the person you want to be and whether you accomplish the things you 3 value. How does this happen? How can a simple belief have the power to transform your psychology and, as a result, your life? Believing that your qualities are carved in stone––the fixed mindset––creates an urgency to prove yourself over and over. If you have only a certain amount of intelligence, a certain personality, and a certain moral character-well, then you'd better prove that you have a healthy dose of them. It simply wouldn't do to look or feel deficient in these most basic characteristics. Some of us are trained in this mindset from an early age. Even as a child, I was focused on being smart, but the fixed mindset was really stamped in by Mrs.Wilson, my sixth-grade teacher. Unlike Alfred Binet, she believed that people's IQ scores told the whole story of who they were. We were seated around the room in IQ order, and only the highest-IQ students could be trusted to carry the flag, clap the erasers, or take a note to the principal. Aside from the daily stomachaches she provoked with her judgmental stance, she was creating a mindset in which everyone in the class hid one consuming goal––look smart, don't look dumb. Who cared about or enjoyed learning when our whole being was at stake every time she gave us a test or called on us in class? I've seen so many people with this one consuming goal of proving themselves––in the classroom, in their careers, and in their relationships. Every situation calls for a confirmation of their intelligence, personality, or character. Every situation is evaluated: Will I succeed or fail? Will I look smart or dumb? Will I be accepted or rejected? Will I feel like a winner or a loser? But doesn't our society value intelligence, personality, and character? Isn't it normal to want these traits? Yes, but... There's another mindset in which these traits are not simply a hand you're dealt and have to live with, always trying to convince yourself and others that you have a royal flush when you're secretly worried it's a pair of tens. In this mindset, the hand you're dealt is just the starting point for development. This growth mindset is based on the belief that your basic qualities are things you can cultivate through your efforts, your strategies, and help from others. Although people may differ in every which way––in their initial talents and aptitudes, interests, or temperaments ––everyone can change and grow through application and experience. Do people with this mindset believe that anyone can be anything, that anyone with proper motivation or education can become Einstein or Beethoven? No, but they believe that a person's true potential is unknown (and unknowable); that it's impossible to foresee what can be accomplished with years of passion, toil, and training. Did you know that Darwin and Tolstoy were considered ordinary children? That Ben Hogan, one of the greatest golfers of all time, was completely uncoordinated and graceless as a child? That the photographer Cindy Sherman, who has been on virtually every list of the most important artists of the twentieth century, failed her first photography course? That Geraldine Page, one of our greatest actresses, was advised to give it up for lack of talent? You can see how the belief that cherished qualities can be developed creates a passion for learning. Why waste time proving over and over how great you are, when you could be getting better? Why hide deficiencies instead of overcoming them? Why look for friends or partners who will just shore up your self-esteem instead of ones who will also challenge you to grow? And why seek out the tried and true, instead of experiences that will stretch you? The passion for stretching yourself and sticking to it, even (or especially) when it's not going well, is the hallmark of the growth mindset. This is the mindset that allows people to thrive during some of the most challenging times in their lives.

A VIEW FROM THE TWO MINDSETS To give you a better sense of how the two mindsets work, imagine-as vividly as you can-that you are a young adult having a really bad day: One day, you go to a class that is really important to you and that you like a lot. The professor returns the midterm papers to the class. You got a C+. You're very disappointed. That evening on the way back to your home, you find that you've gotten a parking ticket. Being really frustrated, you call your best friend to share your experience but are sort of brushed off. What would you think? What would you feel? What would you do? When I asked people with the fixed mindset, this is what they said: "I'd feel like a reject." "I'm a total failure." "I'm an idiot." "I'm a loser." "I'd feel worthless and dumb––everyone's better than me." "I'm slime." In other words, they'd see what happened as a direct measure of their competence and worth. This is what they'd think about their lives: "My life is pitiful." "I have no life." "Somebody upstairs doesn't like me." "The world is out to get me." "Someone is out to destroy me." "Nobody loves me, everybody hates me." "Life is unfair and all efforts are useless." "Life stinks. I'm stupid. Nothing good ever happens to me." "I'm the most unlucky person on this earth." Excuse me, was there death and destruction, or just a grade, a ticket, and a bad phone call? Are these just people with low self-esteem? Or card-carrying pessimists? No. When they aren't coping with failure, they feel just as worthy and optimistic––and bright and attractive––as people with the growth mindset. So how would they cope? "I wouldn't bother to put so much time and effort into doing well in anything." (In other words, don't let anyone measure you again.) "Do nothing." "Stay in bed." "Get drunk." "Eat." "Yell at someone if I get a chance to." "Eat chocolate." "Listen to music and pout." "Go into my closet and sit there." "Pick a fight with somebody." "Cry." "Break something." "What is there to do?" What is there to do! You know, when I wrote the vignette, I intentionally made the grade a C+, not an F. It was a midterm rather than a final. It was a parking ticket, not a car wreck. They were "sort of brushed off," not rejected outright. Nothing catastrophic or irreversible happened. Yet from this raw material the fixed mindset created the feeling of utter failure and paralysis. When I gave people with the growth mindset the same vignette, here's what they said. They'd think: "I need to try harder in class, be more careful when parking the car, and wonder if my friend had a bad day." "The C+ would tell me that I'd have to work a lot harder in the class, but I have the rest of the semester to pull up my grade." There were many, many more like this, but I think you get the idea. Now, how would they cope? Directly. "I'd start thinking about studying harder (or studying in a different way) for my next test in that class, I'd pay the ticket, and I'd work things out with my best friend the next time we speak." 5 "I'd look at what was wrong on my exam, resolve to do better, pay my parking ticket, and call my friend to tell her I was upset the day before." "Work hard on my next paper, speak to the teacher, be more careful where I park or contest the ticket, and find out what's wrong with my friend." You don't have to have one mindset or the other to be upset. Who wouldn't be? Things like a poor grade or a rebuff from a friend or loved one—–these are not fun events. No one was smacking their lips with relish. Yet those people with the growth mindset were not labeling themselves and throwing up their hands. Even though they felt distressed, they were ready to take the risks, confront the challenges, and keep working at them. SO, WHAT'S NEW? ls this such a novel idea? We have lots of sayings that stress the importance of risk and the power of persistence, such as "Nothing ventured, nothing gained" and "If at first you don't succeed, try, try again'" or "Rome wasn't built in a day." (By the way, I was delighted to learn that the Italians have the same expression.) What is truly amazing is that people with the fixed mindset would not agree. For them, it's "Nothing ventured, nothing lost." "If at first you don't succeed, you probably don't have the ability." "If Rome wasn't built in a day, maybe it wasn't meant to be." In other words, risk and effort are two things that might reveal your inadequacies and show that you were not up to the task. In fact, it's startling to see the degree to which people with the fixed mindset do not believe in putting in effort or getting help. What's also new is that people's ideas about risk and effort grow out of their more basic mindset. It's not just that some people happen to recognize the value of challenging themselves and the importance of effort. Our research has shown that this comes directly from the growth mindset. When we teach people the growth mindset, with its focus on development, these ideas about challenge and effort follow. Similarly, it's not just that some people happen to dislike challenge and effort. When we (temporarily) put people in a fixed mindset, with its focus on permanent traits, they quickly fear challenge and devalue effort. We often see books with titles like The Ten Secrets of the World's Most Successful People crowding the shelves of bookstores, and these books may give many useful tips. But they're usually a list of unconnected pointers, like "Take more risks!" or "Believe in yourself!" While you're left admiring people who can do that, it's never clear how these things fit together or how you could ever become that way. So you're inspired for a few days, but basically the world's most successful people still have their secrets. Instead, as you begin to understand the fixed and growth mindsets, you will see exactly how one thing leads to another—how a belief that your qualities are carved in stone leads to a host of thoughts and actions, and how a belief that your qualities can be cultivated leads to a host of different thoughts and actions, taking you down an entirely different road. It's what we psychologists call an Aha! experience. Not only have I seen this in my research when we teach people a new mindset, but I get letters all the time from people who have read my work. They recognize themselves: "As I read your article I literally found myself saying over and over again, 'This is me, this is me!'" They see the connections: "Your article completely blew me away. I felt I had discovered the secret of the universe!" They feel their mindsets reorienting: "I can certainly report a kind of personal revolution happening in my own thinking, and this is an exciting feeling." And they can put this new thinking into practice for themselves and others: "Your work has allowed me to transform my work with children and see education through a different lens," or "I just wanted to let you know what an impact—on a personal and practical level—your outstanding research has had for hundreds of students." I get lots of these letters from coaches and business leaders, too. SELF-INSIGHT: WHO HAS ACCURATE VIEWS OF THEIR ASSETS AND LIMITATIONS? Well, maybe the people with the growth mindset don't think they're Einstein or Beethoven, but aren't they more likely to have inflated views of their abilities and try for things they're not capable of? In fact, studies show that people are terrible at estimating their abilities. Recently, we set out to see who is most likely to do this. Sure, we found that people greatly misestimated their performance and their ability. But it was those with the fixed mindset who accounted for almost all the inaccuracy. The people with the growth mindset were amazingly accurate. When you think about it, this makes sense. If, like those with the growth mindset, you believe you can develop yourself, then you're open to accurate information about your current abilities, even if it's unflattering. What's more, if you're oriented toward learning, as they are, you need accurate information about your current abilities in order to learn effectively. However, if everything is either good news or bad news about your precious traits—as it is with fixed-mindset people—distortion almost inevitably enters the picture. Some outcomes are magnified, others are explained away, and before you know it you don't know yourself at all. Howard Gardner, in his book Extraordinary Minds, concluded that exceptional individuals have "a special talent for identifying their own strengths and weaknesses." It's interesting that those with the growth mindset seem to have that talent. WHAT'S IN STORE The other thing exceptional people seem to have is a special talent for converting life's setbacks into future successes. Creativity researchers concur. In a poll of 143 creativity researchers, there was wide agreement about the number one ingredient in creative achievement. And it was exactly the kind of perseverance and resilience produced by the growth mindset. You may be asking again, How can one belief lead to all this––the love of challenge, belief in effort, resilience in the face of setbacks, and greater (more creative!) success? In the chapters that follow, you'll see exactly how this happens: how the mindsets change what people strive for and what they see as success. How they change the definition, significance, and impact of failure. And how they change the deepest meaning of effort. You'll see how these mindsets play out in school, in sports, in the workplace, and in relationships. You'll see where they come from and how they can be changed. Grow Your Mindset Which mindset do you have? Answer these questions about intelligence. Read each statement and decide whether you mostly agree with it or disagree with it. 7 1. Your intelligence is something very basic about you that you can't change very much. 2. You can learn new things, but you can't really change how intelligent you are. 3. No matter how much intelligence you have, you can always change it quite a bit. 4. You can always substantially change how intelligent you are. Questions 1 and 2 are the fixed-mindset questions. Questions 3 and 4 reflect the growth mindset. Which mindset did you agree with more? You can be a mixture, but most people lean toward one or the other. You also have beliefs about other abilities. You could substitute "artistic talent," "sports ability," or "business skill" for "intelligence." Try it. It's not only your abilities; it's your personal qualities too. Look at these statements about personality and character and decide whether you mostly agree or mostly disagree with each one. 1. You are a certain kind of person, and there is not much that can be done to really change that. 2. No matter what kind of person you are, you can always change substantially. 3. You can do things differently, but the important parts of who you are can't really be changed. 4. You can always change basic things about the kind of person you are. Here, questions 1 and 3 are the fixed-mindset questions and questions 2 and 4 reflect the growth mindset. Which did you agree with more? Did it differ from your intelligence mindset? It can. Your "intelligence mindset" comes into play when situations involve mental ability. Your "personality mindset" comes into play in situations that involve your personal qualities––for example, how dependable, cooperative, caring, or socially skilled you are. The fixed mindset makes you concerned with how you'll be judged; the growth mindset makes you concerned with improving. Here are some more ways to think about mindsets: • Think about someone you know who is steeped in the fixed mindset. Think about how they're always trying to prove themselves and how they're supersensitive about being wrong or making mistakes. Did you ever wonder why they were this way? (Are you this way?) Now you can begin to understand why. • Think about someone you know who is skilled in the growth mindset––someone who understands that important qualities can be cultivated. Think about the ways they confront obstacles. Think about the things they do to stretch themselves. What are some ways you might like to change or stretch yourself?

Okay, now imagine you've decided to learn a new language and you've signed up for a class. A few sessions into the course, the instructor calls you to the front of the room and starts throwing questions at you one after another. Put yourself in a fixed mindset. Your ability is on the line. Can you feel everyone's eyes on you? Can you see the instructor's face evaluating you? Feel the tension, feel your ego bristle and waver. What else are you thinking and feeling? Now put yourself in a growth mindset. You're a novice––that's why you're here. You're here to learn. The teacher is a resource for learning. Feel the tension leave you; feel your mind open up. The message is: You can change your mindset.

When she was a young woman, she wanted a prince-like mate. Very handsome, very successful. A big cheese. she wanted a glamorous career, but nothing too hard or risky. And she wanted it all to come to me as validation of who I was. It would be many years before she was satisfied. she got a great guy, but he was a work in progress. she have a great career, but boy, is it a constant challenge. Nothing was easy. So why am I satisfied? she changed her mindset. she changed it because of her work. One day my doctoral student, Mary Bandura, and I were trying to understand why some students were so caught up in proving their ability, while others could just let go and learn. Suddenly we realized that there were two meanings to ability, not one: a fixed ability that needs to be proven, and a changeable ability that can be developed through learning. That's how the mindsets were born. I knew instantly which one I had. I realized why I'd always been so concerned about mistakes and failures. And I recognized for the first time that I had a choice. When you enter a mindset, you enter a new world. In one world––the world of fixed traits–– success is about proving you're smart or talented. Validating yourself. In the other––the world of changing qualities––it's about stretching yourself to learn something new. Developing yourself. In one world, failure is about having a setback. Getting a bad grade. Losing a tournament. Getting fired. Getting rejected. It means you're not smart or talented. In the other world, failure is about not growing. Not reaching for the things you value. It means you're not fulfilling your potential.In one world, effort is a bad thing. It, like failure, means you're not smart or talented. If you were, you wouldn't need effort. In the other world, effort is what makes you smart or talented. You have a choice. Mindsets are just beliefs. They're powerful beliefs, but they're just something in your mind, and you can change your mind. As you read, think about where you'd like to go and which mindset will take you there. IS SUCCESS ABOUT LEARNING – OR PROVING YOU'RE SMART? Benjamin Barber, an eminent political theorist, once said, "I don't divide the world into the weak and the strong, or the successes and the failures... . I divide the world into the learners and nonlearners." What on earth would make someone a nonlearner? Everyone is born with an intense drive to learn. Infants stretch their skills daily. Not just ordinary skills, but the most difficult tasks of a lifetime, like learning to walk and talk. They never decide it's too hard or not worth the effort. 10 Babies don't worry about making mistakes or humiliating themselves. They walk, they fall, they get up. They just barge forward. What could put an end to this exuberant learning? The fixed mindset. As soon as children become able to evaluate themselves, some of them become afraid of challenges. They become afraid of not being smart. I have studied thousands of people from preschoolers on, and it's breathtaking how many reject an opportunity to learn. We offered four-year-olds a choice: They could redo an easy jigsaw puzzle or they could try a harder one. Even at this tender age, children with the fixed mindset––the ones who believed in fixed traits––stuck with the safe one. Kids who are born smart "don't do mistakes," they told us. Children with the growth mindset––the ones who believed you could get smarter––thought it was a strange choice. Why are you asking me this, lady? Why would anyone want to keep doing the same puzzle over and over? They chose one hard one after another. "I'm dying to figure them out!" exclaimed one little girl. So children with the fixed mindset want to make sure they succeed. Smart people should always succeed. But for children with the growth mindset, success is about stretching themselves. It's about becoming smarter. One seventh-grade girl summed it up. "I think intelligence is something you have to work for ... it isn't just given to you... . Most kids, if they're not sure of an answer, will not raise their hand to answer the question. But what I usually do is raise my hand, because if I'm wrong, then my mistake will be corrected. Or I will raise my hand and say, 'How would this be solved?' or 'I don't get this. Can you help me?' Just by doing that I'm increasing my intelligence." Beyond Puzzles It's one thing to pass up a puzzle. It's another to pass up an opportunity that's important to your future. To see if this would happen, we took advantage of an unusual situation. At the University of Hong Kong, everything is in English. Classes are in English, textbooks are in English, and exams are in English. But some students who enter the university are not fluent in English, so it would make sense for them to do something about it in a hurry. As students arrived to register for their freshman year, we knew which ones were not skilled in English. And we asked them a key question: If the faculty offered a course for students who need to improve their English skills, would you take it? We also measured their mindset. We did this by asking them how much they agreed with statements like this: "You have a certain amount of intelligence, and you can't really do much to change it." People who agree with this kind of statement lean toward a fixed mindset. Those who lean toward a growth mindset agree that: "You can always substantially change how intelligent you are." Later, we looked at who said yes to the English course. Students with the growth mindset said an emphatic yes. But those with the fixed mindset were not very interested. Believing that success is about learning, students with the growth mindset seized the chance. But those with the fixed mindset didn't want to expose their deficiencies. Instead, to feel smart in the short run, they were willing to put their college careers at risk. This is how the fixed mindset makes people into nonlearners.

You can even see the difference in people's brain waves. People with both mindsets came into our brain-wave lab at Columbia. As they answered hard questions and got feedback, we were curious about when their brain waves would show them to be interested and attentive. People with a fixed mindset were only interested when the feedback reflected on their ability. Their brain waves showed them paying close attention when they were told whether their answers were right or wrong. But when they were presented with information that could help them learn, there was no sign of interest.

Even when they'd gotten an answer wrong, they were not interested in learning what the right answer was. Only people with a growth mindset paid close attention to information that could stretch their knowledge. Only for them was learning a priority. What's Your Priority? If you had to choose, which would it be? Loads of success and validation or lots of challenge? It's not just on intellectual tasks that people have to make these choices. People also have to decide what kinds of relationships they want: ones that bolster their egos or ones that challenge them to grow? Who is your ideal mate? We put this question to young adults, and here's what they told us. People with the fixed mindset said the ideal mate would: Put them on a pedestal. Make them feel perfect. Worship them. In other words, the perfect mate would enshrine their fixed qualities. My husband says that he used to feel this way, that he wanted to be the god of a one-person (his partner's) religion. Fortunately, he chucked this idea before he met me. People with the growth mindset hoped for a different kind of partner. They said their ideal mate was someone who would: See their faults and help them to work on them. Challenge them to become a better person. Encourage them to learn new things. Certainly, they didn't want people who would pick on them or undermine their self-esteem, but they did want people who would foster their development. They didn't assume they were fully evolved, flawless beings who had nothing more to learn. Are you already thinking, Uh-oh, what if two people with different mindsets get together? A growth-mindset woman tells about her marriage to a fixed-mindset man: I had barely gotten all the rice out of my hair when I began to realize I made a big mistake. Every time I said something like "Why don't we try to go out a little more?" or "I'd like it if you consulted me before making decisions," he was devastated. Then instead of talking about the issue I raised, I'd have to spend literally an hour repairing the damage and making him feel good again. Plus he would then run to the phone to call his 12 mother, who always showered him with the constant adoration he seemed to need. We were both young and new at marriage. I just wanted to communicate. So the husband's idea of a successful relationship––total, uncritical acceptance––was not the wife's. And the wife's idea of a successful relationship––confronting problems––was not the husband's. One person's growth was the other person's nightmare. CEO Disease Speaking of reigning from atop a pedestal and wanting to be seen as perfect, you won't be surprised that this is often called "CEO disease." Lee Iacocca had a bad case of it. After his initial success as head of Chrysler Motors, Iacocca looked remarkably like our four-year-olds with the fixed mindset. He kept bringing out the same car models over and over with only superficial changes. Unfortunately, they were models no one wanted anymore. Meanwhile, Japanese companies were completely rethinking what cars should look like and how they should run. We know how this turned out. The Japanese cars rapidly swept the market. CEOs face this choice all the time. Should they confront their shortcomings or should they create a world where they have none? Lee Iacocca chose the latter. He surrounded himself with worshipers, exiled the critics––and quickly lost touch with where his field was going. Lee Iacocca had become a nonlearner. But not everyone catches CEO disease. Many great leaders confront their shortcomings on a regular basis. Darwin Smith, looking back on his extraordinary performance at Kimberly-Clark, declared, "I never stopped trying to be qualified for the job." These men, like the Hong Kong students with the growth mindset, never stopped taking the remedial course. CEOs face another dilemma. They can choose short-term strategies that boost the company's stock and make themselves look like heroes. Or they can work for long-term improvement–– risking Wall Street's disapproval as they lay the foundation for the health and growth of the company over the longer haul. Albert Dunlap, a self-professed fixed mindsetter, was brought in to turn around Sunbeam. He chose the short-term strategy of looking like a hero to Wall Street. The stock soared but the company fell apart. Lou Gerstner, an avowed growth mindsetter, was called in to turn around IBM. As he set about the enormous task of overhauling IBM culture and policies, stock prices were stagnant and Wall Street sneered. They called him a failure. A few years later, however, IBM was leading its field again. Stretching People in a growth mindset don't just seek challenge, they thrive on it. The bigger the challenge, the more they stretch. And nowhere can it be seen more clearly than in the world of sports. You can just watch people stretch and grow. Mia Hamm, the greatest female soccer star of her time, says it straight out. "All my life I've been playing up, meaning I've challenged myself with players older, bigger, more skillful, more 13 experienced––in short, better than me." First she played with her older brother. Then at ten, she joined the eleven-year-old boys' team. Then she threw herself into the number one college team in the United States. "Each day I attempted to play up to their level ... and I was improving faster than I ever dreamed possible." Patricia Miranda was a chubby, unathletic high school kid who wanted to wrestle. After a bad beating on the mat, she was told, "You're a joke." First she cried, then she felt: "That really set my resolve ... I had to keep going and had to know if effort and focus and belief and training could somehow legitimize me as a wrestler." Where did she get this resolve? Miranda was raised in a life devoid of challenge. But when her mother died of an aneurysm at age forty, ten-year-old Miranda came up with a principle. "When you're lying on your deathbed, one of the cool things to say is, 'I really explored myself.' This sense of urgency was instilled when my mom died. If you only go through life doing stuff that's easy, shame on you." So when wrestling presented a challenge, she was ready to take it on. Her effort paid off. At twenty-four, Miranda was having the last laugh. She won the spot for her weight group on the U.S. Olympic team and came home from Athens with a bronze medal. And what was next? Yale Law School. People urged her to stay where she was already on top, but Miranda felt it was more exciting to start at the bottom again and see what she could grow into this time. Stretching Beyond the Possible Sometimes people with the growth mindset stretch themselves so far that they do the impossible. In 1995, Christopher Reeve, the actor, was thrown from a horse. His neck was broken, his spinal cord was severed from his brain, and he was completely paralyzed below the neck. Medical science said, So sorry. Come to terms with it. Reeve, however, started a demanding exercise program that involved moving all parts of his paralyzed body with the help of electrical stimulation. Why couldn't he learn to move again? Why couldn't his brain once again give commands that his body would obey? Doctors warned that he was in denial and was setting himself up for disappointment. They had seen this before and it was a bad sign for his adjustment. But, really, what else was Reeve doing with his time? Was there a better project? Five years later, Reeve started to regain movement. First it happened in his hands, then his arms, then legs, and then torso. He was far from cured, but brain scans showed that his brain was once more sending signals to his body that the body was responding to. Not only did Reeve stretch his abilities, he changed the entire way science thinks about the nervous system and its potential for recovery. In doing so, he opened a whole new vista for research and a whole new avenue of hope for people with spinal cord injuries. Thriving on the Sure Thing Clearly, people with the growth mindset thrive when they're stretching themselves. When do people with the fixed mindset thrive? When things are safely within their grasp. If things get too challenging––when they're not feeling smart or talented––they lose interest.I watched it happen as we followed pre-med students through their first semester of chemistry. For many students, this is what their lives have led up to: becoming a doctor. And this is the course that decides who gets to be one. It's one heck of a hard course, too. The average grade on each exam is C+, for students who've rarely seen anything less than an A. Most students started out pretty interested in chemistry. Yet over the semester, something happened. Students with the fixed mindset stayed interested only when they did well right away. Those who found it difficult showed a big drop in their interest and enjoyment. If it wasn't a testimony to their intelligence, they couldn't enjoy it. "The harder it gets," reported one student, "the more I have to force myself to read the book and study for the tests. I was excited about chemistry before, but now every time I think about it, I get a bad feeling in my stomach." In contrast, students with the growth mindset continued to show the same high level of interest even when they found the work very challenging. "It's a lot more difficult for me than I thought it would be, but it's what I want to do, so that only makes me more determined. When they tell me I can't, it really gets me going." Challenge and interest went hand in hand. We saw the same thing in younger students. We gave fifth graders intriguing puzzles, which they all loved. But when we made them harder, children with the fixed mindset showed a big plunge in enjoyment. They also changed their minds about taking some home to practice. "It's okay, you can keep them. I already have them," fibbed one child. In fact, they couldn't run from them fast enough. This was just as true for children who were the best puzzle solvers. Having "puzzle talent" did not prevent the decline. Children with the growth mindset, on the other hand, couldn't tear themselves away from the hard problems. These were their favorites and these were the ones they wanted to take home. "Could you write down the name of these puzzles," one child asked, "so my mom can buy me some more when these ones run out?" Not long ago I was interested to read about Marina Semyonova, a great Russian dancer and teacher, who devised a novel way of selecting her students. It was a clever test for mindset. As a former student tells it, "Her students first have to survive a trial period while she watches to see how you react to praise and to correction. Those more responsive to the correction are deemed worthy." In other words, she separates the ones who get their thrill from what's easy—–what they've already mastered—–from those who get their thrill from what's hard. I'll never forget the first time I heard myself say, "This is hard. This is fun." That's the moment I knew I was changing mindsets. When Do You Feel Smart: When You're Flawless or When You're Learning? The plot is about to thicken, for in the fixed mindset it's not enough just to succeed. It's not enough just to look smart and talented. You have to be pretty much flawless. And you have to be flawless right away. We asked people, ranging from grade schoolers to young adults, "When do you feel smart?" The differences were striking. People with the fixed mindset said: "It's when I don't make any mistakes." 15 "When I finish something fast and it's perfect." "When something is easy for me, but other people can't do it." It's about being perfect right now. But people with the growth mindset said: "When it's really hard, and I try really hard, and I can do something I couldn't do before." Or "[When] I work on something a long time and I start to figure it out." For them it's not about immediate perfection. It's about learning something over time: confronting a challenge and making progress. If You Have Ability, Why Should You Need Learning? Actually, people with the fixed mindset expect ability to show up on its own, before any learning takes place. After all, if you have it you have it, and if you don't you don't. I see this all the time. Out of all the applicants from all over the world, my department at Columbia admitted six new graduate students a year. They all had amazing test scores, nearly perfect grades, and rave recommendations from eminent scholars. Moreover, they'd been courted by the top grad schools. It took one day for some of them to feel like complete imposters. Yesterday they were hotshots; today they're failures. Here's what happens. They look at the faculty with our long list of publications. "Oh my God, I can't do that. "They look at the advanced students who are submitting articles for publication and writing grant proposals. "Oh my God, I can't do that." They know how to take tests and get As but they don't know how to do this—–yet. They forget the yet. Isn't that what school is for, to teach? They're there to learn how to do these things, not because they already know everything. I wonder if this is what happened to Janet Cooke and Stephen Glass. They were both young reporters who skyrocketed to the top—–on fabricated articles. Janet Cooke won a Pulitzer Prize for her Washington Post articles about an eight-year-old boy who was a drug addict. The boy did not exist, and she was later stripped of her prize. Stephen Glass was the whiz kid of The New Republic, who seemed to have stories and sources reporters only dream of. The sources did not exist and the stories were not true. Did Janet Cooke and Stephen Glass need to be perfect right away? Did they feel that admitting ignorance would discredit them with their colleagues? Did they feel they should already be like the big-time reporters before they did the hard work of learning how? "We were stars—–precocious stars," wrote

Stephen Glass, "and that was what mattered." The public understands them as cheats, and cheat they did. But I understand them as talented young people––desperate young people––who succumbed to the pressures of the fixed mindset. There was a saying in the 1960s that went: "Becoming is better than being." The fixed mindset does not allow people the luxury of becoming. They have to already be. A Test Score Is Forever Let's take a closer look at why, in the fixed mindset, it's so crucial to be perfect right now. It's because one test––or one evaluation––can measure you forever.

Twenty years ago, at the age of five, Loretta and her family came to the United States. A few days later, her mother took her to her new school, where they promptly gave her a test. The next thing she knew, she was in her kindergarten class––but it was not the Eagles, the elite kindergarten class. As time passed, however, Loretta was transferred to the Eagles and she remained with that group of students until the end of high school, garnering a bundle of academic prizes along the way. Yet she never felt she belonged. That first test, she was convinced, diagnosed her fixed ability and said that she was not a true Eagle. Never mind that she had been five years old and had just made a radical change to a new country. Or that maybe there hadn't been room in the Eagles for a while. Or that maybe the school decided she would have an easier transition in a more low-key class. There are so many ways to understand what happened and what it meant. Unfortunately, she chose the wrong one. For in the world of the fixed mindset, there is no way to become an Eagle. If you were a true Eagle, you would have aced the test and been hailed as an Eagle at once. Is Loretta a rare case, or is this kind of thinking more common than we realize? To find out, we showed fifth graders a closed cardboard box and told them it had a test inside. This test, we said, measured an important school ability. We told them nothing more. Then we asked them questions about the test. First, we wanted to make sure that they'd accepted our description, so we asked them: How much do you think this test measures an important school ability? All of them had taken our word for it. Next we asked: Do you think this test measures how smart you are? And: Do you think this test measures how smart you'll be when you grow up? Students with the growth mindset had taken our word that the test measured an important ability, but they didn't think it measured how smart they were. And they certainly didn't think it would tell them how smart they'd be when they grew up. In fact, one of them told us, "No way! Ain't no test can do that." But the students with the fixed mindset didn't simply believe the test could measure an important ability. They also believed––just as strongly––that it could measure how smart they were. And how smart they'd be when they grew up. They granted one test the power to measure their most basic intelligence now and forever. They gave this test the power to define them. That's why every success is so important. Another Look at Potential This leads us back to the idea of "potential" and to the question of whether tests or experts can tell us what our potential is, what we're capable of, what our future will be. The fixed mindset says yes. You can simply measure the fixed ability right now and project it into the future. Just give the test or ask the expert. No crystal ball needed. So common is the belief that potential can be known right now that Joseph P. Kennedy felt confident in telling Morton Downey Jr. that he would be a failure. What had Downey––later a famous television personality and author––done? Why, he had worn red socks and brown shoes to the Stork Club, a fancy New York nightclub. "Morton," Kennedy told him, "I don't know anybody I've ever met in my life wearing red socks and brown shoes who ever succeeded. Young man, let me tell you now, you do stand out, but you don't stand out in a way that people will ever admire you."Many of the most accomplished people of our era were considered by experts to have no future. Jackson Pollock, Marcel Proust, Elvis Presley, Ray Charles, Lucille Ball, and Charles Darwin were all thought to have little potential for their chosen fields. And in some of these cases, it may well have been true that they did not stand out from the crowd early on. But isn't potential someone's capacity to develop their skills with effort and coaching over time? And that's just the point. How can we know where effort, coaching, and time will take someone? Who knows––maybe the experts were right about Jackson, Marcel, Elvis, Ray, Lucille, and Charles––in terms of their skills at the time. Maybe they were not yet the people they were to become. I once went to an exhibit in London of Paul Cézanne's early paintings. On my way there, I wondered who Cézanne was and what his paintings were like before he was the painter we know today. I was intensely curious because Cézanne is one of my favorite artists and the man who set the stage for much of modern art. Here's what I found: Some of the paintings were pretty bad. They were overwrought scenes, some violent, with amateurishly painted people. Although there were some paintings that foreshadowed the later Cézanne, many did not. Was the early Cézanne not talented? Or did it just take time for Cézanne to become Cézanne? People with the growth mindset know that it takes time for potential to flower. Recently, I got an angry letter from a teacher who had taken one of our surveys. The survey portrays a hypothetical student, Jennifer, who had gotten 65 percent on a math exam. It then asks teachers to tell us how they would treat her. Teachers with the fixed mindset were more than happy to answer our questions. They felt that by knowing Jennifer's score, they had a good sense of who she was and what she was capable of. Their recommendations abounded. Mr. Riordan, by contrast, was fuming. Here's what he wrote. To Whom It May Concern: Having completed the educator's portion of your recent survey, I must request that my results be excluded from the study. I feel that the study itself is scientifically unsound... . Unfortunately, the test uses a faulty premise, asking teachers to make assumptions about a given student based on nothing more than a number on a page... . Performance cannot be based on one assessment. You cannot determine the slope of a line given only one point, as there is no line to begin with. A single point in time does not show trends, improvement, lack of effort, or mathematical ability... . Sincerely, Michael D. Riordan I was delighted with Mr. Riordan's critique and couldn't have agreed with it more. An assessment at one point in time has little value for understanding someone's ability, let alone their potential to succeed in the future. It was disturbing how many teachers thought otherwise, and that was the point of our study.

The idea that one evaluation can measure you forever is what creates the urgency for those with the fixed mindset. That's why they must succeed perfectly and immediately. Who can afford the luxury of trying to grow when everything is on the line right now? Is there another way to judge potential? NASA thought so. When they were soliciting applications for astronauts, they rejected people with pure histories of success and instead selected people who had had significant failures and bounced back from them. Jack Welch, the celebrated CEO of General Electric, chose executives on the basis of "runway," their capacity for growth. And remember Marina Semyonova, the famed ballet teacher, who chose the students who were energized by criticism. They were all rejecting the idea of fixed ability and selecting instead for mindset. Proving You're Special When people with the fixed mindset opt for success over growth, what are they really trying to prove? That they're special. Even superior. When we asked them, "When do you feel smart?" so many of them talked about times they felt like a special person, someone who was different from and better than other people. Until I discovered the mindsets and how they work, I, too, thought of myself as more talented than others, maybe even more worthy than others because of my endowments. The scariest thought, which I rarely entertained, was the possibility of being ordinary. This kind of thinking led me to need constant validation. Every comment, every look was meaningful––it registered on my intelligence scorecard, my attractiveness scorecard, my likability scorecard. If a day went well, I could bask in my high numbers. One bitter cold winter night, I went to the opera. That night, the opera was everything you hope for, and everyone stayed until the very end-not just the end of the opera, but through all the curtain calls. Then we all poured into the street, and we all wanted taxis. I remember it clearly. It was after midnight, it was seven degrees, there was a strong wind, and, as time went on, I became more and more miserable. There I was, part of an undifferentiated crowd. What chance did I have? Suddenly, a taxi pulled up right next to me. The handle of the back door lined up perfectly with my hand, and as I entered, the driver announced, "You were different." I lived for these moments. Not only was I special. It could be detected from a distance. The self-esteem movement encourages this kind of thinking and has even invented devices to help you confirm your superiority. I recently came across an ad for such a product. Two of my friends send me an illustrated list each year of the top ten things they didn't get me for Christmas. From January through November, they clip candidate items from catalogs or download them from the Internet. In December, they select the winners. One of my all-time favorites is the pocket toilet, which you fold up and return to your pocket after using. This year my favorite was the I LOVE ME mirror, a mirror with I LOVE ME in huge capital letters written across the bottom half. By looking into it, you can administer the message to yourself and not wait for the outside world to announce your specialness. Of course, the mirror is harmless enough. The problem is when special begins to mean better than others. A more valuable human being. A superior person. An entitled person. 19 Special, Superior, Entitled John McEnroe had a fixed mindset: He believed that talent was all. He did not love to learn. He did not thrive on challenges; when the going got rough, he often folded. As a result, by his own admission, he did not fulfill his potential. But his talent was so great that he was the number one tennis player in the world for four years. Here he tells us what it was like to be number one. McEnroe used sawdust to absorb the sweat on his hands during a match. This time the sawdust was not to his liking, so he went over to the can of sawdust and knocked it over with his racket. His agent, Gary, came dashing over to find out what was wrong. "You call that sawdust?" I said.

I was actually screaming at him: The sawdust was ground too fine! "This looks like rat poison. Can't you get anything right?" So Gary ran out and, twenty minutes later, came back with a fresh can of coarser sawdust ... and twenty dollars less in his pocket: He'd had to pay a union employee to grind up a twoby-four. This is what it was like to be number one. He goes on to tell us about how he once threw up all over a dignified Japanese lady who was hosting him. The next day she bowed, apologized to him, and presented him with a gift. "This," McEnroe proclaims, "is also what it was like to be number one." "Everything was about you ... 'Did you get everything you need? Is everything okay? We'll pay you this, we'll do that, we'll kiss your behind.' You only have to do what you want; your reaction to anything else is, 'Get the hell out of here.' For a long time I didn't mind it a bit. Would you?" So let's see. If you're successful, you're better than other people. You get to abuse them and have them grovel. In the fixed mindset, this is what can pass for self-esteem. As a contrast, let's look at Michael Jordan––growth-minded athlete par excellence––whose greatness is regularly proclaimed by the world: "Superman," "God in person," "Jesus in tennis shoes." If anyone has reason to think of himself as special, it's he. But here's what he said when his return to basketball caused a huge commotion: "I was shocked with the level of intensity my coming back to the game created... . People were praising me like I was a religious cult or something. That was very embarrassing. I'm a human being like everyone else." Jordan knew how hard he had worked to develop his abilities. He was a person who had struggled and grown, not a person who was inherently better than others. Tom Wolfe, in The Right Stuff, describes the elite military pilots who eagerly embrace the fixed mindset. Having passed one rigorous test after another, they think of themselves as special, as people who were born smarter and braver than other people. But Chuck Yeager, the hero of The Right Stuff, begged to differ. "There is no such thing as a natural-born pilot. Whatever my aptitude or talents, becoming a proficient pilot was hard work, really a lifetime's learning experience... . The best pilots fly more than the others; that's why they're the best." Like Michael Jordan, he was a human being. He just stretched himself farther than most. In short, people who believe in fixed traits feel an urgency to succeed, and when they do, they may feel more than pride. They may feel a sense of superiority, since success means that their fixed traits are better than other people's. However, lurking behind that self-esteem of the fixed mindset is a simple question: If you're somebody when you're successful, what are you when you're unsuccessful?

MINDSETS CHANGE THE MEANING OF FAILURE The Martins worshiped their three-year-old Robert and always bragged about his feats. There had never been a child as bright and creative as theirs. Then Robert did something unforgivable—–he didn't get into the number one preschool in New York. After that, the Martins cooled toward him. They didn't talk about him the same way, and they didn't treat him with the same pride and affection. He was no longer their brilliant little Robert. He was someone who had discredited himself and shamed them. At the tender age of three, he was a failure. As a New York Times article points out, failure has been transformed from an action (I failed) to an identity (I am a failure). This is especially true in the fixed mindset. When I was a child, I, too, worried about meeting Robert's fate. In sixth grade, I was the best speller in my school. The principal wanted me to go to a citywide competition, but I refused. In ninth grade, I excelled in French, and my teacher wanted me to enter a citywide competition. Again, I refused. Why would I risk turning from a success into a failure? From a winner into a loser? Ernie Els, the great golfer, worried about this too. Els finally won a major tournament after a five-year dry spell, in which match after match slipped away from him. What if he had lost this tournament, too? "I would have been a different person," he tells us. He would have been a loser. Each April when the skinny envelopes—–the rejection letters—–arrive from colleges, countless failures are created coast to coast. Thousands of brilliant young scholars become "The Girl Who Didn't Get into Princeton" or the "The Boy Who Didn't Get into Stanford." Defining Moments Even in the growth mindset, failure can be a painful experience. But it doesn't define you. It's a problem to be faced, dealt with, and learned from. Jim Marshall, former defensive player for the Minnesota Vikings, relates what could easily have made him into a failure. In a game against the San Francisco 49ers, Marshall spotted the football on the ground. He scooped it up and ran for a touchdown as the crowd cheered. But he ran the wrong way. He scored for the wrong team and on national television. It was the most devastating moment of his life. The shame was overpowering. But during halftime, he thought, "If you make a mistake, you got to make it right. I realized I had a choice. I could sit in my misery or I could do something about it." Pulling himself together for the second half, he played some of his best football ever and contributed to his team's victory. Nor did he stop there. He spoke to groups. He answered letters that poured in from people who finally had the courage to admit their own shameful experiences. He heightened his concentration during games. Instead of letting the experience define him, he took control of it. He used it to become a better player and, he believes, a better person. In the fixed mindset, however the loss of one's self to failure can be a permanent, haunting trauma. Bernard Loiseau was one of the top chefs in the world. Only a handful of restaurants in all of France receive the supreme rating of three stars from the Guide Michelin, the most respected restaurant guide in Europe. His was one of them. Around the publication of the 2003 Guide Michelin, however, Mr. Loiseau committed suicide. He had lost two points in another 21 guide, going from a nineteen (out of twenty) to a seventeen in the GaultMillau. And there were rampant rumors that he would lose one of his three stars in the new Guide. Although he did not, the idea of failure had possessed him. Loiseau had been a pioneer. He was one of the first to advance the "nouvelle cuisine," trading the traditional butter and cream sauces of French cooking for the brighter flavors of the foods themselves. A man of tremendous energy, he was also an entrepreneur. Besides his threestar restaurant in Burgundy, he had created three eateries in Paris, numerous cookbooks, and a line of frozen foods. "I'm like Yves Saint Laurent," he told people. "I do both haute couture and ready to-wear." A man of such talent and originality could easily have planned for a satisfying future, with or without the two points or the third star. In fact, the director of the GaultMillau said it was unimaginable that their rating could have taken his life. But in the fixed mindset, it is imaginable. Their lower rating gave him a new definition of himself: Failure. Has-been. It's striking what counts as failure in the fixed mindset. So, on a lighter note ... My Success Is Your Failure Last summer my husband and I went to a dude ranch, something very novel since neither of us had ever made contact with a horse. One day, we signed up for a lesson in fly fishing. It was taught by a wonderful eighty-year-old cowboy-type fisherman who showed us how to cast the fishing line, and then turned us loose. We soon realized that he had not taught us how to recognize when the trout bit the lure (they don't tug on the line; you have to watch for a bubble in the water), what to do when the trout bit the lure (tug up- ward), or how to reel the trout in if by some miracle we got that far (pull the fish along the water; do not hoist it into the air). Well, time passed, the mosquitoes bit, but not so the trout. None of the dozen or so of us made the slightest progress. Suddenly, I hit the jackpot. Some careless trout bit hard on my lure and the fisherman, who happened to be right there, talked me through the rest. I had me a rainbow trout. Reaction #1: My husband, David, came running over beaming with pride and saying, “Life with you is so exciting!” Reaction #2: That evening when we came into the dining room for dinner, two men came up to my husband and said, “David, how’re you coping?” David looked at them blankly; he had no idea what they were talking about. Of course he didn’t. He was the one who thought my catching the fish was exciting. But I knew exactly what they meant. They had expected him to feel diminished, and they went on to make it clear that that’s exactly what my success had done to them. Shirk, Cheat, Blame: Not a Recipe for Success Beyond how traumatic a setback can be in the fixed mindset, this mindset gives you no good recipe for overcoming it. If failure means you lack competence or potential—–that you are a failure—–where do you go from there? In one study, seventh graders told us how they would respond to an academic failure—–a poor test grade in a new course. Those with the growth mindset, no big surprise, said they would 22 study harder for the next test. But those with the fixed mindset said they would study less for the next test. If you don’t have the ability, why waste your time? And, they said, they would seriously consider cheating! If you don’t have the ability, they thought, you just have to look for another way. What’s more, instead of trying to learn from and repair their failures, people with the fixed mindset may simply try to repair their self-esteem. For example, they may go looking for people who are even worse off than they are. College students, after doing poorly on a test, were given a chance to look at tests of other students. Those in the growth mindset looked at the tests of people who had done far better than they had. As usual, they wanted to correct their deficiency. But students in the fixed mindset chose to look at the tests of people who had done really poorly. That was their way of feeling better about themselves. Jim Collins tells in Good to Great of a similar thing in the corporate world. As Procter & Gamble surged into the paper goods business, Scott Paper—–which was then the leader—–just gave up. Instead of mobilizing themselves and putting up a fight, they said, “Oh, well ... at least there are people in the business worse off than we are.” Another way people with the fixed mindset try to repair their self-esteem after a failure is by assigning blame or making excuses. Let’s return to John McEnroe. It was never his fault. One time he lost a match because he had a fever. One time he had a backache. One time he fell victim to expectations, another time to the tabloids. One time he lost to a friend because the friend was in love and he wasn’t. One time he ate too close to the match. One time he was too chunky, another time too thin. One time it was too cold, another time too hot. One time he was undertrained, another time overtrained. His most agonizing loss, and the one that still keeps him up nights, was his loss in the 1984 French Open. Why did he lose after leading Ivan Lendl two sets to none? According to McEnroe, it wasn't his fault. An NBC cameraman had taken off his headset and a noise started coming from the side of the court. Not his fault. So he didn't train to improve his ability to concentrate or his emotional control. John Wooden, the legendary basketball coach, says you aren't a failure until you start to blame. What he means is that you can still be in the process of learning from your mistakes until you deny them. When Enron, the energy giant, failed––toppled by a culture of arrogance––whose fault was it? Not mine, insisted Jeffrey Skilling, the CEO and resident genius. It was the world's fault. The world did not appreciate what Enron was trying to do. What about the Justice Department's investigation into massive corporate deception? A "witch hunt." Jack Welch, the growth-minded CEO, had a completely different reaction to one of General Electric's fiascos. In 1986, General Electric bought Kidder, Peabody, a Wall Street investment banking firm. Soon after the deal closed, Kidder, Peabody was hit with a big insider trading scandal. A few years later, calamity struck again in the form of Joseph Jett, a trader who made a bunch of fictitious trades, to the tune of hundreds of millions, to pump up his bonus. Welch phoned fourteen of his top GE colleagues to tell them the bad news and to apologize personally. "I blamed myself for the disaster," Welch said. 23 Mindset and Depression Maybe Bernard Loiseau, the French chef, was just depressed. Were you thinking that? As a psychologist and an educator, I am vitally interested in depression. It runs wild on college campuses, especially in February and March. The winter is not over, the summer is not in sight, work has piled up, and relationships are often frayed. Yet it's been clear to me for a long time that different students handle depression in dramatically different ways. Some let everything slide. Others, though feeling wretched, hang on. They drag themselves to class, keep up with their work, and take care of themselves––so that when they feel better, their lives are intact. Not long ago, we decided to see whether mindsets play a role in this difference. To find out, we measured students' mindsets and then had them keep an online "diary" for three weeks in February and March. Every day they answered questions about their mood, their activities, and how they were coping with problems. Here's what we discovered. First, the students with the fixed mindset had higher levels of depression. Our analyses showed that this was because they ruminated over their problems and setbacks, essentially tormenting themselves with the idea that the setbacks meant they were incompetent or unworthy: "It just kept circulating in my head: You're a dope." "I just couldn't let go of the thought that this made me less of a man." Again, failures labeled them and left them no route to success. And the more depressed they felt, the more they let things go; the less they took action to solve their problems. For example, they didn't study what they needed to, they didn't hand in their assignments on time, and they didn't keep up with their chores. Although students with the fixed mindset showed more depression, there were still plenty of people with the growth mindset who felt pretty miserable, this being peak season for depression. And here we saw something really amazing. The more depressed people with the growth mindset felt (short of severe depression), the more they took action to confront their problems, the more they made sure to keep up with their schoolwork, and the more they kept up with their lives. The worse they felt, the more determined they became! In fact, from the way they acted, it might have been hard to know how despondent they were. Here is a story a young man told me. I was a freshman and it was the first time I had been away from home. Everyone was a stranger, the courses were hard, and as the year wore on I felt more and more depressed. Eventually, it reached a point where I could hardly get out of bed in the morning. But every day I forced myself to get up, shower, shave, and do whatever it was I needed to do. One day I really hit a low point and I decided to ask for help, so I went to the teaching assistant in my psychology course and asked for her advice. "Are you going to your classes?" she asked. "Yes," I replied. "Are you keeping up with your reading?" "Yes." "'Are you doing okay on your exams?" "Yes." "Well," she informed me, "then you're not depressed." 24 Yes, he was depressed, but he was coping the way people in the growth mindset tend to cope––with determination. Doesn't temperament have a lot to do with it? Aren't some people sensitive by nature, while others just let things roll off their backs? Temperament certainly plays a role, but mindset is an important part of the story. When we taught people the growth mindset, it changed the way they reacted to their depressed mood. The worse they felt, the more motivated they became and the more they confronted the problems that faced them. In short, when people believe in fixed traits, they are always in danger of being measured by a failure. It can define them in a permanent way. Smart or talented as they may be, this mindset seems to rob them of their coping resources. When people believe their basic qualities can be developed, failures may still hurt, but failures don't define them.

And if abilities can be expanded––if change and growth are possible––then there are still many paths to success. MINDSETS CHANGE THE MEANING OF EFFORT As children, we were given a choice between the talented but erratic hare and the plodding but steady tortoise. The lesson was supposed to be that slow and steady wins the race. But, really, did any of us ever want to be the tortoise? No, we just wanted to be a less foolish hare. We wanted to be swift as the wind and a bit more strategic––say, not taking quite so many snoozes before the finish line. After all, everyone knows you have to show up in order to win. The story of the tortoise and the hare, in trying to put forward the power of effort, gave effort a bad name. It reinforced the image that effort is for the plodders and suggested that in rare instances, when talented people dropped the ball, the plodder could sneak through. The little engine that could, the saggy, baggy elephant, and the scruffy tugboat––they were cute, they were often overmatched, and we were happy for them when they succeeded. In fact, to this day I remember how fond I was of those little creatures (or machines), but no way did I identify with them. The message was: If you're unfortunate enough to be the runt of the litter––if you lack endowment––you don't have to be an utter failure. You can be a sweet, adorable little slogger, and maybe (if you really work at it and withstand all the scornful onlookers) even a success. Thank you very much, I'll take the endowment. The problem was that these stories made it into an either-or. Either you have ability or you expend effort. And this is part of the fixed mindset. Effort is for those who don't have the ability. People with the fixed mindset tell us, "If you have to work at something, you must not be good at it." They add, "Things come easily to people who are true geniuses."

It never occurred to me that they might be just as smart and more hardworking! For me it was either-or. And it was clear I valued the either over the or. Malcolm Gladwell, the author and New Yorker writer, has suggested that as a society we value natural, effortless accomplishment over achievement through effort. We endow our heroes with superhuman abilities that led them inevitably toward their greatness. It's as if Midori popped out of the womb fiddling, Michael Jordan dribbling, and Picasso doodling. This captures the fixed mindset perfectly. And it's everywhere. A report from researchers at Duke University sounds an alarm about the anxiety and depression among female undergraduates who aspire to "effortless perfection." They believe they should display perfect beauty, perfect womanhood, and perfect scholarship all without trying (or at least without appearing to try). Americans aren't the only people who disdain effort. French executive Pierre Chevalier says, "We are not a nation of effort. After all, if you have savoir-faire [a mixture of know-how and cool], you do things effortlessly." People with the growth mindset, however, believe something very different. For them, even geniuses have to work hard for their achievements. And what's so heroic, they would say, about having a gift? They may appreciate endowment, but they admire effort, for no matter what your ability is, effort is what ignites that ability and turns it into accomplishment. Seabiscuit Here was a horse who was so broken, he was supposed to be put to sleep. In fact, here was a whole team of people––the jockey, the owner, the trainer––who were damaged in one way or another. Yet through their dogged determination and against all odds, they transformed themselves into winners. A down-and-out nation saw this horse and rider as a symbol of what could be accomplished through grit and spirit. 26 Equally moving is the parallel story about Seabiscuit's author, Laura Hillenbrand. Felled in her college years by severe, recurrent chronic fatigue that never went away, she was often unable to function. Yet something in the story of the "horse who could" gripped and inspired her, so that she was able to write a heartfelt, magnificent story about the triumph of will. The book was a testament to Seabiscuit's triumph and her own, equally. Seen through the lens of the growth mindset, these are stories about the transformative power of effort––the power of effort to change your ability and to change you as a person. But filtered through the fixed mindset, it's a great story about three men and a horse, all with deficiencies, who had to try very hard. High Effort: The Big Risk From the point of view of the fixed mindset, effort is only for people with deficiencies. And when people already know they're deficient, maybe they have nothing to lose by trying. But if your claim to fame is not having any deficiencies––if you're considered a genius, a talent, or a natural––then you have a lot to lose. Effort can reduce you. Nadja Salerno-Sonnenberg made her violin debut at the age of ten with the Philadelphia Orchestra. Yet when she arrived at Juilliard to study with Dorothy DeLay, the great violin teacher, she had a repertoire of awful habits. Her fingerings and bowings were awkward and she held her violin in the wrong position, but she refused to change. After several years, she saw the other students catching up and even surpassing her, and by her late teens she had a crisis of confidence. "I was used to success, to the prodigy label in newspapers, and now I felt like a failure." This prodigy was afraid of trying. "Everything I was going through boiled down to fear. Fear of trying and failing... . If you go to an audition and don't really try, if you're not really prepared, if you didn't work as hard as you could have and you don't win, you have an excuse.... Nothing is harder than saying, 'I gave it my all and it wasn't good enough.'" The idea of trying and still failing—of leaving yourself without excuses—is the worst fear within the fixed mindset, and it haunted and paralyzed her. She had even stopped bringing her violin to her lesson! Then, one day, after years of patience and understanding, DeLay told her, "Listen, if you don't bring your violin next week, I'm throwing you out of my class." Salerno-Sonnenberg thought she was joking, but DeLay rose from the couch and calmly informed her, I'm not kidding. If you are going to waste your talent, I don't want to be a part of it. This has gone on long enough." Why is effort so terrifying? There are two reasons. One is that in the fixed mindset, great geniuses are not supposed to need it. So just needing it casts a shadow on your ability. The second is that, as Nadja suggests, it robs you of all your excuses. Without effort, you can always say, "I could have been ____ [fill in the blank]." But once you try, you can't say that anymore. Someone once said to me, "I could have been Yo-Yo Ma." If she had really tried for it, she wouldn't have been able to say that. Salerno-Sonnenberg was terrified of losing DeLay. She finally decided that trying and failing—an honest failure—was better than the course she had been on, and so she began training with DeLay for an upcoming competition. For the first time she went all out, and, by the way,won. Now she says, "This is something I know for a fact: You have to work hardest for the things you love most. And when it's music you love, you're in for the fight of your life." Fear of effort can happen in relationships, too, as it did with Amanda, a dynamic and attractive young woman. I had a lot of crazy boyfriends. A lot. They ranged from unreliable to inconsiderate. "How about a nice guy for once?" my best friend Carla always said. It was like, "You deserve better." So then Carla fixed me up with Rob, a guy from her office. He was great, and not just on day one. I loved it. It was like, "Oh, my God, a guy who actually shows up on time. "Then it became serious and I freaked. I mean, this guy really liked me, but I couldn't stop thinking about how, if he really knew me, he might get turned off. I mean, what if I really, really tried and it didn't work? I guess I couldn't take that risk. Low Effort: The Big Risk In the growth mindset, it's almost inconceivable to want something badly, to think you have a chance to achieve it, and then do nothing about it. When it happens, the I could have been is heartbreaking, not comforting. There were few American women in the 1930s through 1950s who were more successful than Clare Boothe Luce. She was a famous author and playwright, she was elected to Congress twice, and she was ambassador to Italy. "I don't really understand the word 'success,'" she has said. "I know people use it about me, but I don't understand it." Her public life and private tragedies kept her from getting back to her greatest love: writing for the theater. She'd had great success with plays like The Women, but it just wouldn't do for a political figure to keep penning tart, sexy comedies. For her, politics did not provide the personal creative effort she valued most, and looking back she couldn't forgive herself for not pursuing her passion for theater. "I often thought," she said, "that if l were to write an autobiography, my title would be The Autobiography of a Failure." Billie Jean King says it's all about what you want to look back and say. I agree with her. You can look back and say, "I could have been ... ," polishing your unused endowments like trophies. Or you can look back and say, "I gave my all for the things I valued." Think about what you want to look back and say. Then choose your mindset. Turning Knowledge into Action Sure, people with the fixed mindset have read the books that say: Success is about being your best self, not about being better than others; failure is an opportunity, not a condemnation; effort is the key to success. But they can't put this into practice because their basic mindset––their belief in fixed traits––is telling them something entirely different: that success is about being more gifted than others, that failure does measure you, and that effort is for those who can't make it on talent.

At this point, you probably have questions. Let me see if I can answer some of them. Question: If people believe their qualities are fixed, and they have shown themselves to be smart or talented, why do they have to keep proving it? After all, when the prince proved his bravery, he and the princess lived happily ever after. He didn't have to go out and slay a dragon every day. Why don't people with the fixed mindset prove themselves and then live happily ever after? Because every day new and larger dragons come along and, as things get harder, maybe the ability they proved yesterday is not up to today's task. Maybe they were smart enough for algebra but not calculus. Maybe they were a good enough pitcher for the minor leagues but not the majors. Maybe they were a good enough writer for their school newspaper but not The New York Times. So they're racing to prove themselves over and over, but where are they going? To me they're often running in place, amassing countless affirmations, but not necessarily ending up where they want to be. You know those movies where the main character wakes up one day and sees that his life has not been worthwhile—–he has always been besting people, not growing, learning, or caring. My favorite is Groundhog Day, which I didn't see for a long time because I couldn't get past the name. At any rate, in Groundhog Day, Bill Murray doesn't just wake up one day and get the message; he has to repeat the same day over and over until he gets the message. Phil Connors (Murray) is a weatherman for a local station in Pittsburgh who is dispatched to Punxsutawney, Pennsylvania, to cover the Groundhog Day ceremony. On February 2, a groundhog is taken out of his little house; if he is judged to have seen his shadow, there will be another six weeks of winter. If not, there will be an early spring. Phil, considering himself to be a superior being, has complete contempt for the ceremony, the town, and the people ("hicks" and "morons"), and after making that perfectly clear, he plans to get out of Punxsutawney as quickly as possible. But this is not to be. A blizzard hits the town, he is forced to remain, and when he wakes up the next morning, it's Groundhog Day again. The same Sonny and Cher song, "I Got You Babe," wakes him up on the clock radio and the same groundhog festival is gearing up once again. And again. And again. At first, he uses the knowledge to further his typical agenda, making fools out of other people. Since he is the only one reliving the day, he can talk to a woman on one day, and then use the information to deceive, impress, and seduce her the next. He is in fixed-mindset heaven. He can prove his superiority over and over. But after countless such days, he realizes it's all going nowhere and he tries to kill himself. He crashes a car, he electrocutes himself, he jumps from a steeple, he walks in front of a truck. With no way out, it finally dawns on him. He could be using this time to learn. He goes for piano lessons. He reads voraciously. He learns ice sculpting. He finds out about people who need help that day (a boy who falls from a tree, a man who chokes on his steak) and starts to help them, and care about them. Pretty soon the day is not long enough! Only when this change of mindset is complete is he released from the spell.

Question: Are mindsets a permanent part of your makeup or can you change them? Mindsets are an important part of your personality, but you can change them. Just by knowing about the two mindsets, you can start thinking and reacting in new ways. People tell me they start to catch themselves when they are in the throes of the fixed mindset—–passing up a chance for learning, feeling labeled by a failure, or getting discouraged when something requires a lot of effort. And then they switch themselves into the growth mindset—–making sure they take the challenge, learn from the failure, or continue their effort. When my graduate students and I first discovered the mindsets, they would catch me in the fixed mindset, smile kindly, and let me know it. It's also important to realize that even if people have a fixed mindset, they're not always in that mindset. In fact, in many of our studies, we put people into a growth mindset. We tell them that an ability can be learned and that the task will give them a chance to do that. Or we have them read a scientific article that teaches them the growth mindset. The article describes people who did not have natural ability, but who developed exceptional skills. These experiences make our research participants into growth-minded thinkers, at least for the moment––and they act like growth-minded thinkers, too. Later, there's a chapter all about change. There I describe people who have changed and programs we've developed to bring about change. Question: Can I be half-and-half? I recognize both mindsets in myself. All of us have elements of both-we're all a mixture of fixed and growth mindsets. I'm talking about it as a simple either-or right now for the sake of simplicity. People can also have different mindsets in different areas. I might think that my artistic skills are fixed but that my intelligence can be developed. Or that my personality is fixed, but my creativity can be developed. We've found that whatever mindset people have in a particular area will guide them in that area. Question: With all your belief in effort, are you saying that when people fail, it\ always their fault-they didn't try hard enough? No! It's true that effort is crucial––no one can succeed for long without it––but it's certainly not the only thing. People have different resources and opportunities. For example, people with money (or rich parents) have a safety net. They can take more risks and keep going longer until they succeed. People with easy access to a good education, people with a network of influential friends, people who know how to be in the right place at the right time––all stand a better chance of having their effort pay off. Rich, educated, connected effort works better. People with fewer resources, in spite of their best efforts, can be de-railed so much more easily. The hometown plant you've worked in all of your life suddenly shuts down. What now? Your child falls ill and plunges you into debt. There goes the house. Your spouse runs off with the nest egg and leaves you with the children and bills. Forget the night school classes. Before we judge, let's remember that effort isn't quite everything and that all effort is not created equal.

Question: You keep talking about how the growth mindset makes people number one, the best, the most successful. Isn't the growth mindset about personal development, not besting others? I use examples of people who made it to the top to show how far the growth mindset can take you: Believing talents can be developed allows people to fulfill their potential. In addition, examples of laid-back people having a good time would not be as convincing to people with a fixed mindset. It doesn't provide a compelling alternative for them because it makes it look like a choice between fun and excellence. However, this point is crucial: The growth mindset does allow people to love what they're doing––and to continue to love it in the face of difficulties. The growth-minded athletes, CEOs, musicians, or scientists all loved what they did, whereas many of the fixed-minded ones did not. Many growth-minded people didn't even plan to go to the top. They got there as a result of doing what they love. It's ironic: The top is where the fixed-mindset people hunger to be, but it's where many growth-minded people arrive as a by-product of their enthusiasm for what they do. This point is also crucial. In the fixed mindset, everything is about the outcome. If you fail––or if you're not the best––it's all been wasted. The growth mindset allows people to value what they're doing regardless of the outcome. They're tackling problems, charting new courses, working on important issues. Maybe they haven't found the cure for cancer, but the search was deeply meaningful. A lawyer spent seven years fighting the biggest bank in his state on behalf of people who felt they'd been cheated. After he lost, he said, "Who am I to say that just because I spent seven years on something I am entitled to success? Did I do it for the success, or did I do it because I thought the effort itself was valid? "I do not regret it. I had to do it. I would not do it differently." Question: I know a lot of workaholics on the fast track who seem to have a fixed mindset. They're always trying to prove how smart they are, but they do work hard and they do take on challenges. How does this fit with your idea that people with a fixed mindset go in for low effort and easy tasks? On the whole, people with a fixed mindset prefer effortless success, since that's the best way to prove their talent. But you're right, there are also plenty of high-powered people who think their traits are fixed and are looking for constant validation. These may be people whose life goal is to win a Nobel Prize or become the richest person on the planet––and they're willing to do what it takes. We'll meet people like this in the chapter on business and leadership. These people may be free of the belief that high effort equals low ability, but they have the other parts of the fixed mindset. They may constantly put their talent on display. They may feel that their talent makes them superior to other people. And they may be intolerant of mistakes, criticism, or setbacks. Incidentally, people with a growth mindset might also like a Nobel Prize or a lot of money. But they are not seeking it as a validation of their worth or as something that will make them better than others.

Question: What if I like my fixed mindset? If I know what my abilities and talents are, I know where I stand, and I know what to expect. Why should I give that up? If you like it, by all means keep it. This book shows people they have a choice by spelling out the two mindsets and the worlds they create. The point is that people can choose which world they want to inhabit. The fixed mindset creates the feeling that you can really know the permanent truth about yourself. And this can be comforting: You don't have to try for such-and-such because you don't have the talent. You will surely succeed at thus-and-such because you do have the talent. It's just important to be aware of the drawbacks of this mindset. You may be robbing yourself of an opportunity by underestimating your talent in the first area. Or you may be undermining your chances of success in the second area by assuming that your talent alone will take you there. By the way, having a growth mindset doesn't force you to pursue something. It just tells you that you can develop your skills. It's still up to you whether you want to. Question: Can everything about people be changed, and should people try to change everything they can? The growth mindset is the belief that abilities can be cultivated. But it doesn't tell you how much change is possible or how long change will take. And it doesn't mean that everything, like preferences or values, can be changed. I was once in a taxi, and the driver had an opera on the radio. Thinking to start a conversation, I said, "Do you like opera?" "No," he replied, "I hate it. I've always hated it." "I don't mean to pry," I said, "but why are you listening to it?" He then told me how his father had been an opera buff, listening to his vintage records at every opportunity. My cabdriver, now well into middle age, had tried for many years to cultivate a rapturous response to opera. He played the disks, he read the scores––all to no avail. "Give yourself a break," I advised him. "There are plenty of cultured and intelligent people who can't stand opera. Why don't you just consider yourself one of them?" The growth mindset also doesn't mean everything that can be changed should be changed. We all need to accept some of our imperfections, especially the ones that don't really harm our lives or the lives of others. The fixed mindset stands in the way of development and change. The growth mindset is a starting point for change, but people need to decide for themselves where their efforts toward change would be most valuable. Question: Are people with the fixed mindset simply lacking in confidence? No. People with the fixed mindset can have just as much confidence as people with the growth mindset––before anything happens, that is. But as you can imagine, their confidence is more fragile since setbacks and even effort can undermine it. Joseph Martocchio conducted a study of employees who were taking a short computer training course. Half of the employees were put into a fixed mindset. He told them it was all a matter of how much ability they possessed. The other half were put in a growth mindset. He 32 told them that computer skills could be developed through practice. Everyone, steeped in these mindsets, then proceeded with the course. Although the two groups started off with exactly equal confidence in their computer skills, by the end of the course they looked quite different. Those in the growth mindset gained considerable confidence in their computer skills as they learned, despite the many mistakes they inevitably made. But, because of those mistakes, those with the fixed mindset actually lost confidence in their computer skills as they learned! The same thing happened with Berkeley students. Richard Robins and Jennifer Pals tracked students at the University of California at Berkeley over their years of college. They found that when students had the growth mindset, they gained confidence in themselves as they repeatedly met and mastered the challenges of the university. However, when students had the fixed mindset, their confidence eroded in the face of those same challenges. That's why people with the fixed mindset have to nurse their confidence and protect it. That's what John McEnroe's excuses were for: to protect his confidence. Michelle Wie was a teenage golfer when she decided to go up against the big boys. She entered the Sony Open, a PGA tournament that features the best male players in the world. Coming from a fixed-mindset perspective, everyone rushed to warn her that she could do serious damage to her confidence if she did poorly––that "taking too many early lumps against superior competition could hurt her long-range development." "It's always negative when you don't win," warned Vijay Singh, a prominent golfer on the tour. But Wie disagreed. She wasn't going there to groom her confidence. "Once you win junior tournaments, it's easy to win multiple times. What I'm doing now is to prepare for the future." It's the learning experience she was after––what it was like to play with the world's best players in the atmosphere of a tournament. After the event, Wie's confidence had not suffered one bit. She had exactly what she wanted. "I think I learned that I can play here." It would be a long road to the winner's circle, but she now had a sense of what she was shooting for. Some years ago, I got a letter from a world-class competitive swimmer.

I've always had a problem with confidence. My coaches always told me to believe in myself 100%. They told me not to let any doubts enter my mind and to think about how I'm better than everyone else. I couldn't do it because I'm always so aware of my defects and the mistakes I make in every meet. Trying to think I was perfect made it even worse. Then I read your work and how it's so important to focus on learning and improving. It turned me around. My defects are things I can work on! Now a mistake doesn't seem so important. I wanted to write you this letter for teaching me how to have confidence. Thank you

What I mean is that even when you think you're not good at something, you can still plunge into it wholeheartedly and stick to it. Actually, sometimes you plunge into something because you're not good at it. This is a wonderful feature of the growth mindset. You don't have to think you're already great at something to want to do it and to enjoy doing it. This book is one of the hardest things I've ever done. I read endless books and articles. The information was overwhelming. I'd never written in a popular way. It was intimidating. Does it seem easy for me? Way back when, that's exactly what I would have wanted you to think. Now I want you to know the effort it took––and the joy it brought. Grow Your Mindset • People are all born with a love of learning, but the fixed mindset can undo it. Think of a time you were enjoying something––doing a crossword puzzle, playing a sport, learning a new dance. Then it became hard and you wanted out. Maybe you suddenly felt tired, dizzy, bored, or hungry. Next time this happens, don't fool yourself . It's the fixed mindset. Put yourself in a growth mindset. Picture your brain forming new connections as you meet the challenge and learn. Keep on going. • It's tempting to create a world in which we're perfect. (Ah, I remember that feeling from grade school.) We can choose partners, make friends, hire people who make us feel faultless. But think about it––do you want to never grow? Next time you're tempted to surround yourself with worshipers, go to church. In the rest of your life, seek constructive criticism. • Is there something in your past that you think measured you? A test score? A dishonest or callous action? Being fired from a job? Being rejected? Focus on that thing. Feel all the emotions that go with it. Now put it in a growth-mindset perspective. Look honestly at your role in it, but understand that it doesn't define your intelligence or personality. Instead, ask: What did I (or can I) learn from that experience? How can I use it as a basis for growth? Carry that with you instead. • How do you act when you feel depressed? Do you work harder at things in your life or do you let them go? Next time you feel low, put yourself in a growth mindset––think about learning, challenge, confronting obstacles. Think about effort as a positive, constructive force, not as a big drag. Try it out. • Is there something you've always wanted to do but were afraid you weren't good at? Make a plan to do it.

THE TRUTH ABOUT ABILITY AND ACCOMPLISHMENT Try to picture Thomas Edison as vividly as you can. Think about where he is and what he's doing. Is he alone? I asked people, and they always said things like this: "He's in his workshop surrounded by equipment. He's working on the phonograph, trying things. He succeeds! [Is he alone?] Yes, he's doing this stuff alone because he's the only one who knows what he's after." "He's in New Jersey. He's standing in a white coat in a lab-type room. He's leaning over a lightbulb. Suddenly, it works! [Is he alone?] Yes. He's kind of a reclusive guy who likes to tinker on his own." In truth, the record shows quite a different fellow, working in quite a different way. Edison was not a loner. For the invention of the lightbulb, he had thirty assistants, including well-trained scientists, often working around the clock in a corporate-funded state-of-the-art laboratory! It did not happen suddenly. The lightbulb has become the symbol of that single moment when the brilliant solution strikes, but there was no single moment of invention. In fact, the lightbulb was not one invention, but a whole network of time-consuming inventions each requiring one or more chemists, mathematicians, physicists, engineers, and glass- blowers. Edison was no naive tinkerer or unworldly egghead. The "Wizard of Menlo Park" was a savvy entrepreneur, fully aware of the commercial potential of his inventions. He also knew how to cozy up to the press––sometimes beating others out as the inventor of something because he knew how to publicize himself. Yes, he was a genius. But he was not always one. His biographer, Paul Israel, sifting through all the available information, thinks he was more or less a regular boy of his time and place. Young Tom was taken with experiments and mechanical things (perhaps more avidly than most), but machines and technology were part of the ordinary midwestern boy's experience. What eventually set him apart was his mindset and drive. He never stopped being the curious, tinkering boy looking for new challenges. Long after other young men had taken up their roles in society, he rode the rails from city to city learning everything he could about telegraphy, and working his way up the ladder of telegraphers through nonstop self-education and invention. And later, much to the disappointment of his wives, his consuming love remained self-improvement and invention, but only in his field. There are many myths about ability and achievement, especially about the lone, brilliant person suddenly producing amazing things. Yet Darwin's masterwork, The Origin of Species, took years of teamwork in the field, hundreds of discussions with colleagues and mentors, several preliminary drafts, and half a lifetime of dedication before it reached fruition. 35 Mozart labored for more than ten years until he produced any work that we admire today. Before then, his compositions were not that original or interesting. Actually, they were often patched-together chunks taken from other composers. This chapter is about the real ingredients in achievement. It's about why some people achieve less than expected and why some people achieve more. MINDSET AND SCHOOL ACHIEVEMENT Let's step down from the celestial realm of Mozart and Darwin and come back to earth to see how mindsets create achievement in real life. It's funny, but seeing one student blossom under the growth mindset has a greater impact on me than all the stories about Mozarts and Darwins. Maybe because it's more about you and me—–about what's happened to us and why we are where we are now. And about children and their potential. Back on earth, we measured students' mindsets as they made the transition to junior high school: Did they believe their intelligence was a fixed trait or something they could develop? Then we followed them for the next two years. The transition to junior high is a time of great challenge for many students. The work gets much harder, the grading policies toughen up, the teaching becomes less personalized. And all this happens while students are coping with their new adolescent bodies and roles. Grades suffer, but not everyone's grades suffer equally. No. In our study, only the students with the fixed mindset showed the decline. The students with the growth mindset showed an increase in their grades over the two years. When the two groups had entered junior high, their past records were indistinguishable. In the more benign environment of grade school, they'd earned the same grades and achievement test scores. Only when they hit the challenge of junior high did they begin to pull apart. Here's how students with the fixed mindset explained their poor grades. Many maligned their abilities: "I am the stupidest" or "I suck in math." And many covered these feelings by blaming someone else: "[The math teacher] is a fat male slut ... and [the English teacher] is a slob with a pink ass." "Because the teacher is on crack." These interesting analyses of the problem hardly provide a road map to future success. With the threat of failure looming, students with the growth mindset instead mobilized their resources for learning. They told us that they, too, sometimes felt overwhelmed, but their response was to dig in and do what it takes. They were like George Danzig. Who? George Danzig was a graduate student in math at Berkeley. One day, as usual, he rushed in late to his math class and quickly copied the two homework problems from the blackboard. When he later went to do them, he found them very difficult, and it took him several days of hard work to crack them open and solve them. They turned out not to be homework problems at all. They were two famous math problems that had never been solved. The Low-Effort Syndrome Our students with the fixed mindset who were facing the hard transition saw it as a threat. It threatened to unmask their flaws and turn them from winners into losers. In fact, in the fixed 36 mindset, adolescence is one big test. Am I smart or dumb? Am I good-looking or ugly? Am I cool or nerdy? Am I a winner or a loser? And in the fixed mindset, a loser is forever. It's no wonder that many adolescents mobilize their resources, not for learning, but to protect their egos. And one of the main ways they do this (aside from providing vivid portraits of their teachers) is by not trying. This is when some of the brightest students, just like Nadja SalernoSonnenberg, simply stop working. In fact, students with the fixed mindset tell us that their main goal in school––aside from looking smart––is to exert as little effort as possible. They heartily agree with statements like this: "In school my main goal is to do things as easily as possible so I don't have to work very hard." This low-effort syndrome is often seen as a way that adolescents assert their independence from adults, but it is also a way that students with the fixed mindset protect themselves. They view the adults as saying, "Now we will measure you and see what you've got." And they are answering, "No you won't." John Holt, the great educator, says that these are the games all human beings play when others are sitting in judgment of them. "The worst student we had, the worst I have ever encountered, was in his life outside the classroom as mature, intelligent, and interesting a person as anyone at the school. What went wrong? ... Somewhere along the line, his intelligence became disconnected from his schooling." For students with the growth mindset, it doesn't make sense to stop trying. For them, adolescence is a time of opportunity: a time to learn new subjects, a time to find out what they like and what they want to become in the future. Later, I'll describe the project in which we taught junior high students the growth mindset. What I want to tell you now is how teaching them this mindset unleashed their effort. One day, we were introducing the growth mindset to a new group of students. All at once Jimmy––the most hard-core turned-off low-effort kid in the group––looked up with tears in his eyes and said, "You mean I don't have to be dumb?" From that day on, he worked. He started staying up late to do his homework, which he never used to bother with at all. He started handing in assignments early so he could get feedback and revise them. He now believed that working hard was not something that made you vulnerable, but something that made you smarter. Finding Your Brain A close friend of mine recently handed me something he'd written, a poem-story that reminded me of Jimmy and his unleashed effort. My friend's second-grade teacher, Mrs. Beer, had had each student draw and cut out a paper horse. She then lined up all the horses above the blackboard and delivered her growth-mindset message: "Your horse is only as fast as your brain. Every time you learn something, your horse will move ahead." My friend wasn't so sure about the "brain" thing. His father had always told him, "You have too much mouth and too little brains for your own good." Plus, his horse seemed to just sit at the starting gate while "everyone else's brain joined the learning chase," especially the brains of Hank and Billy, the class geniuses, whose horses jumped way ahead of everyone else's. But my friend kept at it. To improve his skills, he kept reading the comics with his mother and he kept adding up the points when he played gin rummy with his grandmother. 37 And soon my sleek stallion bolted forward like Whirlaway, and there was no one who was going to stop him. Over the weeks and months he flew forward overtaking the others one by one. In the late spring homestretch Hank's and Billy's mounts were ahead by just a few subtraction exercises, and when the last bell of school rang, my horse won––"By a nose!" Then I knew I had a brain: I had the horse to prove it. –– PAUL WORTMAN Of course, learning shouldn't really be a race. But this race helped my friend discover his brain and connect it up to his schooling. The College Transition Another transition, another crisis. College is when all the students who were the brains in high school are thrown together. Like our graduate students, yesterday they were king of the hill, but today who are they? Nowhere is the anxiety of being dethroned more palpable than in pre-med classes. In the last chapter, I mentioned our study of tense but hopeful undergraduates taking their first college chemistry course. This is the course that would give them––or deny them––entree to the premed curriculum, and it's well known that students will go to almost any lengths to do well in this course. At the beginning of the semester, we measured students' mindsets, and then we followed them through the course, watching their grades and asking about their study strategies. Once again we found that the students with the growth mindset earned better grades in the course. Even when they did poorly on a particular test, they bounced back on the next ones. When students with the fixed mindset did poorly, they often didn't make a comeback. In this course, everybody studied. But there are different ways to study. Many students study like this: They read the textbook and their class notes. If the material is really hard, they read them again. Or they might try to memorize everything they can, like a vacuum cleaner. That's how the students with the fixed mindset studied. If they did poorly on the test, they concluded that chemistry was not their subject. After all, "I did everything possible, didn't I?" Far from it. They would be shocked to find out what students with the growth mindset do. Even I find it remarkable. The students with growth mindset completely took charge of their learning and motivation. Instead of plunging into unthinking memorization of the course material, they said: "I looked for 38 themes and underlying principles across lectures," and "I went over mistakes until I was certain I understood them." They were studying to learn, not just to ace the test. And, actually, this was why they got higher grades––not because they were smarter or had a better background in science. Instead of losing their motivation when the course got dry or difficult, they said: "I maintained my interest in the material." "I stayed positive about taking chemistry." "I kept myself motivated to study." Even if they thought the textbook was boring or the instructor was a stiff, they didn't let their motivation evaporate. That just made it all the more important to motivate themselves. I got an e-mail from one of my undergraduate students shortly after I had taught her the growth mindset. Here's how she used to study before: "When faced with really tough material I tend[ed] to read the material over and over." After learning the growth mindset, she started using better strategies––that worked: Professor Dweck: When Heidi [the teaching assistant] told me my exam results today I didn't know whether to cry or just sit down. Heidi will tell you, I looked like I won the lottery (and I feel that way, too)! I can't believe I did SO WELL. I expected to "scrape" by. The encouragement you have given me will serve me well in life... . I feel that I've earned a noble grade, but I didn't earn it alone. Prof Dweck, you not only teach [your] theory, you SHOW it. Thank you for the lesson. It is a valuable one, perhaps the most valuable I've learned at Columbia. And yeah, I'll be doing THAT [using these strategies] before EVERY exam! Thank you very, very much (and you TOO Heidi)! No longer helpless, June Because they think in terms of learning, people with the growth mindset are clued in to all the different ways to create learning. It's odd. Our pre-med students with the fixed mindset would do almost anything for a good grade––except take charge of the process to make sure it happens. Created Equal? Does this mean that anyone with the right mindset can do well? Are all children created equal? Let's take the second question first. No, some children are different. In her book Gifted Children, Ellen Winner offers incredible descriptions of prodigies. These are children who seem to be born with heightened abilities and obsessive interests, and who, through relentless pursuit of these interests, become amazingly accomplished. Michael was one of the most precocious. He constantly played games involving letters and numbers, made his parents answer endless questions about letters and numbers, and spoke, read, and did math at an unbelievably early age. Michael's mother reports that at four months old, he 39 said, "Mom, Dad, what's for dinner?" At ten months, he astounded people in the supermarket by reading words from the signs. Everyone assumed his mother was doing some kind of ventriloquism thing. His father reports that at three, he was not only doing algebra, but discovering and proving algebraic rules. Each day, when his father got home from work, Michael would pull him toward math books and say, "Dad, let's go do work." Michael must have started with a special ability, but, for me, the most outstanding feature is his extreme love of learning and challenge. His parents could not tear him away from his demanding activities. The same is true for every prodigy Winner describes. Most often people believe that the "gift" is the ability itself. Yet what feeds it is that constant, endless curiosity and challenge seeking. Is it ability or mindset? Was it Mozart's musical ability or the fact that he worked till his hands were deformed? Was it Darwin's scientific ability or the fact that he collected specimens nonstop from early childhood? Prodigies or not, we all have interests that can blossom into abilities. As a child, I was fascinated by people, especially adults. I wondered: What makes them tick? In fact, a few years back, one of my cousins reminded me of an episode that took place when we were five years old. We were at my grandmother's house, and he'd had a big fight with his mother over when he could eat his candy. Later, we were sitting outside on the front steps and I said to him: "Don't be so stupid. Adults like to think they're in charge. Just say yes, and then eat your candy when you want to." Were those the words of a budding psychologist? All I know is that my cousin told me this advice served him well. (Interestingly, he became a dentist.) Can Everyone Do Well? Now back to the first question. Is everyone capable of great things with the right mindset? Could you march into the worst high school in your state and teach the students college calculus? If you could, then one thing would be clear: With the right mindset and the right teaching, people are capable of a lot more than we think. Garfield High School was one of the worst schools in Los Angeles. To say that the students were turned off and the teachers burned out is an understatement. But without thinking twice, Jaime Escalante (of Stand and Deliver fame) taught these inner-city Hispanic students collegelevel calculus. With his growth mindset, he asked, "How can I teach them?" not "Can I teach them?" and "How will they learn best?" not "Can they learn?" But not only did he teach them calculus, he (and his colleague, Benjamin Jimenez) took them to the top of the national charts in math. In 1987, only three other public schools in the country had more students taking the Advanced Placement Calculus test. Those three included Stuyvesant High School and the Bronx High School of Science, both elite math-and-scienceoriented schools in New York. What's more, most of the Garfield students earned test grades that were high enough to gain them college credits. In the whole country that year, only a few hundred Mexican American students passed the test at this level. This means there's a lot of intelligence out there being wasted by underestimating students' potential to develop. 40 Marva Collins Most often when kids are behind––say, when they're repeating a grade––they're given dumbeddown material on the assumption that they can't handle more. That idea comes from the fixed mindset: These students are dim-witted, so they need the same simple things drummed into them over and over. Well, the results are depressing. Students repeat the whole grade without learning any more than they knew before. Instead, Marva Collins took inner-city Chicago kids who had failed in the public schools and treated them like geniuses. Many of them had been labeled "learning disabled," "retarded," or "emotionally disturbed." Virtually all of them were apathetic. No light in the eyes, no hope in the face. Collins's second-grade public school class started out with the lowest-level reader there was. By June, they reached the middle of the fifth-grade reader, studying Aristotle, Aesop, Tolstoy, Shakespeare, Poe, Frost, and Dickinson along the way. Later when she started her own school, Chicago Sun-Times columnist Zay Smith dropped in. He saw four-year-olds writing sentences like "See the physician'" and "Aesop wrote fables," and talking about "diphthongs" and "diacritical marks." He observed second graders reciting passages from Shakespeare, Longfellow, and Kipling. Shortly before, he had visited a rich suburban high school where many students had never heard of Shakespeare. "Shoot," said one of Collins's students, "you mean those rich high school kids don't know Shakespeare was born in 1564 and died in 1616?" Students read huge amounts, even over the summer. One student, who had entered as a "retarded" six-year-old, now four years later had read twenty-three books over the summer, including A Tale of Two Cities and Jane Eyre. The students read deeply and thoughtfully. As the three- and four-year-olds were reading about Daedalus and Icarus, one four- year-old exclaimed, "Mrs. Collins, if we do not learn and work hard, we will take an Icarian flight to nowhere." Heated discussions of Macbeth were common. Alfred Binet believed you could change the quality of someone's mind. Clearly you can. Whether you measure these children by the breadth of their knowledge or by their performance on standardized tests, their minds had been transformed. Benjamin Bloom, an eminent educational researcher, studied 120 outstanding achievers. They were concert pianists, sculptors, Olympic swimmers, world-class tennis players, mathematicians, and research neurologists. Most were not that remarkable as children and didn't show clear talent before their training began in earnest. Even by early adolescence, you usually couldn't predict their future accomplishment from their current ability. Only their continued motivation and commitment, along with their network of support, took them to the top. Bloom concludes, "After forty years of intensive research on school learning in the United States as well as abroad, my major conclusion is: What any person in the world can learn, almost all persons can learn, if provided with the appropriate prior and current conditions of learning." He's not counting the 2 to 3 percent of children who have severe impairments, and he's not counting the top 1 to 2 percent of children at the other extreme that include children like Michael. He is counting everybody else.

Ability Levels and Tracking But aren't students sorted into different ability levels for a reason? Haven't their test scores and past achievement shown what their ability is? Remember, test scores and measures of achievement tell you where a student is, but they don't tell you where a student could end up. Falko Rheinberg, a researcher in Germany, studied schoolteachers with different mindsets. Some of the teachers had the fixed mindset. They believed that students entering their class with different achievement levels were deeply and permanently different: "According to my experience students' achievement mostly remains constant in the course of a year." "If I know students' intelligence I can predict their school career quite well." "As a teacher I have no influence on students' intellectual ability." Like my sixth-grade teacher, Mrs. Wilson, these teachers preached and practiced the fixed mindset. In their classrooms, the students who started the year in the high-ability group ended the year there, and those who started the year in the low-ability group ended the year there. But some teachers preached and practiced a growth mindset. They focused on the idea that all children could develop their skills, and in their classrooms a weird thing happened. It didn't matter whether students started the year in the high- or the low-ability group. Both groups ended the year way up high. It's a powerful experience to see these findings. The group differences had simply disappeared under the guidance of teachers who taught for improvement, for these teachers had found a way to reach their "low-ability" students. How teachers put a growth mindset into practice is the topic of a later chapter, but here's a preview of how Marva Collins, the renowned teacher, did it. On the first day of class, she approached Freddie, a left-back second grader, who wanted no part of school. "Come on, peach," she said to him, cupping his face in her hands, "we have work to do. You can't just sit in a seat and grow smart... . I promise, you are going to do, and you are going to produce. I am not going to let you fail."

The fixed mindset limits achievement. It fills people's minds with interfering thoughts, it makes effort disagreeable, and it leads to inferior learning strategies. What's more, it makes other people into judges instead of allies. Whether we're talking about Darwin or college students, important achievements require a clear focus, all-out effort, and a bottomless trunk full of strategies. Plus allies in learning. This is what the growth mindset gives people, and that's why it helps their abilities grow and bear fruit. IS ARTISTIC ABILITY A GIFT? Despite the widespread belief that intelligence is born, not made, when we really think about it, it's not so hard to imagine that people can develop their intellectual abilities. The intellect is so multifaceted. You can develop verbal skills or mathematical-scientific skills or logical thinking skills, and so on. But when it comes to artistic ability, it seems more like a God-given gift. For example, people seem to naturally draw well or poorly.

Even I believed this. While some of my friends seemed to draw beautifully with no effort and no training, my drawing ability was arrested in early grade school. Try as I might, my attempts were primitive and disappointing. I was artistic in other ways. I can design, I'm great with colors, I have a subtle sense of composition. Plus I have really good eye-hand coordination. Why couldn't I draw? I must not have the gift. I have to admit that it didn't bother me all that much. After all, when do you really have to draw? I found out one evening as the dinner guest of a fascinating man. He was an older man, a psychiatrist, who had escaped from the Holocaust. As a ten-year-old child in Czechoslovakia, he and his younger brother came home from school one day to find their parents gone. They had been taken. Knowing there was an uncle in England, the two boys walked to London and found him. A few years later, lying about his age, my host joined the Royal Air Force and fought for Britain in the war. When he was wounded, he married his nurse, went to medical school, and established a thriving practice in America. Over the years, he developed a great interest in owls. He thought of them as embodying characteristics he admired, and he liked to think of himself as owlish. Besides the many owl statuettes that adorned his house, he had an owl-related guest book. It turned out that whenever he took a shine to someone, he asked them to draw an owl and write something to him in this book. As he extended this book to me and explained its significance, I felt both honored and horrified. Mostly horrified. All the more because my creation was not to be buried somewhere in the middle of the book, but was to adorn its very last page. I won't dwell on the intensity of my discomfort or the poor quality of my artwork, although both were painfully clear. I tell this story as a prelude to the astonishment and joy I felt when I read Drawing on the Right Side of the Brain. On the opposite page are the before-and-after self-portraits of people who took a short course in drawing from the author, Betty Edwards. That is, they are the self-portraits drawn by the students when they entered her course and five days later when they had completed it. Aren't they amazing? At the beginning, these people didn't look as though they had much artistic ability. Most of their pictures 43 reminded me of my owl. But only a few days later, everybody could really draw! And Edwards swears that this is a typical group. It seems impossible. Edwards agrees that most people view drawing as a magical ability: that only a select few possess, and that only a select few will ever possess. But this is because people don't understand the components––the learnable components––of drawing. Actually, she informs us, they are; not drawing skills at all, but seeing skills. They are the ability to perceive edges, spaces, relationships, lights and shadows, and the whole. Drawing requires us to learn each component skill and then combine them into one process. Some people simply pick up these skills in the natural course of their lives, whereas others have to work to learn them and put them together. But as we can see from the "after" self-portraits, everyone can do it. Here's what this means: Just because some people can do something with little or no training, it doesn't mean that others can't do it (and sometimes do it even better) with training. This is so important, because many, many people with the fixed mindset think that someone's early performance tells you all you need to know about their talent and their future. Jackson Pollock It would have been a real shame if people discouraged Jackson Pollock for that reason. Experts agree that Pollock had little native talent for art, and when you look at his early products, it showed. They also agree that he became one of the greatest American painters of the twentieth century and that he revolutionized modern art. How did he go from point A to point B? Twyla Tharp, the world-famous choreographer and dancer, wrote a book called The Creative Habit. As you can guess from the title, she argues that creativity is not a magical act of inspiration. It's the result of hard work and dedication. Even for Mozart. Remember the movie Amadeus? Remember how it showed Mozart easily churning out one masterpiece after another while Salieri, his rival, is dying of envy? Well, Tharp worked on that movie and she says: Hogwash! Nonsense! "There are no 'natural' geniuses." Dedication is how Jackson Pollock got from point A to point B. Pollock was wildly in love with the idea of being an artist. He thought about art all the time, and he did it all the time. Because he was so gung ho, he got others to take him seriously and mentor him until he mastered all there was to master and began to produce startlingly original works. His "poured" paintings, each completely unique, allowed him to draw from his unconscious mind and convey a huge range of feeling. Several years ago, I was privileged to see a show of these paintings at the Museum of Modern Art in New York. I was stunned by the power and beauty of each work. Can anyone do anything? I don't really know. However, I think we can now agree that people can do a lot more than first meets the eye. THE DANGER OF PRAISE AND POSITIVE LABELS If people have such potential to achieve, how can they gain faith in their potential? How can we give them the confidence they need to go for it? How about praising their ability in order to convey that they have what it takes? In fact, more than 80 percent of parents told us it was necessary to praise children's ability so as to foster their confidence and achievement. You know, it makes a lot of sense. 44 But then we began to worry. We thought about how people with the fixed mindset already focus too much on their ability: "Is it high enough?" "Will it look good?" Wouldn't praising people's ability focus them on it even more? Wouldn't it be telling them that that's what we value and, even worse, that we can read their deep, underlying ability from their performance? Isn't that teaching them the fixed mindset? Adam Guettel has been called the crown prince and savior of musical theater. He is the grandson of Richard Rodgers, the man who wrote the music to such classics as Oklahoma! and Carousel. Guettel's mother gushes about her son's genius. So does everyone else. "The talent is there and it's major," raved a review in The New York Times. The question is whether this kind of praise encourages people. What's great about research is that you can ask these kinds of questions and then go get the answers. So we conducted studies with hundreds of students, mostly early adolescents. We first gave each student a set of ten fairly difficult problems from a nonverbal IQ test. They mostly did pretty well on these, and when they finished we praised them. We praised some of the students for their ability. They were told: "Wow, you got [say] eight right. That's a really good score. You must be smart at this." They were in the Adam Guettel you're-so-talented position. We praised other students for their effort: "Wow, you got [say] eight right. That's a really good score. You must have worked really hard." They were not made to feel that they had some special gift; they were praised for doing what it takes to succeed. Both groups were exactly equal to begin with. But right after the praise, they began to differ. As we feared, the ability praise pushed students right into the fixed mindset, and they showed all the signs of it, too: When we gave them a choice, they rejected a challenging new task that they could learn from. They didn't want to do anything that could expose their flaws and call into question their talent. When Guettel was thirteen, he was all set to star in a Metropolitan Opera broadcast and TV movie of Amahl and the Night Visitors. He bowed out, saying that his voice had broken. "I kind of faked that my voice was changing... . I didn't want to handle the pressure." In contrast, when students were praised for effort, 90 percent of them wanted the challenging new task that they could learn from. Then we gave students some hard new problems, which they didn't do so well on. The ability kids now thought they were not smart after all. If success had meant they were intelligent, then less-than-success meant they were deficient. Guettel echoes this. "In my family, to be good is to fail. To be very good is to fail... . The only thing not a failure is to be great." The effort kids simply thought the difficulty meant "Apply more effort or try new strategies." They didn't see it as a failure, and they didn't think it reflected on their intellect. What about the students' enjoyment of the problems? After the success, everyone loved the problems, but after the difficult problems, the ability students said it wasn't fun anymore. It can't be fun when your claim to fame, your special talent, is in jeopardy. Here's Adam Guettel: "I wish I could just have fun and relax and not have the responsibility of that potential to be some kind of great man." As with the kids in our study, the burden of talent was killing his enjoyment. The effort-praised students still loved the problems, and many of them said that the hard problems were the most fun. 45 We then looked at the students' performance. After the experience with difficulty, the performance of the ability-praised students plummeted, even when we gave them some more of the easier problems. Losing faith in their ability, they were doing worse than when they started. The effort kids showed better and better performance. They had used the hard problems to sharpen their skills, so that when they returned to the easier ones, they were way ahead. Since this was a kind of IQ test, you might say that praising ability lowered the students' IQs. And that praising their effort raised them. Guettel was not thriving. He was riddled with obsessive-compulsive tics and bitten, bleeding fingers. "Spend a minute with him––it takes only one––and a picture of the terror behind the tics starts to emerge," says an interviewer. Guettel has also fought serious, recurrent drug problems. Rather than empowering him, the "gift" has filled him with fear and doubt. Rather than fulfilling his talent, this brilliant composer has spent most of his life running from it. One thing is hopeful––his recognition that he has his own life course to follow that is not dictated by other people and their view of his talent. One night he had a dream about his grandfather. "I was walking him to an elevator. I asked him if I was any good. He said, rather kindly, 'You have your own voice.'" Is that voice finally emerging? For the score of The Light in the Piazza, an intensely romantic musical, Guettel won the 2005 Tony Award. Will he take it as praise for talent or praise for effort? I hope it's the latter. There was one more finding in our study that was striking and depressing at the same time. We said to each student: "You know, we're going to go to other schools, and I bet the kids in those schools would like to know about the problems." So we gave students a page to write out their thoughts, but we also left a space for them to write the scores they had received on the problems. Would you believe that almost 40 percent of the ability-praised students lied about their scores? And always in one direction. In the fixed mindset, imperfections are shameful–– especially if you're talented––so they lied them away. What's so alarming is that we took ordinary children and made them into liars, simply by telling them they were smart. Right after I wrote these paragraphs, I met with a young man who tutors students for their College Board exams. He had come to consult with me about one of his students. This student takes practice tests and then lies to him about her score. He is supposed to tutor her on what she doesn't know, but she can't tell him the truth about what she doesn't know! And she is paying money for this. So telling children they're smart, in the end, made them feel dumber and act dumber, but claim they were smarter. I don't think this is what we're aiming for when we put positive labels––"gifted," "talented," "brilliant"––on people. We don't mean to rob them of their zest for challenge and their recipes for success. But that's the danger.

Everyone knows negative labels are bad, so you'd think this would be a short section. But it isn't a short section, because psychologists are learning how negative labels harm achievement. No one knows about negative ability labels like members of stereotyped groups. For example, African Americans know about being stereotyped as lower in intelligence. And women know about being stereotyped as bad at math and science. But I'm not sure even they know how creepy these stereotypes are. Research by Claude Steele and Joshua Aronson shows that even checking a box to indicate your race or sex can trigger the stereotype in your mind and lower your test score. Almost anything that reminds you that you're black or female before taking a test in the subject you're supposed to be bad at will lower your test score––a lot. In many of their studies, blacks are equal to whites in their performance, and females are equal to males, when no stereotype is evoked. But just put more males in the room with a female before a math test, and down goes the female's score. This is why. When stereotypes are evoked, they fill people's minds with distracting thoughts––with secret worries about confirming the stereotype. People usually aren't even aware of it, but they don't have enough mental power left to do their best on the test. This doesn't happen to everybody, however. It mainly happens to people who are in a fixed mindset. It's when people are thinking in terms of fixed traits that the stereotypes get to them. Negative stereotypes say: "You and your group are permanently inferior." Only people in the fixed mindset resonate to this message. So in the fixed mindset, both positive and negative labels can mess with your mind. When you're given a positive label, you're afraid of losing it, and when you're hit with a negative label, you're afraid of deserving it. When people are in a growth mindset, the stereotype doesn't disrupt their performance. The growth mindset takes the teeth out of the stereotype and makes people better able to fight back. They don't believe in permanent inferiority. And if they are behind––well, then they'll work harder, seek help, and try to catch up. 47 The growth mindset also makes people able to take what they can and what they need even from a threatening environment. We asked African American students to write an essay for a competition. They were told that when they finished, their essays would be evaluated by Edward Caldwell III, a distinguished professor with an Ivy League pedigree. That is, a representative of the white establishment. Edward Caldwell Ill's feedback was quite critical, but also helpful––and students' reactions varied greatly. Those with a fixed mindset viewed it as a threat, an insult, or an attack. They rejected Caldwell and his feedback. Here's what one student with the fixed mindset thought: "He's mean, he doesn't grade right, or he's obviously biased. He doesn't like me." Said another: "He is a pompous asshole... . It appears that he was searching for anything to discredit the work." And another, deflecting the feedback with blame: "He doesn't understand the conciseness of my points. He thought it was vague because he was impatient when he read it. He dislikes creativity." None of them will learn anything from Edward Caldwell's feedback. The students with the growth mindset may also have viewed him as a dinosaur, but he was a dinosaur who could teach them something. "Before the evaluation, he came across as arrogant and overdemanding. [After the evaluation?] 'Fair' seems to be the first word that comes to mind... . It seems like a new challenge." "He sounded like an arrogant, intimidating, and condescending man. [What are your feelings about the evaluation?] The evaluation was seemingly honest and specific. In this sense, the evaluation could be a stimulus ... to produce better work." "He seems to be proud to the point of arrogance. [The evaluation?]. He was intensely critical... . His comments were helpful and clear, however. I feel I will learn much from him." The growth mindset allowed African American students to recruit Edward Caldwell III for their own goals. They were in college to get an education and, pompous asshole or not, they were going to get it. Do I Belong Here? Aside from hijacking people's abilities, stereotypes also do damage by making people feel they don't belong. Many minorities drop out of college and many women drop out of math and science because they just don't feel they fit in. To find out how this happens, we followed college women through their calculus course. This is often when students decide whether math, or careers involving math, are right for them. Over the semester, we asked the women to report their feelings about math and their sense of belonging in math. For example, when they thought about math, did they feel like a full-fledged member of the math community or did they feel like an outsider; did they feel comfortable or did they feel anxious; did they feel good or bad about their math skills? The women with the growth mindset––those who thought math ability could be improved–– felt a fairly strong and stable sense of belonging. And they were able to maintain this even when they thought there was a lot of negative stereotyping going around. One student described it this way: "In a math class, [female] students were told they were wrong when they were not (they 48 were in fact doing things in novel ways). It was absurd, and reflected poorly on the instructor not to 'see' the students' good reasoning. It was alright because we were working in groups and we were able to give & receive support among us students... . We discussed our interesting ideas among ourselves." The stereotyping was disturbing to them (as it should be), but they could still feel comfortable with themselves and confident about themselves in a math setting. They could fight back. But women with the fixed mindset, as the semester wore on, felt a shrinking sense of belonging. And the more they felt the presence of stereotyping in their class, the more their comfort with math withered. One student said that her sense of belonging fell because "I was disrespected by the professor with his comment, 'that was a good guess,' whenever I made a correct answer in class." The stereotype of low ability was able to invade them––to define them––and take away their comfort and confidence. I'm not saying it's their fault by any means. Prejudice is a deeply ingrained societal problem, and I do not want to blame the victims of it. I am simply saying that a growth mindset helps people to see prejudice for what it is––someone else's view of them–– and to confront it with their confidence and abilities intact. Trusting People's Opinions Many females have a problem not only with stereotypes, but with other people's opinions of them in general. They trust them too much. One day, I went into a drugstore in Hawaii to buy dental floss and deodorant, and, after fetching my items, I went to wait in line. There were two women together in front of me waiting to pay. Since I am an incurable time stuffer, at some point I decided to get my money ready for when my turn came. So I walked up, put the items way on the side of the counter, and started to gather up the bills that were strewn throughout my purse. The two women went berserk. I explained that in no way was I trying to cut in front of them. I was just preparing for when my turn came. I thought the matter was resolved, but when I left the store, they were waiting for me. They got in my face and yelled, "You're a bad-mannered person!" My husband, who had seen the whole thing from beginning to end, thought they were nuts. But they had a strange and disturbing effect on me, and I had a hard time shaking off their verdict. This vulnerability afflicts many of the most able, high-achieving females. Why should this be? When they're little, these girls are often so; perfect, and they delight in everyone's telling them so. They're so well behaved, they're so cute, they're so helpful, and they're so precocious. Girls learn to trust people's estimates of them. "Gee, everyone's so nice to me; if they criticize me, it must be true." Even females at the top universities in the country say that other people's opinions are a good way to know their abilities. Boys are constantly being scolded and punished. When we observed in grade school classrooms, we saw that boys got eight times more criticism than girls for their conduct. Boys are also constantly calling each other slobs and morons. The evaluations lose a lot of their power. 49 A male friend once called me a slob. He was over to dinner at my house and, while we were eating, I dripped some food on my blouse. "That's because you're such a slob," he said. I was shocked. It was then that I realized no one had ever said anything like that to me. Males say it to each other all the time. It may not be a kind thing to say, even in jest, but it certainly makes them think twice before buying into other people's evaluations. Even when women reach the pinnacle of success, other people's attitudes can get them. Frances Conley is one of the most eminent neurosurgeons in the world. In fact, she was the first woman ever given tenure in neurosurgery at an American medical school. Yet careless comments from male colleagues––even assistants––could fill her with self-doubt. One day during surgery, a man condescendingly called her "honey." Instead of returning the compliment, she questioned herself. "Is a honey," she wondered, "especially this honey, good enough and talented enough to be doing this operation?" The fixed mindset, plus stereotyping, plus women's trust in other people's assessments of them: All of these contribute to the gender gap in math and science. That gap is painfully evident in the world of high tech. Julie Lynch, a budding techie, was already writing computer code when she was in junior high school. Her father and two brothers worked in technology, and she loved it, too. Then her computer programming teacher criticized her. She had written a computer program and the program ran just fine, but he didn't like a shortcut she had taken. Her interest evaporated. Instead, she went on to study recreation and public relations. Math and science need to be made more hospitable places for women. And women need all the growth mindset they can get to take their rightful places in these fields. When Things Go Right But let's look at the times the process goes right. The Polgar family has produced three of the most successful female chess players ever. How? Says Susan, one of the three, "My father believes that innate talent is nothing, that [success] is 99 percent hard work. I agree with him." The youngest daughter, Judit, is now considered the best woman chess player of all time. She was not the one with the most talent. Susan reports, "Judit was a slow starter, but very hardworking." A colleague of mine has two daughters who are math whizzes. One is a graduate student in math at a top university. The other was the first girl to rank number one in the country on an elite math test, won a nationwide math contest, and is now a neuroscience major at a top university. What's their secret? Is it passed down in the genes? I believe it's passed down in the mindset. It's the most growth-mindset family I've ever seen. In fact, their father applied the growth mindset to everything. I'll never forget a conversation we had some years ago. I was single at the time, and he asked me what my plan was for finding a partner. He was aghast when I said I didn't have a plan. "You wouldn't expect your work to get done by itself," he said. "Why is this any different?" It was inconceivable to him that you could have a goal and not take steps to make it happen. In short, the growth mindset lets people––even those who are targets of negative labels-use and develop their minds fully. Their heads are not filled with limiting thoughts, a fragile sense of belonging, and a belief that other people can define them. 50 Grow Your Mindset • Think about your hero. Do you think of this person as someone with extraordinary abilities who achieved with little effort? Now go find out the truth. Find out the tremendous effort that went into their accomplishment––and admire them more. • Think of times other people outdid you and you just assumed they were smarter or more talented. Now consider the idea that they just used better strategies, taught themselves more, practiced harder, and worked their way through obstacles. You can do that, too, if you want to. • Are there situations where you get stupid––where you disengage your intelligence? Next time you're in one of those situations, get yourself into a growth mindset––think about learning and improvement, not judgment––and hook it back up. • Do you label your kids? This one is the artist and that one is the scientist. Next time, remember that you're not helping them––even though you may be praising them. Remember our study where praising kids' ability lowered their IQ scores. Find a growth-mindset way to compliment them. • More than half of our society belongs to a negatively stereotyped group. First you have all the women, and then you have all the other groups who are not supposed to be good at something or other. Give them the gift of the growth mindset. Create an environment that teaches the growth mindset to the adults and children in your life, especially the ones who are targets of negative stereotypes. Even when the negative label comes along, they'll remain in charge of their learning.

End Matter And Strategies For Changing Mindset

Tenth graders were 3x more likely to score in the top fifth on a national achievement test if they had a growth mindset (if they believed that intelligence is something you can grow). Teachers suspended 50% fewer students if they adopted an empathic mindset about discipline (if they believed teachers should try to understand the perspective of a misbehaving student). Those are just two examples of the dramatic ways in which our mindsets can affect our behavior and our lives in meaningful ways.

Our mindsets also affect whether we seek out and persist through challenges, whether we think others should be given opportunities to learn, whether we get depressed, even whether we act prejudiced. In short, mindsets are important.

How do you help people develop mindsets that bring out their best?

People's intuitions about how to change mindsets are often wrong. I've been studying mindsets at Stanford for the last 10 years, and I've seen numerous well-intentioned efforts to change mindsets fall flat or backfire because they ignored the psychology of persuasion.

Persuaders (those trying to change someone else's mindset) sometimes err by approaching mindsets as if they were "facts" to be memorized rather than habits of mind to be internalized. Or they ignore the personal and emotionally charged nature of many mindsets, which means changing them calls for special sensitivity to the perspective of the persuadee (the person whose mindset you're trying to change).

Imparting a new mindset successfully requires a careful application of persuasion principles. I listed just a few of these principles below, and I oversimplified for the sake of brevity. My goal is just to whet your appetite. For a more nuanced and comprehensive account of these processes, read books or take classes on "attitudes and persuasion" or "social influence;" read Greg Walton's (2014) paper on wise interventions; or pursue a Ph.D. in social psychology (it's pretty fun).

1. Social modeling — provide a positive example of the transformation you seek

If you want someone to transform — to adopt a new mindset or behavior — provide positive social models for the transformation you hope to see (Bandura, 1962). For example, if you want a teacher to invest more in building strong relationships with students, given them the opportunity to hear from teachers who invested more in building strong relationships and had positive experiences as a result. That will help them envision what change could look like for them and why it might be attractive.

2. Social norms — use the bandwagon

To get someone to do something new, convey the idea that most "people like them" are already doing it — or that there is a growing trend towards people doing it (Lewin, 1943). For example, Schultz and colleagues (2007) got people to use less electricity by showing them that others in their own community, on average, use less electricity than they do. Whereas "social modeling" provides a narrative account of the transformational process, "social norms" focus on the number of people who are enacting a desired behavior, or subscribing to the desired mindset.

3. Signal credibility — use a trusted messenger

People are more likely to be persuaded by messengers whose opinion seems credible on the topic at hand (e.g., Heesacker, Petty, & Cacioppo, 1983). Keep in mind that credibility is not necessarily about credentials or prestige. For example, a student might find a peer to be a more credible source of information than a teacher when it comes to deciding what's "cool."

4. Respect autonomy — being patronized elicits resistance, not persuasion

People don't like it when somebody else tells them how to think, especially if it's "for their own good." If the persuadee suspects you're trying to manipulate them, they are more likely to become defensive and to resist your persuasion attempts. This is a phenomenon called reactance (Brehm, 1966). To avoid reactance, don't talk down to people or tell them they're "thinking about it the wrong way." Instead, create situations in which a person will discover the new mindset for themselves.

5. Avoid blame and focus on growth

People want to see themselves (and others they care about) in a positive light, and they resist persuasion if it paints them in a negative light. (This is an example of "cognitive dissonance" in action, see Festinger, 1957; Festinger, 1962). To get around this problem while still inducing change, find a way to pardon the persuadee's past behavior while increasing pressure to change future behavior. That is, try to help them "save face" for past transgressions, but not for future transgressions. For example, imagine you were trying to convince parents to stop using corporal punishment:

"Historically, many parents used corporal punishment to discipline kids, but corporal punishment is rapidly disappearing as more and more parents learn about new research on the long-term effects of corporal punishment. This new research shows that corporal punishment can cause toxic stress which impedes kids' cognitive development and predisposes them to aggression and domestic violence later in life — an unintended consequence that few parents were aware of until very recently."

Conclusion

Changing mindsets isn't easy, but social psychology points us towards many effective strategies. Of course, there are lots of factors to think about. Above all, try to empathize with the person whose mindset you're trying to change. Why do they hold a counterproductive mindset right now? If you held that counterproductive mindset, ask yourself what might convince you to change your mind (hint: probably neither nagging nor sanctimony).

Happy mindset changing!